day trips to the
oregon coast

D0877829

7-20

day trips® series

day trips® to the
oregon coast

>>> getaway ideas for the local traveler

kim cooper findling

Globe
Pequot

Guilford, Connecticut

Globe Pequot

An imprint of The Rowman & Littlefield Publishing Group, Inc.
4501 Forbes Blvd., Ste. 200
Lanham, MD 20706
www.rowman.com

Distributed by NATIONAL BOOK NETWORK

Copyright © 2020 Kim Cooper Findling
Maps by Melissa Baker

British Library Cataloguing in Publication Information available

Library of Congress Cataloging-in-Publication Data available

ISBN 978-1-4930-4504-4 (paper : alk. paper)
ISBN 978-1-4930-4505-1 (electronic)

♾™ The paper used in this publication meets the minimum requirements of American National Standard for Information Sciences—Permanence of Paper for Printed Library Materials, ANSI/NISO Z39.48-1992.

contents

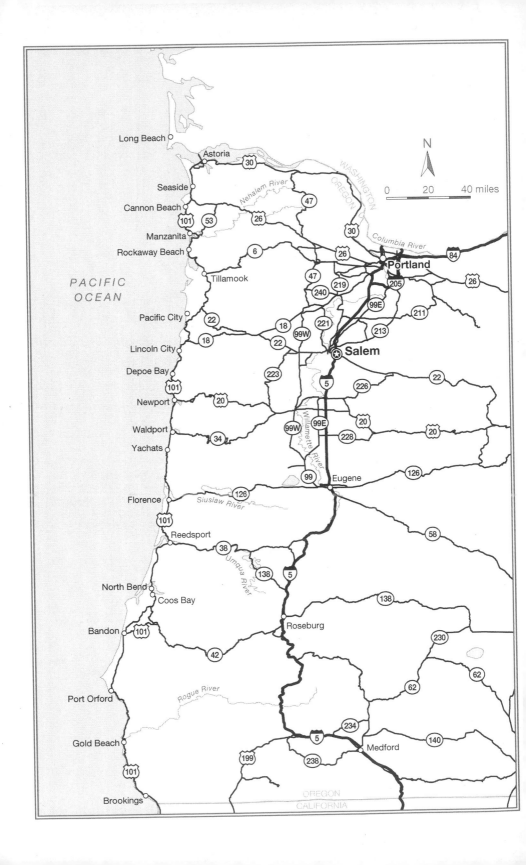

acknowledgments

Some kids dream of leaving home and never looking back; others spend a lifetime trying to return home. I'm in the second category, and this book is my homecoming. Growing up on the Oregon Coast meant always being surrounded by a rugged and incredibly beautiful landscape. I extend appreciation to the coast itself first, for inspiration and my very roots. Next to thank are the many others who help me in my work. I owe thank-yous to dozens of tourism professionals and longtime colleagues who contributed ideas to these pages. Personal thanks to friends and acquaintances who regularly offer travel destination ideas. Finally, I extend endless gratitude to my traveling companions, Todd, Libby, Maris, and Carson. You are the best road-trip sidekicks on the planet, and I am so very lucky.

about the author

Fifth-generation Oregonian and award-winning author Kim Cooper Findling grew up on the Oregon Coast, spent several years in the Willamette Valley, and has lived in Central Oregon for 25 years. She is the author of *The Sixth Storm* (with coauthor and daughter Libby Findling); *Bend, Oregon Daycations: Day Trips for Curious Families*; *Day Trips from Portland: Getaway Ideas for the Local Traveler*; and *Chance of Sun: An Oregon Memoir*. Her work has appeared in many publications including *Bend Magazine*, *Travel Oregon*, *The Oregonian*, *Horizon Air*, *Alaska Air*, *Oregon Quarterly*, *1859 Oregon's Magazine*, *The Best Places to Kiss NW*, and *High Desert Journal*. See kimcooperfindling.com.

introduction

Hey, Oregon Coast Lovers! As you already know or are about to find out, the Oregon Coast is extremely lovable. This place of incredible natural beauty and endless recreational opportunities is one of the most marvelous destinations on the planet. Here you can marvel at the magnificence of nature, relax with a view of the sea, wander on beaches and in the woods, feel the coastal breeze on your skin, eat local foods, bike, surf, hike, learn, explore, and play.

From the stately historic northern city of Astoria perched on the Columbia River to the rugged rural southernmost city of Brookings on the California border, there are dozens of delights per mile to soak up along the way. The 363 miles of the Oregon Coast have one thing in common—each is incredibly scenic. Beyond that, there is a lot more diversity than you might imagine to be found on the Oregon Coast. The northern coast, closer to urban metropolitan areas, is denser, trendier, and experiences higher residential and visitation rates. The southern coast is rural, rugged, lightly populated, and begging for exploration. The central coast is a mixture of the two. This book covers all three regions, and helps you find the best of the best in each location.

Maybe you've never been to the Oregon Coast at all or maybe you are an Oregon Coast devotee, ready to explore towns and destinations you have not yet discovered. You've seen the beach, you've watched the waves, you've flown a kite, you've spooned up the clam chowder. Now you're ready to dig a little deeper. You want to know more. You want to hit a new town with knowledge and a plan that will take you to new places to explore, new insights to be had, new flavors and experiences to savor.

Here you'll find 21 day-trip destinations. Some visit one action-packed town and help you narrow down what to see there. Other trips cover two or three smaller towns, some more action-packed than others. Each trip is just a little bit different; each destination offers its own unique flavor. We suggest attractions, restaurants, shops, and outdoor destinations that might tickle your fancy. You'll find more options than you could possibly cover in one day, so pick and choose as you please. Should you find you want more of a certain city, check out the lodgings section—each trip has one, if appropriate.

Our intention is that in these pages you'll find nearly everything you need to visit each Oregon Coast destination for a daylong adventure. A few words of wisdom to the savvy traveler, however. First—take a map. Even if your car is equipped with a GPS system or your smartphone is loaded with maps, these systems aren't foolproof and don't always include smaller or newer roads. In these cases, a paper map is an invaluable tool. If you have time, it's also a good idea to highlight the places you really want to see in your chosen day trip ahead of time and call ahead to check on hours of operation, necessary reservations, and the like. The Oregon Coast is wildly seasonal—hours vary greatly over the course of a year, and shops and restaurants change their schedules accordingly and even sometimes close for winter months.

With that in mind—hit the beach! Take a hike, fly a kite, try some seafood, climb a sand dune, eat some ice cream, go windsurfing, hug a tree, hit the surf. Whatever you do, have a great time day-trippin'!

using this guide

Day Trips to the Oregon Coast is organized differently than other books in this series, which typically send day-trippers out from a centrally located city. The Oregon Coast is 363 miles long, each section easily accessed from Oregon's I-5 corridor, but not necessarily from a starting point of a single city. Most of the towns on the Oregon Coast sit along US 101, also called Highway 101, and often (especially by longtime Oregon residents) simply referred to as "the 101." This guide is divided into three sections: Northern, Central, and Southern Oregon Coast. Directions are provided from the most appropriate large city on I-5 from which to access each destination.

Listings in the Where to Go, Where to Shop, Where to Eat, and Where to Stay sections are arranged in alphabetical order, unless otherwise specified. If several places in a given town offer similar opportunities, listing titles highlight broad categories (e.g., "antiques") rather than the names of specific businesses or locations. Each stop on every day trip includes a Where to Go listing, but Where to Shop, Where to Eat, and Where to Stay are only included when there are appropriate listings worth visiting.

scheduling your day trip

Half the fun of day-tripping is planning. Many a workday can be endured by imagining what fun you'll have come the weekend and an unencumbered day—just you and the open road, maybe a pal or two along for the ride, nowhere to go and all day to get there. As you fantasize about your next day trip, keep these things in mind:

The Oregon Coast is highly seasonal. The coast can get up to 80 inches of rain a year, most of it in winter and spring. Summers are much more likely to be sunny and clear, albeit wind is common all year long. That means that summers are very busy in terms of tourism; winters are very quiet. It's going to be a lot easier to get a table or a room in February, but the weather may be wet and wild, and many destinations may not be open every day of the week.

Especially in the off-season, be aware that many tourist-dependent businesses in smaller towns choose to close shop midweek, often on Monday or Tuesday, to accommodate the majority of travelers and yet still have a break themselves. Sundays can be hit-and-miss too. Hours vary widely summer-to-winter on any day of the week.

Many Oregon Coast towns are small and rural, which is part of the charm but can mean inconsistency in services from place to place. If your heart is set on a certain destination, call in advance to check on hours and plan your trip accordingly. That said, winter is an increasingly popular time to visit the coast for spectacular storm watching, whale watching, and beating the crowds.

hours of operation

Many businesses change their hours frequently or seasonally. Hours of operation are sometimes included in these pages, but be aware that this information may change without notice. In many cases, hours of operation vary so widely over the course of the year that they've been omitted in these pages—call ahead before visiting. Phone numbers and, when possible, websites for each listing are included here so that you can access current information on your own. Also, small businesses can be known to change location or phone number at whim. If a phone number turns out to be out of service, call information or try a web search. Keep in mind, too, that many businesses close on major holidays, even though that information may not be indicated in these pages.

pricing key

The price codes for accommodations and restaurants are represented as a scale of one to three dollar signs ($). Most businesses take credit cards these days, but you can't always be guaranteed of this convenience. Should a business require cash only, in most cases they can direct you to a nearby ATM to access cash, which will sometimes assess a small banking fee. You will only pay sales tax in Washington (the percentage varies by area), not Oregon, and some Washington attractions may have already factored sales tax into their pricing schema.

restaurants

The price code used here is based on the average price of dinner entrees for two, excluding drinks, appetizers, dessert, tax, and tip. (Oregon has no sales tax; Washington does and it varies by county and city.) You can typically expect to pay a little less for lunch and/or breakfast, where applicable. If the business only serves lunch and/or breakfast, the code has been applied to those meals.

$ Less than $25

$$ $25 to $40

$$$ More than $40

accommodations

This book is intended primarily for those who wish to venture to the coast for just a day or half day. However, overnight accommodations are included in many sections for those who wish to explore an area further. You wouldn't be the first to find yourself at the beach and not ready to leave yet. Accommodations included here are almost all local hotels and bed-and-breakfasts. Large national chains are typically not included, though many of the larger cities in this book do have chain hotels. Other cities in this book are too small for a chain—some are too small for any other lodging. In that case the Where to Stay section has been omitted. Each day trip does not include accommodation listings for every stop, though typically at least one stop per day trip includes a suggested overnight lodging. With few exceptions, most towns in each trip aren't more than 40 minutes apart, and many are much closer.

The following price code is used for accommodations throughout this book. It is based on the average price of a onenight stay in a standard, double-occupancy room, before taxes. This price does not include state and city hotel taxes, which vary but are typically around 8 percent. City taxes vary, and are typically lower in smaller towns. Keep in mind that lodging prices often change seasonally or between the weekend and midweek. Summer pricing is almost always higher, and weekends are very frequently more expensive as well.

$ Less than $125

$$ $125 to $225

$$$ More than $225

driving tips

In general, Oregon and Washington have good signage, and navigation between towns should be fairly straightforward. That said, especially in more-rural areas, signage is more intermittent and roads are narrower, more winding, and not as well lit. Drive cautiously and keep your eyes open for road changes and directional signage.

In the winter, many of the destinations included in this book can be subject to stormy weather. It is rare for the Oregon Coast itself to get snow, but you may encounter snow or ice in the Coast Range en route to the beach. Occasionally some of the roads in this book are closed due to weather conditions. The beach can be windy and incredibly rainy—make sure your windshield wipers are in good working order before heading to the coast.

For road closures and weather information, call the **Oregon Department of Transportation Trip Check** at (800) 977-ODOT or check it online at tripcheck.com.

A few trips in these pages will lead to Forest Service roads en route to hikes or waterfalls, but follow directions and always stay on marked roads. If you aren't sure where you are or which way to go, ask for directions. It doesn't hurt to carry water, blankets, and food when traveling in the Pacific Northwest in the winter. A cell phone is always handy—charge it up before you leave, and be aware that coverage is intermittent in rural, forested, and mountainous areas.

Oregon is one of the last states in the nation in which travelers are not allowed to pump their own gas, except in fairly rare locations. Wait for an attendant and ask him or her for the gas type and quantity you desire. In Washington, gas is pumpyourown. Oregonians might find this an uncomfortable practice—ask for help if you aren't sure how to operate a gas pump.

Maximum highway speeds vary by state. Oregon's I-5 tops out at 65 mph, while Washington's I-5 allows speeds up to 70 mph. State highway top speeds vary too. In Oregon, you won't see many allowed speeds over 55 mph on rural highways; Washington may allow higher speeds. The best practice is to stay alert, pay attention, and obey the posted signs.

Keep in mind that speed limits can change abruptly from one town or stretch of highway to the next. While it's important to heed speed limits at all times when driving, be particularly cautious when passing through construction zones, where speeding ticket fines can be double the normal (already high) fine. Many smaller highways in these trips pass directly through small towns, necessitating a speed limit change on either end. Respect the residents of these towns, and slow down appropriately to avoid getting pulled over by a police officer.

Be prepared for a leisurely drive. US 101 as it runs north–south along the coastline is in many cases only a two-lane highway with winding curves and frequent pullouts for views and attractions. Traffic can be thick in the summer; weather can be intense in the winter. This is to say that US 101 is not a high-speed journey, ever. Fill up the gas tank, plan for enough time to get from place to place, enjoy the journey, and stop to smell the roses and take in the drop-dead gorgeous views.

Public transportation is intermittent at the still-small-and-rural coast. Uber and Lyft exist in a few of the region's towns, but don't count on it. Bicycle touring the Oregon Coast, on the other hand, is very popular. Many of the smaller more-rural roads and destinations in this book are simply perfect for road biking. Be safe and wear a helmet, please.

highway designations

For consistency's sake, this book typically refers to state highways as "OR" or "WA" followed by the highway number (e.g., OR 20). In many cases, that number will be followed by a cardinal designation (e.g., OR 20 E). In other cases, the same highway may have more than one name. US 101, while often referred to verbally as Highway 101 or "the 101" by locals, is still listed at US 101 in the text in this book in order to be consistent with address listings. Another factor to take into consideration is that an address may be listed as N US 101 or S US 101 no matter its location on the greater Oregon Coast, but instead its cardinal direction within each particular town. As an example, in Lincoln City, you'll find N US 101 and S US 101 addresses, based on which side of the D River each is located, the north or the south. This system is repeated in many of the cities in this book.

area codes

The northwest corner of Oregon uses the area code 503. This area extends south to Salem, southwest to Pacific City, east to Mount Hood, and southeast to Detroit. Beyond those parameters, in Oregon, the 541 area code is the most prevalent, though you will also see the area code 458. In Washington, the areas covered in this book almost all use 564. Cell phone prefixes, obviously, vary widely.

where to get more information

Day Trips to the Oregon Coast attempts to cover a variety of interests and destinations, but those looking for additional travel information can contact the following agencies by phone, mail, or the web. Keep in mind that online reviews can be contradictory, as everyone experiences places differently. Call directly or stick with advice from respected travel organizations.

for general travel information:

Oregon Coast Visitors Association
555 SW Coast Hwy.
Newport, OR 97365
(541) 265-8801
visittheoregoncoast.com

Oregon Department of Transportation
Intelligent Transportation Systems
800 Airport Rd. SE, Rm. 81
Salem, OR 97301
(800) 977-ODOT
tripcheck.com (for road condition information)

Oregon State Tourism
Travel Oregon
319 SW Washington, Ste. 700
Portland, OR 97204
(503) 967-1560
traveloregon.com
Request a copy of the Travel Oregon Visitor Guide.

Washington State Tourism
(800) 544-1800
tourism@cted.wa.gov
experiencewa.com

AAA Oregon
600 SW Market St.
Portland, OR 97201
(503) 222-6767 or (800) 452-1643
aaaorid.com

AAA Washington
4301 E Fourth Plain Blvd.
Vancouver, WA 98661
(360) 696-4081
aaawa.com

for camping & recreation information:

Oregon Parks and Recreation Department, State Parks
725 Summer St. NE, Ste. C
Salem, OR 97301
(503) 986-0707 (main); (800) 452-5687 (reservations); (800) 551-6949 (information)
park.info@state.or.us
oregon.gov/OPRD

Washington State Parks and Recreation Commission
1111 Israel Rd. SW
Olympia, WA 98504-2650
(360) 902-8844 (main); (888) CAMP-OUT (reservations)
parks.wa.gov

north coast

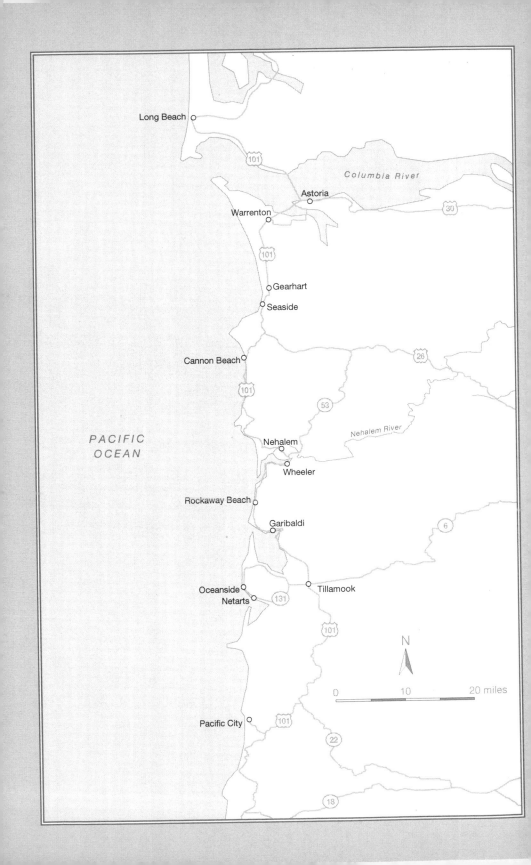

day trip 01

north coast

wild waters & wooden boardwalks:
long beach peninsula, wa

long beach peninsula, wa

The title of this book is *Day Trips to the Oregon Coast*, and yet our first chapter is a location in Washington State. The 28-mile Long Beach Peninsula juts out of Washington's southwest corner, just north across the bridge from Astoria, Oregon. Long, narrow, and picturesque, the peninsula is bounded on the west by the Pacific Ocean, the south by the Columbia River, and the east by Willapa Bay. The peninsula is most definitely in Washington State, but in terms of geography, accessibility, and aesthetics, it's akin to the beaches and beach towns of Oregon, and has long been thought of by many locals as an extension of such.

On the Pacific Ocean side, a sandy beach stretches continuously for 28 miles. This wide strip of beach is great for kite flying, walking, clam digging, sandcastle building, and more, but not so great for swimming. The water is cold and dangerous. In fact, the confluence of the Columbia River and the Pacific Ocean, just south of the peninsula, is some of the most dangerous water on the West Coast.

Many small communities dot the Long Beach Peninsula, each a bit different. Downtown Long Beach offers the most festive atmosphere, with kite, candy, ice cream, and T-shirt shops, and a wonderful kite festival in August. Oysterville is known for its historic homes; Ilwaco for the Port of Ilwaco, the comings and goings of a working marina, and a summertime Saturday Market. Only Ilwaco and Long Beach are incorporated, and the residents of the peninsula think of themselves as one community, called the Long Beach Peninsula. The

3

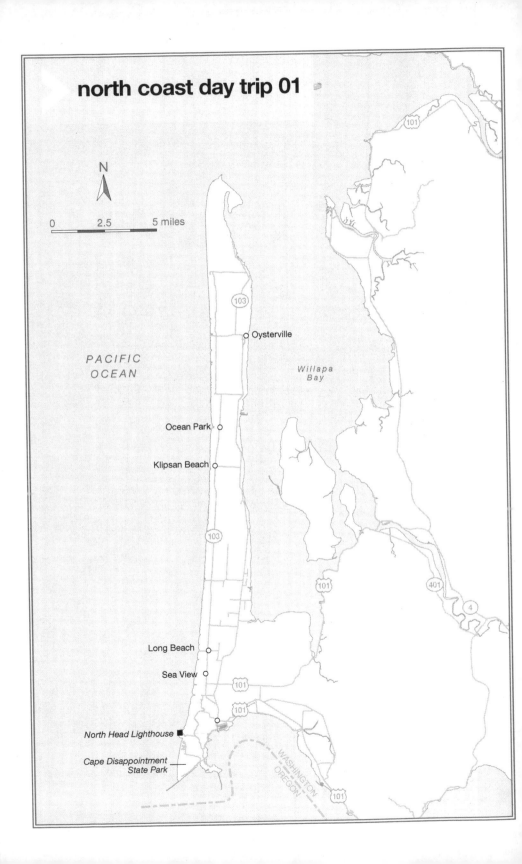

principal industry is tourism, though fishing, crabbing, oyster farming, and cranberry farming are also important components of the local economy.

From spring break through mid-October, the peninsula is hopping with visitors, festivals, and activity. The rest of the year, it's awfully quiet. Winter can still be a great time to visit, especially if you are interested in clam digging or want to get a glimpse of some of the epic winter storms that strike the Cape Disappointment headlands from the Pacific.

getting there

From Portland: Take US 26 W / OR 26 W out of Portland and continue 74 miles to the coast. At the US 101 junction, go north for 36 miles, crossing the Astoria-Megler Bridge into Washington State. US 101 will turn into WA 103 / Pacific Avenue S, which traverses the entire Long Beach Peninsula.

where to go

Cape Disappointment State Park. South end of peninsula, south of Ilwaco off WA 100. Cape Disappointment State Park is the most visited park in the Washington State Parks system. Here you can walk a sandy beach, explore bunkers of an old military fort, wander through coastal forests, have a picnic, camp, take in spectacular vistas, and visit a beach called Dead Man's Cove. The park has an old-growth forest, lakes, freshwater and saltwater marshes, streams, ocean tidelands, lots of watchable wildlife, and a working Coast Guard station that specializes in search-and-rescue training. "Cape D" encompasses 1,882 acres and is fronted by both the Pacific Ocean and Baker Bay. The park is open year-round for camping and day use, 6:30 a.m. to dusk.

Within its boundaries are these highlights:

Cape Disappointment Lighthouse. On the southeast tip of the peninsula, off WA 100. Pretty, but not open to the public. Take the easy walk from the interpretive center to the site and enjoy Cape Disappointment Lighthouse from the outside, knowing that it's the oldest operating lighthouse on the West Coast.

Columbia Pacific Heritage Museum. 115 SE Lake St., Ilwaco; (360) 642-3446; columbiapacificheritagemuseum.org. Explore the history of the region where the Columbia River meets the Pacific Ocean. Artifacts, images, and stories interpret the Chinook Indians, European explorers, 19th-century pioneers, fishermen, cranberry growers, loggers, and summer people who have made the Long Beach Peninsula what it is today. Open 10 a.m. to 4 p.m. Tues through Sat. Free admission for children ages 12 and under.

Discovery Trail. North end access is off 26th St. NW in Long Beach; south end access is off the corner of Elizabeth Avenue and Waterfront Way in Ilwaco. The Discovery Trail was created to commemorate the Lewis and Clark Expedition and parallels Capt. William Clark's hike to the Pacific Ocean in November 1805. Stretching 8.3 miles between Long Beach and Ilwaco, the trail is closed to motor vehicles and horses and offers peaceful, scenic passage to pedestrians and cyclists. Interpretive markers and several bronze statues can be found on the route. The trail is relatively easy and flat from the northern terminus to Beard's Hollow. It gets more challenging at that point, rising in elevation as much as 300 feet between Beard's Hollow and the southern terminus at the Port of Ilwaco. A spur trail takes you to North Head Lighthouse.

Lewis and Clark Interpretive Center. Cape Disappointment State Park, off WA 100 on the south end of the peninsula; (360) 642-3029. Perched on a cliff 200 feet above the mouth of the Columbia River, the Lewis and Clark Interpretive Center tells the story of the journey of the Corps of Discovery, focusing particularly on their Pacific Coast stay. Exhibits featuring Lewis's journal entries bring home the arduous journey Lewis, Clark, and their crew made, ending with the stories of what happened to each member after their return home. During winter and spring, volunteers help visitors spot migrating gray whales; year-round, views of the Columbia Bar are truly spectacular from this vantage point on the tip of the cape. Open year-round from 10 a.m. to 5 p.m. daily.

North Head Lighthouse. North Head Lighthouse Road, off WA 100 in Ilwaco; (360) 642-3078. The 65-foot North Head Lighthouse was completed in 1898. Tours include history and gorgeous panoramic views of the peninsula and Pacific Ocean. Incidentally, North Head is the windiest lighthouse area on the West Coast and the second windiest in the nation. Winds of 120 miles per hour have been recorded at the site. The lighthouse grounds are open year-round, dawn until dusk, at no charge on foot; those driving will need a Washington State Parks Discover Pass to park in all parts of Cape Disappointment State Park. Call for tour hours, which change seasonally.

Waikiki Beach. On the southern end of the peninsula off WA 100. Waikiki Beach is considered the only swim-safe beach on the peninsula. Still, whether or not you actually want to venture into the water will depend on your fortitude and/or the air temperature—the water here isn't exactly as warm as the other Waikiki, in Hawaii. During the summer, concerts are held near the beach on Sat nights at 7 p.m.

Green Angel Gardens Farm Store. 6807 Sandridge Rd., Long Beach; (360) 642-4018; greenangelgardening.com. Stocked with organic greens grown on-site, local fresh eggs, and a variety of certified organic produce obtained from regional growers. The Green Angel Farm promotes education and is family-friendly, encouraging kids and adults to come and learn how quality food is grown. Open daily 10 a.m. to 4 p.m.

water rescue school

On the southern tip of the Long Beach Peninsula is the **National Motor Lifeboat School,** *run by the US Coast Guard. The location is no accident—the waters off the peninsula are considered some of the most treacherous in the world and make for ideal training ground for wild and woolly ocean rescues. Known as the Graveyard of the Pacific, the stretch of water where the Pacific Ocean meets the Columbia River has claimed more than 2,000 ships since the late 1700s. Students come to the Lifeboat School from all over the United States, Mexico, and Canada to learn how to perform in some of the harshest maritime conditions on the planet. The school is at the Coast Guard station en route to the Lewis and Clark Interpretive Center—peer through the chain-link fence or from the overlook at the interpretive center to see the students in action on the grounds and in the water.*

Knappton Cove Heritage Center. Right on WA 401 northeast of the Astoria-Megler Bridge; (503) 738-5206; knapptoncoveheritagecenter.org. Everything that happened at New York's famous Ellis Island happened at other US ports during the waves of immigration in the 1800s and early 1900s, only on a smaller scale. In Astoria, boats from overseas anchored and were boarded by an inspector. If fumigation for infestation and disease was deemed necessary, the boats were sent here, across the Columbia River to the US Columbia River Quarantine Station, the only point for federal quarantine on the West Coast north of San Francisco. Today it's a National Historic Site, set on preserving the history of this unique location and the role of the US Public Health Service. Hours are "most summer weekends" or by appointment.

Long Beach Boardwalk. Access at Bolstad Avenue and Sid Snyder Drive in Long Beach. The *Today Show* named the Long Beach Boardwalk one of the top five in the nation, calling it the "most unique." That's because, unlike many US boardwalks, the half-mile boardwalk in Long Beach isn't lined with hot dog stands and sunglasses vendors, but instead surrounded by grassy dunes and wide-open vistas. Interpretive exhibits dot the route, and spectacular views of the ocean, beach, and North Head Lighthouse make this a must-walk. The boardwalk makes for a great place to watch the Fourth of July fireworks show or the summertime Kite Festival each summer.

North Jetty Brewing. 4200 Pacific Way, Seaview; (360) 642-4234; northjettybrew.com. This sweet little taproom opened in April 2014 and immediately became a community gathering place and tourist must-stop. The on-site 10-barrel brewhouse produces a wide array of beers, distributed by 18 taps. Try the Cape D IPA or the Yellow Boots Kolsch. No food, except for all the shelled peanuts you can eat. Open Sun and Mon noon to 7 p.m., Wed and Thurs noon to 9 p.m., Fri and Sat noon to 10 p.m.

Pacific Coast Cranberry Research Foundation Museum and Gift Shop. 2907 Pioneer Rd., Long Beach; (360) 642-5553; cranberrymuseum.com. Cranberry farming in the southwest corner of Washington State has a more than 100-year history and remains an important part of the local economy. This 1,200-square-foot facility next to a 10-acre demonstration cranberry farm interprets the history and cultivation of this garnet-colored berry and offers a self-guided walking tour of cranberry bogs year-round. September is the most spectacular month, when the berries are ripening. Open daily 10 a.m. to 5 p.m., Apr through Dec.

Painted Lady Lavender Farm. 1664 US 101, Ilwaco; (360) 642-3531. This charming 2-acre farm grows lavender and also includes a chicken coop, rabbits, and a guest cabin. Open daily until dusk. Call for guided tours of the plantings of lavender and other organic herbs.

where to eat

Bailey's Bakery & Cafe. 26910 Sandridge Rd., Nahcotta; (360) 665-4449; baileysbakery cafe.com. Bailey's is famous for their "Thunder Buns," an amazing cinnamon roll described as "the most outrageous on the planet" that sells out early each day. If you miss out on those, there are lots of other treats to tempt you, including bread, scones, sausage rolls, and fresh soups. Open Wed through Sun 9 a.m. to 3 p.m. $.

The Depot Restaurant. 1208 38th Place, Seaview; (360) 642-7880; depotrestaurant dining.com. Discover great food and a warm and friendly ambience at this restaurant in a 120-year-old depot building at the end of the historic "Clamshell Railroad." After the railroad closed, the depot became a rough-and-tumble Coast Guard bar for a few decades before chef Michael Lalewicz and his wife Nancy renovated the depot into a fine-dining destination. Entrees include "landfood" and "seafood." The Depot's chowder is to die for, with leeks and steamer clams. They offer a regional and international wine list with 6 microbrews on tap. Monthly winemaker dinners have a preset menu. $$–$$$.

42nd Street Cafe. 4201 Pacific Way, Seaview; (360) 642-2323; 2ndstcafe.com. Showcasing the many cuisines of the West Coast in a casual environment, 42nd Street Cafe is a locals' favorite. Seafood is a focus, with special dining events around clam-digging season, mushroom season, and the like. Service is great, and 42nd Street sells their condiments to go. Cafe breakfast and lunch Wed through Sun 8 a.m. to 1:30 p.m.; American bistro dinners Tues through Sat beginning at 4:30 p.m. $–$$.

Lost Roo. 1700 S Pacific Hwy., Long Beach; (360) 642-4329; lostroo.com. This big, welcoming establishment offers drinks and fare for the whole family. A restaurant, outdoor patio, and full bar with plenty of televisions please everyone. A big menu with a (slightly) Australian theme includes burgers, seafood, and "sammies." Open 7 days a week 11:30 a.m. to close. $–$$.

Salt Pub. 147 Howerton Ave., Ilwaco; (360) 642-7258; salt-hotel.com. Tucked into a tiny retro hotel on the Ilwaco Harbor is this little pub with a big heart. The menu is chock-full of delicious food prepared by a Le Cordon Bleu–trained chef. The tuna melt includes local tuna and smoked Tillamook cheese, and you can't go wrong with the Dungeness mac and cheese or the Parmesan-crusted rockfish. The view of the boats in port is charming too; you might just want to get a room and stay the night. Open for lunch and dinner Thurs through Mon (check website for current hours). $$.

Serious Pizza. 243 Robert Gray Dr., Ilwaco; (360) 642-3060; capedisappointmentstore .com. The place doesn't look like much, and is only open seasonally, but the wood-fired artisan pizza is worth the wait here. Calling ahead is a good plan. $–$$.

where to stay

Adrift Hotel. 409 Sid Snyder Dr., Long Beach; (800) 561-2456; adrifthotel.com. This 80-room hotel has a minimalist European feel. There is a spa on-site, and they lend out cruiser bikes so guests can explore the Discovery Trail, which is just outside the front doors. Their restaurant, Pickled Fish, serves specialty cocktails, a farm-and-sea-to-table menu, and live entertainment nightly. $$–$$$.

Boreas Bed & Breakfast Inn. 607 Ocean Beach Blvd. N, Long Beach; (360) 642-8069; boreasinn.com. This oceanfront boutique inn has only 5 rooms, making it peaceful and private. A 3-course award-winning brunch is served daily; expect delicious surprises like fruit soup and handmade pastries and cookies. A hot tub out back has only one key so that

happy as a clam

I took my children clam digging for the first time on the Long Beach Peninsula a few years ago. Recreational digging of the Pacific razor clam is a classic old-time activity that has taken off in recent years, bringing families out during the fall and spring seasons to dig for dinner. It's quick and easy to learn, and very fun for all ages, especially if the catching is good. Watching my girls master the art of the clam gun, work hard at unearthing a clam from the wet sand, and celebrate with a happy dance on the beautiful beach next to the Pacific Ocean was a blast. Bring the kids and your clam gun or shovel and see how much fun this sport can be. Specific times and dates are set for legal harvest, and diggers need to purchase a license to harvest shellfish. See visitlongbeachpeninsula.com.

guests have it all to themselves. Boreas is tucked off of the main road and nestled in the dunes within walking distance of the Discovery Trail and Long Beach Boardwalk. $$–$$$.

The Breakers. WA 103 at 26th Street; (360) 642-4414; breakerslongbeach.com. Four buildings house 122 rooms and suites, making this place a great destination for family lodging. There is an indoor pool and large outdoor hot tub on the property, as well as a children's play area. Beach access is easy; the Breakers is at one end of the Discovery Trail. Walk toward the beach to see *Clark's Tree*, a bronze sculpture emulating a tree that William Clark carved his initials into during Lewis and Clark's visit to Long Beach Peninsula, and which marks the northernmost and westernmost point of their journey. $$.

China Beach Retreat. 222 Robert Gray Dr., Ilwaco; (360) 642-5660; chinabeachretreat .com. China Beach is the perfect place to unwind. Decorated with an eclectic selection of European and Asian antiques and original artwork, and frequently visited by deer, waterfowl, and bald eagles, China Beach Retreat has a view of the mouth of the Columbia River and Baker Bay and offers private spa tubs and gourmet breakfast. With just 3 guest rooms, you may never see another person—aside from the one you bring with you, that is. For even more seclusion, try the Audubon Cottage, a two-story unit that sleeps 2 with an outdoor jetted tub, on the same property. $$$.

Klipsan Beach Cottages. 22617 Pacific Way, Ocean Park; (360) 665-4888; klipsan beachcottages.com. These impeccably kept, classic traditional beach cottages at Klipsan Beach sit on a ridge facing the Pacific Ocean and are surrounded by beautifully landscaped grounds. Well-appointed kitchens, fireplaces, and the ocean nearby—what more do you need? $–$$.

Shelburne Hotel. 4415 Pacific Way, Seaview; (360) 642-2442; theshelburnehotelwa .com. Established in 1896, the Shelburne Hotel is the longest continually operating hotel in Washington State. Four-star dining, a stunning breakfast, and a pub serving fine wines and microbrews distinguish this world-renowned country inn retreat right on the main road up the peninsula. $–$$.

day trip 02

north coast

>>> **three rivers & a sea:**
astoria

astoria

Astoria is the oldest American settlement west of the Rockies. In other words, it's not only the oldest town on the Oregon Coast, but also the oldest in the state and even the entire West Coast. At the same time, it's a forward-thinking and surprisingly hip little city with great culture and dining options. The proximity to Portland means a sense of modernity and cool that, coupled with Astoria's incredible natural beauty, makes this city a charming, atmospheric weekend getaway with many wonderful surprises.

Perched on the Columbia River at one of its widest points, and with two tributary rivers winding around the city limits, Astoria is a hilly city dominated by watery views. The town sits on a steep peninsula, and the 360-degree views of the ocean, rivers, and temperate rain forest that surround Astoria are incredibly beautiful.

Astoria was the first permanent US settlement on the Pacific coast, but eventually Portland, Seattle, and San Francisco surpassed it as the West Coast's main port cities, and Astoria was left to thrive quietly on the pursuits of fishing and logging, albeit with plenty of leftover historical charm. History is all around you in Astoria, which even before the fur trappers was the place that Lewis and Clark overwintered on their overland journey in the early 1800s. Astoria has more historical markers than anywhere else in Oregon and—in a state that isn't very old and is on a rugged coastline with weather that doesn't always treat

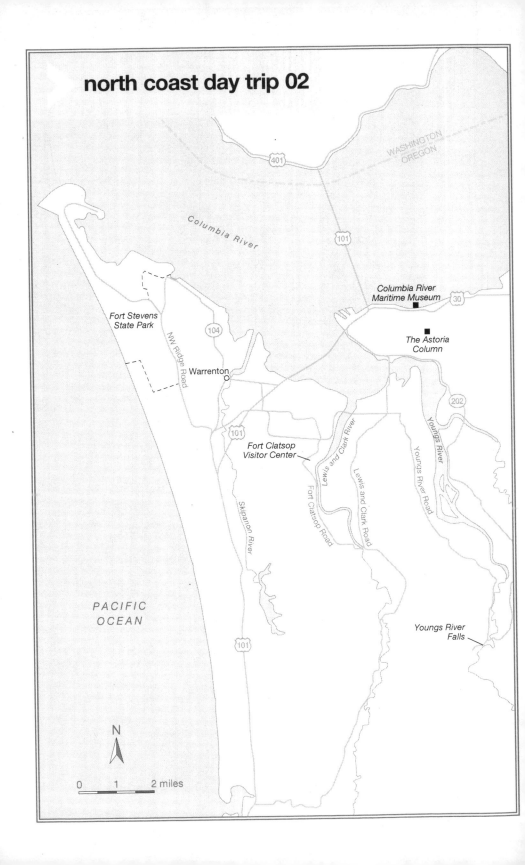

north coast day trip 02

Columbia River

WASHINGTON
OREGON

401

101

Columbia River
Maritime Museum

30

The Astoria
Column

Fort Stevens
State Park

104

NW Ridge Road

Warrenton

202

101

Fort Clatsop
Visitor Center

Lewis and Clark River

Lewis and Clark Road

Youngs River

Youngs River Road

Fort Clatsop Road

Skipanon River

PACIFIC
OCEAN

Youngs River
Falls

101

N

0   1   2 miles

buildings kindly—is known for historic architecture, including hundreds of Victorian homes and a revitalized 1920s-era downtown.

Today, tourism is a primary industry. Lovely shops, all kinds of dining, and many museums dot downtown, which clings to a waterfront that once bustled with salmon fisheries. Walking the Astoria Waterfront is a great way to take in the sweep and scope of the Columbia River. Visit Maritime Memorial Park, the 6th Street Viewing Platform, the 14th Street Pier, and the 17th Street Dock to become familiar with Astoria, a vibrant small city alive with a spectacular landscape, rich past, and classy culture.

getting there

From Portland: Take US 26 W / OR 26 west 73 miles. Merge onto US 101 N toward Seaside/Astoria. Continue north for 22 miles until you reach Astoria.

where to go

Astoria Column. At the top of Coxcomb Drive off 15th Street; (503) 325-2963; astoriacolumn.org. For the best view in town, drive up to the top of Astoria's Coxcomb Drive and then climb another 165 steps on foot to the top of the Astoria Column. The column is an Astoria icon, built in 1926 as the dream child of Ralph Budd, president of the Midwest-based Great Northern Railroad, with support from Vincent Astor, great-grandson of businessman John Jacob Astor, whose Pacific Fur Company settled Astoria. Stunning views of the Columbia River to the north, the Cascade Range to the east, and the Pacific Ocean to the west wow those willing to test their lungs with the climb up the winding staircase. This is a great place to go when you first arrive in Astoria to begin to get the lay of the land. Before you climb, buy a balsawood airplane to fly from the top. Even if you don't choose to climb the column, the views from the parking lot are outstanding. Parking comes with a $5 annual pass; the park is open dawn to dusk.

Astoria Riverfront Trolley. 1 Basin St.; (503) 325-6311; old300.org. Adding to downtown Astoria's charm is this restored 1913 trolley, which makes a 2.6-mile run along the Columbia River. The conductor does his part by narrating to passengers tales of Astoria's history and attractions. You can catch a ride on the trolley from just about anywhere on the riverfront between Basin and 39th Streets. Round-trip ride is $1; an all-day pass is $2. The round-trip takes about an hour. Hours change seasonally and the trolley does not operate in rain; check website.

Clatsop County Historical Society. 714 Exchange St.; (503) 325-2203; cumtux.org. The society has three museums; two are listed here. Call for hours and details.

   The Flavel House. Corner of 8th and Duane Streets. Captain George Flavel was a prominent sea captain and one of the wealthier residents of early Astoria. This quaint Queen Anne Victorian home was built for him in 1885 and features parklike grounds, original Eastlake-style woodwork interiors, and exotic hardwood fire-places with imported tile surrounds.

Heritage Museum. Corner of 16th and Exchange Streets. A historical exhibit includes Chinook and Clatsop Indian baskets and a partially constructed Astoria saloon. Pick up a booklet here to help guide you on a walking tour of Astoria's famous historical homes. The exhibit *The Astor Party and the Founding of Astoria* tells you everything you need to know about Astoria's beginnings.

Columbia River Maritime Museum. 1792 Marine Dr.; (503) 325-2323; crmm.org. Brave souls have been tackling the oceans and rivers by boat for hundreds of years. Here you can explore marine transportation from the age of dugout canoes to sailboats to the present. There are many exhibits: A film introduces the history of life and commerce on the Columbia River. *Crossing the Bar: Perilous Passage* takes an exciting look at the legendary Columbia River entrance, where the forces of the mighty Columbia and the Pacific Ocean meet, creating waves that can exceed 40 feet during bad winter storms. Ancient maps show the ways explorers first envisioned the shape of the world. A massive screen shows NOAA data live. An on-site 3-D theater shows a different film each year. Entry to the *Lightship Columbia* is included with admission; the floating lighthouse is moored outside and offers a glimpse of an early solution to helping seamen navigate the treacherous bar. Open daily 9:30 a.m. to 5 p.m.

Fort Stevens State Park. 100 Peter Iredale Rd., Hammond; (503) 861-3170; oregonstate parks.org. Fort Stevens was the primary military defense installation at the mouth of the Columbia River, serving from the Civil War through World War II. Today the site is a great place to access and walk the beach, as well as catch a glimpse of the wreck of the *Peter Iredale*, an oceangoing ship that was destroyed near the mouth of the Columbia River in the early part of the 20th century. The ship ran aground at Clatsop Beach, striking shore with such force that three masts snapped upon impact. None of the crew of 27 was hurt (including two castaways!), but the ship ended up a total loss. The wreck can still be seen at low tide and makes for a striking scene. Fort Stevens State Park is great for all sorts of recreation, including camping, boating, swimming, picnicking, hiking, and biking. $5 daily fee; camping also available.

Lewis and Clark National Historic Park (Fort Clatsop Unit). 92343 Fort Clatsop Rd.; (503) 861-2471; nps.gov/lewi. Lewis and Clark spent a winter here, hoping that a ship would pass by to return them to their homes on the East Coast. When that didn't happen, in the spring of 1806, they returned the way they'd come—but not before getting a solid taste of a Pacific Northwest winter spent in a fort they built. What will strike you right away, with your own memories of bad weather and close quarters crowding in, is how small the fort is. The facility includes the reconstructed fort, a visitor center and museum, historical exhibits, a canoe landing, a picnic area, trails through the wetlands, and a rain forest of young Sitka

a watery grave

The South Jetty, which sits at the northern tip of **Fort Stevens State Park,** *is a great place to get a view of the infamous* **Columbia River Bar.** *The bar is the place where the Columbia River collides with the Pacific Ocean, and it has taken down hundreds of ships over time. The colliding currents, wind, and massive waves have sunk approximately 2,000 vessels here since 1792, earning the location the nickname* **"Graveyard of the Pacific."** *While you stand on the overlook at the jetty, take a look at the geography around you. Another reason the bar is so treacherous is that the shores of the Columbia River are solid basalt, created from lava flows thousands of years old. These tough rock walls compress and contain the river's flow, forcing it to shoot from the river terminus like water from a fire hose. But all that water does is collide with more water—the incoming tides of the Pacific— hence, the massive waves and terrifying currents that have far too often turned deadly. Massive jetties were constructed over a hundred years ago to try to gain some semblance of control over the water, but the bar remains as dangerous as ever and ships to this day are not allowed to cross without a specially trained and certified bar pilot.*

spruce and western hemlock. During the summer months, experience living-history demonstrations depicting fort activities. Open daily: summer 9 a.m. to 6 p.m.; winter 9 a.m. to 5 p.m.

Oregon Film Museum. 732 Duane St.; (503) 325-2203; oregonfilmmuseum.org. Astoria's beauty and architecture have attracted many to the area, including filmmakers. To celebrate the 25th anniversary of the Steven Spielberg film *The Goonies*, the Oregon Film Museum was born in 2010. Housed in the historic Clatsop County Jail, which was featured in the opening scene of *The Goonies*, the museum is dedicated to preserving the art and legacy of Oregon films and filmmaking. Other movies filmed in Oregon include *Overboard, Short Circuit, The Black Stallion, Kindergarten Cop, Free Willy, Free Willy 2: The Adventure Home, Teenage Mutant Ninja Turtles III, Benji the Hunted, The Ring, The Ring Two, Into the Wild, The Guardian,* and *Cthulhu*. If you happen to be in town on the weekend nearest June 7 of any year, you're in for a special treat: Annually, fans flock to Astoria for the Goonies Day celebration, a weekend of treasure hunting, group truffle shuffles, trivia scavenger hunts, and more. Depending on the year, visitors might experience cast and crew reunions, film screenings, fan gatherings, filming location tours, and much more. Open daily; hours vary seasonally.

where to shop

Astoria Vintage Hardware. 1162 Marine Dr.; (503) 325-1313. The owners met at a flea market, and the rest is history. This business has expanded and moved more than once, always maintaining its immense charm but allowing for even more amazing relics to be displayed. From vintage double front doors to antique furniture to the world's largest "Operation" game, this place is full of fabulous finds. A "Vintage Flea Market" runs the first Sunday of July, Aug, Sept, and Oct.

Chariot Spirit and Home. 1421 Commercial St.; (503) 502-7023; chariothome.com. A combination housewares retailer, interior design studio, and spiritual workshop, Chariot carries vintage and one-of-a-kind housewares for the home and intends to inspire everyone who walks in the door. Classes and workshops are offered here too, in this beautiful space in a classic downtown building storefront.

Josephson's Smokehouse. 106 Marine Dr.; (800) 772-FISH; josephsons.com. For nearly 90 years, Josephson's has sold the finest local smoked, canned, and jerked seafood. At their historic smokehouse, an unequaled variety of seafood is smoked daily, sold at retail fresh from the smokers, packed for individual mail order to customers and restaurants, and shipped worldwide.

Lucy's Books. 348 12th St.; (503) 325-4210; lucys-books.com. Every town needs a charming downtown bookstore, and Lucy's Books is Astoria's answer. Located in the historic Liberty Theater Building, Lucy's welcomes you to linger in two rocking chairs. Whether you are reading or being read to, Lucy's has something for everyone.

who put the "astor" in astoria?

*You know you're a big cheese when a place you've never actually visited is named for you. Without ever setting foot on a single rain-soaked acre of what is now Clatsop County, **John Jacob Astor** founded the Columbia River fur-trading post Fort Astoria in 1811, which also became the first permanent US settlement on the Pacific coast. Astor made quite a lot of money off of the beaver furs of Astoria, but never made a visit himself. Still, his name endures on the map and all over the landscape too. Learn more about John Jacob Astor at the Astoria Column, the Clatsop County Heritage Museum, and the Columbia River Maritime Museum.*

where to eat

Albatross. 1 2nd St.; (503) 325-0033; shipinn-astoria.com. You might just feel like one of Astoria's long-ago mariners here. Cornish pasties, great fish-and-chips, and calamari are served in a true English pub atmosphere. Don't miss the fabulous views of the Columbia River, and, of course, there are lots of great beers on tap. $$.

Astoria Coffeehouse and Bistro. 243 11th St.; (503) 325-1787; astoriacoffeehouse.com. This place looks unassuming, but you will no doubt love your experience here, whether it's for a cup of coffee or an utterly fantastic dinner. Astoria Coffeehouse makes everything from scratch—even the ketchup—and serves Stumptown Roasters coffee; fresh gourmet pastries; homemade soups, salads, and entrees; and a wide variety of hot and cold beverages, plus cocktails, beer, and wine. The decor is funky and cool; don't miss the collection of globes perched on a high shelf around the room. Centrally located right downtown—look for the neon coffee cup on 11th Street. Open 7 days a week for breakfast, lunch, and dinner. $$.

Baked Alaska. 1 12th St.; (503) 325-7414; bakedak.com. Voted "best happy hour" by the locals, this fine dining and public house serves delicious food inspired by the region and the season. Wild, natural, and sustainable fare dominates the menu. Try the wild salmon or the pork shank. Bonus: Baked Alaska overlooks the Columbia River and offers lovely views. Open for lunch and dinner 7 days a week. $$$.

Blue Scorcher Bakery Cafe. 1493 Duane St.; (503) 338-7473; bluescorcher.coop. Operating as a worker collective with the motto "joyful work, delicious food, and strong community," Blue Scorcher creates artisan breads, pastries, and handcrafted seasonal foods using local and organic ingredients. A children's area features a play kitchen and makes this restaurant a natural gathering place for families. Located in the historic Fort George building with views of the Columbia River. (PS: A "scorcher" is a line of bicycles that appeared in the late 1880s, renowned for their speed. Who knew?) Open 7 days a week for breakfast and lunch. $.

Bowpicker. Located across from the Clatsop County Heritage Museum, at the corner of 17th and Duane Streets, in a converted gillnet boat; bowpicker.com. Getting your lunch from this dry-docked but authentic fishing boat will make you feel a bit closer to the sea. Bowpicker is locally famous for their beer-battered albacore tuna and steak fries—the best fish-and-chips in town. Hours vary dramatically, based on the season and the weather. Call ahead. $.

Bridgewater Bistro. 20 Basin St., Ste. A; (503) 325-6777; bridgewaterbistro.com. This well-lit, high-ceilinged, attractive, modern wood-and-metal space in a renovated boatyard on the west end of downtown provides river and bridge views from every table. The menu is composed of creatively prepared seafood, meats, soups, and vegetarian entrees. Choose a table in the family-friendly casual bistro setting or on the fine-dining mezzanine. Open 7 days a week for lunch and dinner; brunch on Sun. $$–$$$.

Buoy Beer Company. 1 8th St.; (503) 325-4540; buoybeer.com. Established in 2013 with a grand opening in 2014, Buoy Beer was the third brewery to open its doors in Astoria. Whether you are a beer drinker or not, Buoy's location in a 90-year-old cannery overlooking the riverfront is worth a visit for the view alone. A floor window in the main dining room gives a view of resting sea lions and is a great distraction for the kids. Try the habanero oyster deviled eggs or chicken Romesco while large vessels passing by keep you company. Open daily at 11 a.m. $–$$.

Carruther's. 1198 Commercial St.; (503) 975-5305; carruthers-restaurant.business.site. This cozy American bistro serves delicious comfort food in a hip environment. From mussels to halibut to peanut butter cheesecake, the dishes are as imaginative as they are delectable. The restaurant is named for the 1920s-era Carruther's Building that it occupies, and the eatery maintains era-appropriate class and style. Open for lunch and dinner daily. $–$$.

Fort George Brewery and Public House. 1483 Duane St.; (503) 325-PINT; fortgeorge brewery.com. Pub food and seafood are served in this popular brewpub built in an incredible old building that was once an auto repair shop. Try the sausage sampler with spicy mustard or the albacore tuna melt. Enjoy live music on some weekends, and outdoor dining season-ally. The beers are plentiful, varied, reliably delicious, and often on tap around the Pacific Northwest, if you don't catch them here. Fort George, by the way, was briefly the name of Astoria, renamed for King George when England seized temporary control during the War of 1812. Open 7 days a week for lunch and dinner. $$.

Frite and Scoop. 175 14th St.; (503) 468-0416; friteandscoop.com. Ice cream and french fries, french fries and ice cream—could there be a better combination? This newish spot on the waterfront makes their own small-batch ice cream and from-scratch Belgian frites from Kennebac potatoes. A large covered seating area makes it easy to stay out of the weather, with a view of the river, while you finish your snack. Hours change seasonally; call ahead. $.

Mo's. 101 15th St.; (971) 704-1750; moschowder.com. Astoria is one of Mo's eight loca-tions, but the only one perched on a pier overlooking the massive Columbia River. The classic Oregon family-owned chowder restaurant delivers meals surrounded by a medley of beach-kitsch decor with a standard but well-prepared seafood-laden menu. Try the hot crab melt or the albacore tuna salad sandwich. Open daily 11 a.m. to 8 p.m. $–$$.

Silver Salmon Grille. 1105 Commercial St.; (503) 338-6640; silversalmongrille.com. The historic Fisher Building that houses this restaurant was built in 1924, but it's got nothing on the bar that sits inside. The Silver Salmon's ornately carved antique bar is 120 years old, is constructed of Scottish cherrywood, and was shipped around Cape Horn in the 1880s. This romantic, historic restaurant in downtown offers great food, drinks, and desserts. Open for lunch and dinner 7 days a week. $$–$$$.

where to stay

Cannery Pier Hotel. 10 Basin St.; (888) 325-4996; cannerypierhotel.com. Built on the site of the former Union Fish Cannery 600 feet over the Columbia River, this hotel is the ultimate in comfort and luxury, Astoria style. Guests, who have up-close and unparalleled views of a real working river, are provided with a list of the ships they should expect to see pass by their windows during their stay, as well as a description of their cargo. Views of the amazing Astoria-Megler Bridge and Cape Disappointment are also impressive. Each room has a private balcony and fireplace; halls are decorated with wonderful historical photographs of Astoria. Complimentary wine and hors d'oeuvres in the evening; continental breakfast in the morning. A free chauffeur-driven limo service uses classic old cars to shuttle you to and from your evening destination, making you feel a bit like royalty. The real star is that big old beautiful river out the window; you'll have a hard time tearing your eyes off of it. Expensive, but worth every penny. $$$+.

Commodore Hotel Astoria. 258 14th St.; (503) 325-4747; commodoreastoria.com. Crisp, modernist rooms are found here in this historic renovated building. The location in the heart of downtown is ideal for exploration. All rooms have a flat-screen TV, radiant heat, and premium bathrobes. Some rooms are pet-friendly. $–$$.

Grandview Bed and Breakfast. 1574 Grand Ave.; (503) 325-5555; grandviewbedandbreakfast.com. This lovely and romantic Victorian house on the Historic Homes Walking Tour features wonderful Columbia River views. Three two-bedroom and 3 one-bedroom lodgings with private baths have lace and floral decor. $–$$.

Hotel Elliott. 357 12th St.; (503) 325-2222; hotelelliott.com. Built in 1924, Hotel Elliott underwent a dramatic 3-year transformation in the early 2000s to expand rooms and glamorize everything, but preserve the classic ambience. This beautifully restored old hotel has a fabulous rooftop terrace, cellar wine bar, and proximity to downtown restaurants. The rooms are designed for relaxed comfort. $$–$$$.

worth more time

The Youngs River is one of the tributary waterways of the Columbia. Ten miles south of Astoria, the river tumbles as a 54-foot waterfall called **Youngs River Falls** into a pool beneath. The trail from the parking lot is short, maybe a 5-minute hike, but be aware that the last stretch down to the pool is steep and rocky. Visitors often swim in the pool in the summer months. This is a great place to witness the immortalization of Oregon places by Oregon-made films, as you might recognize this site from the films *Teenage Mutant Ninja Turtles III* and *Free Willy 2*.

day trip 03

north coast

historic coast:
gearhart, seaside

gearhart

Even back when settlers had barely arrived in the Willamette Valley and hardly recovered from their journey on the Oregon Trail, some were drawn the final 100 miles over the Coast Range to experience the breathtaking beauty of the Oregon Coast. Even the fact that there were no roads didn't daunt these early tourists—vacationers came by water down the Columbia to Astoria and then traveled by stagecoach to the beach.

Gearhart was one of the earliest developments intended mainly for vacationers. Gearhart Park started as a tent town on the other side of Neawanna Creek from Seaside, drawing attention for its quiet, pleasant landscape fun for exploring and picnicking. The charms of tent camping only translated to so many, even back then, and the first hotel was built in 1890, the same year that a passenger railroad was built to connect Astoria to Seaside. Wealthy Portland families traveled eight hours by ferry and rail back then to spend summers at the beach.

Gearhart is rich in Oregon history, though most evidence of past grandeur has been lost to time, or more disastrously, fire. Photos of the first Gearhart Hotel show a grand structure with sweeping covered patios and access directly to the beach. A natatorium stood nearby, and the first golf course, **Gearhart Golf Links,** sprung up in 1892, making it one of the oldest public courses west of the Mississippi. But alas, the beautiful hotel burned to ruin in 1913. Another was built, and then burned just two years later. A third to carry the town

20

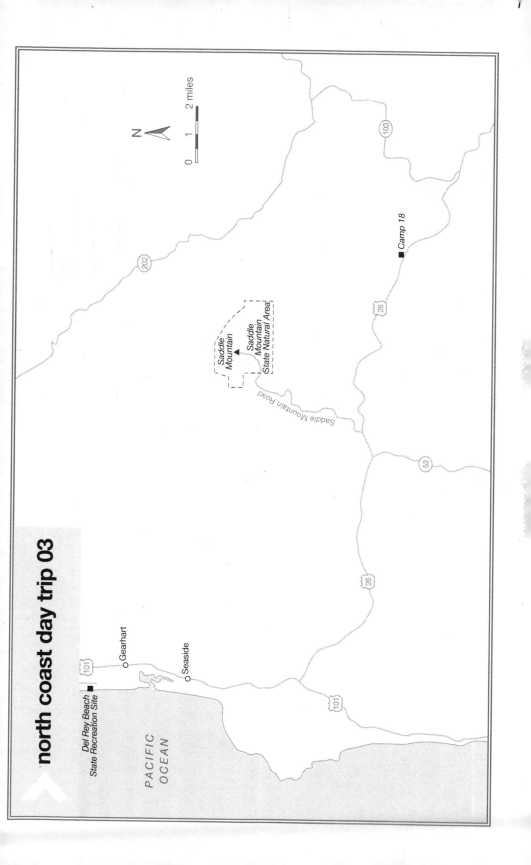

north coast day trip 03

name, and also be connected to the golf club, was built in 1923 and endured until 1972 before being demolished and replaced by condos.

And then Gearhart had no hotel at all, at least not until the McMenamin brothers stepped in. The fourth version of the Hotel Gearhart opened in 2012, adjacent to the golf course. While it is a new building, the McMenamins excel at preserving history, and their hotel and restaurant is the best place in town to see historical photos of the courses and hotels of Gearhart's past.

Gearhart remains the quieter sister to Seaside, drawing families and golfers for peaceful retreats to the sea.

getting there

From Portland: Travel US 26 W 74 miles west out of Portland. Merge with US 101 N / Oregon Coast Highway, traveling north toward Seaside/Astoria. Gearhart is 3 miles north of Seaside on US 101 N.

where to go

Del Rey Beach State Recreation Site. Access at 10th Street, or Fairway Drive and Butterfly Lane. The ocean is just a short walk from Del Rey's quiet, secluded parking area. Or, if you prefer, just drive onto the sand. Motor vehicles are not allowed on all of the beaches in Oregon, which is good news to most people. However, Gearhart is one of the beaches on which you can simply drive right into the fun. From 10th Street north to the jetty of the Columbia River, a 13-mile stretch, is open to vehicles. The first 10 miles, to the Peter Iredale Road exit at Fort Stevens State Park, are open year-round. The remaining miles to the jetty are open mid-September through April. Access begins right in Gearhart. Del Rey is also a great destination for flying a kite, building a sandcastle, picnicking, or catching a divine sunset.

Gearhart Golf Links. 1157 N. Marion Ave.; (503) 738-3538; gearhartgolflinks.com. This exact location is where golf started on the Oregon Coast and, reportedly, anywhere west of the Mississippi. In the late 1800s, a 3-hole links-style golf course was set with tin cans into the seaside meadows. Early visitors to the Hotel Gearhart in the late 1800s crossed the street to play a round. By 1892, golf was a regular pastime for guests and one of the things the hotel was famous for. Gearhart is still known for golf, and the "new" Gearhart Golf Links is a public resort course with 18 holes of spectacular, links-style golf. The course is open 365 days a year.

Highland Golf Course. 33260 Highlands Ln.; (503) 738-5248; highlandsgolfgearhart.com. Nine holes of ocean-view golf are here on this enjoyable course nestled between the dunes and the sea. Easy to walk and play, and a bit more affordable than some golf courses, Highlands is great for the family and for all golf player levels.

where to shop

Gearhart Ironwerks. 1368 Pacific Way; (800) 738-5434; johnemmerlingknives.com. John Emmerling is an artist and metal craftsman with over 25 years' experience in the creative trades. He and his wife moved to Gearhart and opened this little shop, specializing in furniture, lighting, fire screens, and decorative hand-forged work. But it is knives that are Emmerling's specialty, and not just any knives. Stop in the shop just to see his absolutely gorgeous handcrafted chef and hunting knives, raved about by those who purchase and wield them. Call for hours.

A Great Gallery. 576 Pacific Way; (503) 709-2840; agreatgallery.com. Pastel artist Susan Thomas started this gallery after her move from Lake Oswego with her family in 2010, drawn to the quiet community and the sea. The gallery displays and sells her work, which features coastal concepts like the beach; birds including pelicans, puffins, and great blue herons; shells; lighthouses; and more. Hours vary.

Sweet Shop Gearhart. 567 Pacific Way; (503) 739-7338; sweetshopgearhart.com. In a historic building downtown, find this cozy gathering place carrying a few essential provisions—and not just sweets. With an emphasis on local, organic, and homemade items, the shop showcases 32 flavors of ice cream from Cascade Glacier in the Willamette Valley, coffee from Longbottom Coffee (Hillsboro) and Sleepy Monk Organic Coffee (Cannon Beach), and an extensive selection of Oregon and Washington wines. Stop in and pick up some items to take to the beach.

the famous beard

Celebrated chef, author, teacher, and TV personality James Beard grew up in Portland, and his family had a beach house in Gearhart. He was one of the first to celebrate the foods of the Pacific Northwest, including salmon, shellfish, game meats, berries, and wild plants. Beard died in New York City in 1985, but his ashes were spread here in Gearhart, at the childhood getaway he loved so much. In honor of him, taste something harvested or grown locally during your Oregon Coast visit. Many unique foods are not only available but also celebrated here, partly because of Beard's influence. You might never get another chance to try an oyster or a rockfish harvested within sight of the restaurant it's prepared in—dig in!

where to eat

Pacific Way Bakery & Cafe. 601 Pacific Way; (503) 738-0245; pacificwaybakery-cafe
.com. This historic building was constructed in 1929 first as a mom-and-pop grocery story,
and was a post office, realty office, and insurance office over the years. Since 1988, it's
been this little cafe, serving baked goods and pastries in the morning and lunch and dinner
the rest of the day. Charming inside and out, Pacific Way serves salads and sandwiches
for lunch and dinner classics like halibut and pork chops at night. The restaurant is open 5
days a week year-round (typically closed Tues and Wed); the bakery is open 5 days a week
in the summer season only (opening only on Sat and Sun the remainder of the year). $–$$.

where to eat & stay

McMenamins Gearhart Hotel and Sand Trap Pub. 1157 N. Marion Ave.; (503) 717-
8159; mcmenamins.com/gearhart-hotel. The McMenamin brothers took over management
of the Sand Trap Pub on the Gearhart Golf Links course in 2008, serving burgers and beers
to hungry golfers. They then brought a hotel back to Gearhart in 2012 with the addition of
18 guest rooms over the pub. In 2018, they upped the ante again with the construction of
an annex, adding 16 more rooms in an adjacent building. The entire property is new construction, but the classic coastal wooden shingles and white trim mirror the series of historic
Gearhart Hotels of the past. Art throughout the property depicts Gearhart history, including
golf tournaments and night putting. Longtime Gearhart visitor James Beard, author and
international gourmet, is honored in art as well. The hotel overlooks the golf course, in the
meadows inland from the ocean, but it is just a short walk to the beach. The Sand Trap Pub
serves breakfast, lunch, and dinner every day. In season, dine outside by the fire pit. Downstairs on the green is the Pot Bunker Bar, a cozy lair featuring antique golf clubs. $$–$$$.

seaside

As with Gearhart, Seaside sprung into existence largely due to vacationers. The first bunk-
house opened in 1850, and a tourist town was born. Back then, not surprisingly, Seaside
beach vacations were a luxury primarily available to the prosperous. Around the turn of the
century, the wealthy and fashionable alone made the trip to Seaside, and when they did,
they stayed in elegant comfort. The trek was generally made from Portland via train; the
mode of transportation became known as the "Daddy Train," as fathers would use it to join
their families on weekends throughout the summer.

Eventually, roads went in, more people ventured to the ocean, and services began
to pop up for the common family. Today, Seaside continues to be one of the most visited
places on the Oregon Coast, and is also considered one of the most accessible. Everything
is within walking distance and many places are wheelchair accessible, including the 1.5-mile
beachfront Promenade, making it easy for all to explore.

Visitors can still choose pricey accommodations, but there are plenty affordable options available too. Seaside is the rare Oregon Coast city with amenities more common to East Coast beach towns, including a paved walkway or the "Prom," as locals call it, a carousel, and an arcade. In the summer, the streets are packed with families carrying bags of saltwater taffy and ice cream cones, waiting for their turn at the bumper cars.

Of course, the amenities that brought visitors here in the first place remain—the beach and the ocean. For those who require no more than fresh air and sand in their toes for entertainment, Seaside is a great place to visit.

getting there

Seaside is 3 miles south of Gearhart.

where to go

Entertainment centers. When it rains, many Seaside tourists head indoors. In that case, there are a few options—eat, shop, or hit one of the entertainment centers. These three are very popular destinations, rain or shine:

Funland Entertainment Center. 201 Broadway; (503) 738-7361; funlandseaside .com. Just about every video and arcade game you can hope for is here, and then some. Bumper cars and whale racing are here too. On weekends, and throughout the summer, try your hand at Fascination—a game that dates back to the 1920s. Seaside's Fascination parlor is just one of fewer than a dozen remaining in the country. Opens at 9 a.m. daily.

Gearhart Bowl & Fultano's Pizza. 3518 N US 101, Gearhart; (503) 738-5333; gearhartbowl.com. This facility underwent a major renovation project in 2014 and has become a quick hit with locals. Features 12 bowling lanes, arcade games, projection television screens, pizza, and a full-service lounge.

Interstate Amusement Co. 110 Broadway; (503) 738-5540. Bumper cars, tilt-a-whirl, and miniature golf. The snack bar serves "pronto pup" hot dogs, slushies, soft-serve ice cream cones, chips, and other snacks. Hours vary seasonally.

The Times Theatre and Public House. 133 Broadway; (503) 739-7188; timestheatre .com. This downtown Seaside institution originally opened in 1940, closed in 1989, and was brought back to life in 2019 as an independent cinema and craft brewpub. Come and see second-run classics at discounted prices and live sporting events like college and NFL football, while noshing on comfort-food favorites such as fried dill pickle chips, cheese curds, grilled cheese sandwiches, loaded chili dogs, homemade mac and cheese, and a full slate of specialty burgers.

Seaside Aquarium. 200 N Prom; (503) 738-6211; seasideaquarium.com. Founded in 1937, the Seaside Aquarium is one of the oldest on the West Coast. This historic building on the waterfront is full of fun discoveries, including underwater areas that provide a glimpse of a fascinating world of unusual and rare life forms. An underwater viewing tank and a touch tank with sea anemones, sandpaper-textured starfish, and prickly sea urchins are beautiful and full of life. Don't miss the family of harbor seals—which, in some years, includes baby seal pups in the spring. Open daily at 9 a.m. (winter and summer closing hours may vary).

Seaside Museum, Historical Society, and Butterfield Cottage. 570 Necanicum Dr.; (503) 738-7065; seasideoregonmuseum.org. This cool old museum includes exhibits on the history of Native Americans in the Seaside area, logging, and local hotels and tourism. The Seaside Museum is the only beach cottage museum in Oregon, existing in and interpreting the Butterfield Cottage to the era circa 1912. Built in 1880 as a beach cottage for a wealthy Portlander, the Butterfield Cottage sits on beautiful grounds. The adjacent gift shop sells all sorts of fun gifts and souvenirs like historic photos. Open Mon through Sat year-round, but call for specific hours.

Seaside Promenade and Turnaround. Seaside's Broadway Street leads west directly to the Seaside Turnaround, the epicenter of Seaside, with a magnificent view of the Pacific Ocean and a statue of Meriwether Lewis and William Clark that commemorates the explorers' historic expedition. Intersecting the turnaround is the popular Promenade, or Prom, a 1.5-mile paved walkway that leads walkers, runners, and cyclists past grand Seaside homes on one side and gorgeous dunes and beach views on the other. Everybody loves the Prom, which is lined with benches for relaxing.

run, play, party

The **Hood to Coast Relay,** considered to be the world's largest annual relay, begins on the slopes of Mount Hood and finishes on the beach at Seaside. The event brings 12,000 runners, their support teams, race staff, and volunteers to this small city each year—numbers that can total 50,000. In effect, a second city is temporarily created to accommodate the masses. Dozens of tents are erected on the beach, a footbridge is installed over US 101, and local businesses stock way up on beer and hot dogs. Depending on your point of view, race weekend— the last full weekend before Labor Day—might be a great time to visit Seaside or a great time to avoid Seaside. One thing is for sure, with 50,000 extra people in town, this is where the party is. See hoodtocoast.com.

Wheel Fun Rentals. 407 S Holladay Dr.; (503) 738-8447; wheelfunrentals.com. At Wheel Fun, you can rent just about anything. Set yourself loose on the streets of Seaside in an electric fun car, including mini-Hummers, mopeds, and a 1923 Ford Roadster. Pedal-powered options include single, double, and triple surrey bikes, kids' bikes, tandems, coupes, choppers, and cruiser bicycles. You can even rent kayaks, boogie boards, surfboards, baby joggers, and sandcastle kits. Whatever your beach vacation can't live without, these folks have. Rental prices are $10 to $85 per hour. Summer hours: open daily 9 a.m. to sunset. Winter hours: varied, weather permitting.

where to shop

Beach Books. 616 Broadway; (503) 738-3500; beachbooks37.com. While many independent booksellers have closed up shop, this hideaway expanded operations in 2013. Located in the heart of the Gilbert District, with an adjacent bakery and coffee shop and near a sushi bar and two pubs, Beach Books features many regional authors. Complete with lots of natural light, the location's upstairs often holds book signings, art exhibits, and readings. Open 7 days a week; hours vary.

Seaside Carousel Mall. 300 Broadway; (503) 738-6728; seasidecarouselmall.com. Everyone loves a carousel. Twenty unique shops surround a full-size classic carousel in this cheery, colorful mall. Shops offer dining, snacks, coffee, specialty gifts, art, imports, framing, kites, games, clothing, jewelry, toys, candies, ice cream, old-time photos and portraits, and much more. The carousel horses are replicas of original hand-carved vintage carousel horses from the early 1900s. Open 7 days a week, though hours change seasonally.

Seaside Outlet Center. 1111 N. Roosevelt; (503) 717-1603; seasideoutlets.com. A shopping destination featuring designer labels and name-brand merchandise at factory-direct prices. Over 100,000 square feet of saving, shopping, food, fun, and more is located just a few blocks from the beach along US 101 and 12th Avenue. Open 7 days a week; hours can vary during the winter months.

where to eat

The Bridgetender. 554 Broadway; (503) 738-8002. Sometimes there's nothing better than whiling away an afternoon in a classic old-style bar. The Bridgetender is friendly, dark, busy but not too busy, and boasts the twin pleasures of pool tables and inexpensive cold beer. The shingled wood exterior and red wooden sign stand out, and the Necanicum River flows by easily outside. Kick back and stay a while. $.

Dough Dough Bakery and Fermentation Station. 8 N Holladay; (503) 739-7660. With the closure of Harrison's Bakery along Broadway many years ago, Seaside lacked a true local bakery. That changed in 2017 when a local couple opened Dough Dough, much to the delight of locals and visitors. Sitting adjacent to Beach Books and among several other fun shops and restaurants in the Gilbert District, the bakery features sweet treats, daily lunch specials, and a weekend of experimentation with the Fermentation Station on Fri through Sun nights. An in-house pantry also features many can't-find items for the gourmet home chef. Open for breakfast, lunch, and weekend dinner. Closed Wed and Thurs. $–$$$.

Maggie's on the Prom Restaurant. 581 S Prom; (503) 738-6403; theseasideinn.com. Located on the main floor of the Seaside Oceanfront Inn, Maggie's is a favorite for locals and tourists alike. Guests enjoy stunning views of the Pacific Ocean and Tillamook Head. The restaurant decor is Northwest contemporary with a river rock fireplace, solid wood tables and chairs, box-beamed 10-foot ceilings, wrapped windows, and custom millwork. Outdoor dining is available. The seasonal menus offer fresh seafood, salads, sandwiches, chowder and soups, pasta dishes, specialty poultry and meat dishes, vegetarian and gluten-free dishes, and desserts. Maggie's has a large bar. Reservations are recommended. Open for lunch and dinner daily. $$–$$$.

Nonni's Italian Bistro. 831 Broadway; (503) 738-4264; nonnisitalianbistro.com. This little restaurant only seats a few lucky diners at a time—come early to ensure your spot for excellent Italian food inspired by the owner and chef's family. Cannelloni, linguine, and the usuals are accented with plenty of local produce and seafood. Don't miss the panna cotta and tiramisu. Open 7 days a week for dinner. $$–$$$.

Norma's Seafood & Steak. 20 N Columbia St.; (503) 738-4331; normasoceandiner.com. Norma's has been a Seaside standard since 1976. This restaurant's food has been called "best beach fare," "unpretentious," and "best road food." Simply prepared and excellent seafood, steaks, and pasta dishes are served for lunch and dinner daily in a spacious and comfortable room. Dinners include your choice of a cup of Norma's world-famous clam chowder or dinner salad with shrimp. $$–$$$.

Osprey Cafe. 2281 Beach Dr.; (503) 739-7054; facebook.com/ospreycafe. One of Seaside's more popular spots on the quieter south end, Osprey serves breakfast all day and a lunch menu from 11:30 until close. Located just off of Avenue U (at the south end of the Prom), the menu includes items with a Latin American flair. Try *arroz con pollo* and *lomo saltado* or a flavorful omelet. Open 7:30 a.m. to 3 p.m., 7 days a week. $–$$.

Seaside Brewing Company. 851 Broadway; (503) 717-5451; seasidebrewery.com. Seaside Brewing Company opened in June 2012 nearly 100 years after the building it occupies was established as Seaside City Hall and the old city jail. A year after opening, operations expanded from a nano-brewery to a full-fledged barrel system—and it's been uphill ever since. Featuring standard pub food and a minimum of four SBC brews (including the lovely Lockup IPA), the selection of beer also includes many other Oregon suds. Family-friendly, and yet maybe the only place in Oregon where you can hear old-timers boast they were thrown in jail for drinking too much in the same room they are currently drinking in. Open for lunch and dinner 7 days a week. $–$$.

Zinger's Homemade Ice Cream. 210 Broadway; (503) 738-3939; zingersicecream.com. Zinger's is a true mom-and-pop shop, family run and only open seasonally. It's the only place in town that makes its own homemade ice cream with ultra-premium 16 percent butterfat that is fresh, smooth, sweet, and creamy. Twenty-four flavors are made, and rotated, so that visitors can try everything over the course of a season. Try butter brickle, eggnog, blue moon, black walnut . . . and many, many more. Call for hours. Cash only. $.

where to stay

Ashore Hotel. 125 Oceanway St.; (503) 568-7506; ashorehotel.com. Once standing as the old Sundowner hotel, this just-off-the-beach property was completely renovated in 2014. Simple, comfortable, and chic, Ashore is perfect for a couple's getaway and features a small soaking pool, a bar, and evening bites. $–$$.

Gilbert Inn. 341 Beach Dr.; (800) 507-2714; gilbertinn.com. The Gilbert Inn is a romantic Queen Anne Victorian home built in 1892 now functioning as a bed-and-breakfast. Rooms are fancy and floral. Only 300 feet from the Prom and 1 block south of Broadway, the location is as convenient as it is luxurious and beautiful. No children, smokers, or pets. $–$$$.

Inn at the Prom. 341 S Prom; (800) 507-2714; innattheprom.com. Oceanfront rooms on the Promenade with views of the Pacific Ocean and Tillamook Head make this renovated lodging a great place to relax and enjoy your Seaside stay. Fireplaces and Jacuzzi tubs will mellow you out; fall asleep to the sound of the waves. Beach toys and chairs are available on loan. $–$$.

River Inn at Seaside. 531 Avenue A; (503) 717-5744; riverinnatseaside.com. The River Inn at Seaside is the newest property in town and offers 48 rooms ideal for families or couples. Artwork throughout the four-level property was locally curated, with each of the floors dedicated to a different artist. Breakfast is included, and a kids' play area out back complements the family-friendly town. $–$$.

worth more time

As you drive to or from Portland to Seaside, consider a mountain hike and a stop at a classic museum/restaurant commemorating the region's logging history.

    Saddle Mountain (off US 26 W, 8 miles northeast of Necanicum Junction) is the highest point in northwest Oregon and one of the most popular hikes in the state. That's because it's easy to get to, traverses flower-filled meadows unparalleled in this part of the state, and boasts a view on top that stretches from the ocean to the mouth of the Columbia River to the Cascades. A 5.2-mile round-trip hike to the top through rough terrain and steep grades makes for challenging climbing, but you'll be so busy marveling at the natural beauty that you won't mind. As you climb to the rocky summit, gaze upon mature forest and fields of wildflowers. The view from the apex is a floral show that only exists at that elevation. The temperature is very different at the summit than in the parking lot, so come prepared with a jacket.

Stop for a meal and some old-time learning at **Camp 18 Museum and Restaurant** (42362 US 26, Elsie; 800-874-1810; camp18restaurant.com). This massive wood building—part museum, part restaurant—includes an 85-foot ridgepole that's the largest such piece in the US and weighs approximately 25 tons, cool wood carvings, two fireplaces built with approximately 50 tons of rock found locally, and a fireplace mantel of solid black walnut. The logging museum exists inside and out and includes a huge collection of old logging equipment, including multiple steam donkeys, a large bandsaw from a sawmill, a self-propelled Ohio steam crane, and Caterpillar-style tracked vehicles that worked in the woods. If this doesn't do it for you, hit the restaurant, which features log-cabin-like decor including a burl table entirely carved from one hunk of wood. The menu would fill up any logger with rib-sticking dishes like ribs, pork chops, sirloin steak, and fish-and-chips. For breakfast, try one of Camp 18's famous cinnamon rolls. They're so big you're definitely going to need some help.

day trip 04

north coast

>>> **resident artist:**
cannon beach

cannon beach

Cannon Beach is Oregon's resident artist. Galleries abound, in each a plethora of eclectic artistic talent, and this little city has been voted one of the 100 best art towns in the United States. Cannon Beach offers all of the other things a coastal town should too—stunning beach walks, tasty foods and beverages, kites to fly, sandcastles to build, and rooms with a view.

As for the cannons of Cannon Beach, you can catch a glimpse of them too. In 1846, the US Naval schooner *Shark,* part of a surveying fleet, arrived off the mouth of the Columbia River. The ship landed in Astoria and, after a month, disembarked again only to encounter troubled waters and run up against rocks. The captain ordered the jettison of all cannons, and ultimately several washed ashore south of Cannon Beach at Arch Cape. One is displayed at the Cannon Beach History Center and Museum, and in recent years efforts have been made to preserve it from the effects of time and rust.

Interestingly, two more cannons were uncovered. In February 2008 after an especially low tide, the sand had been washed away from the beach at Arch Cape to reveal two cannons, presumably also from the wreck of the *Shark.* Not only did the event underscore Cannon Beach's name, but it also proved that history has a way of staking its claim on even the most modern and artistic city.

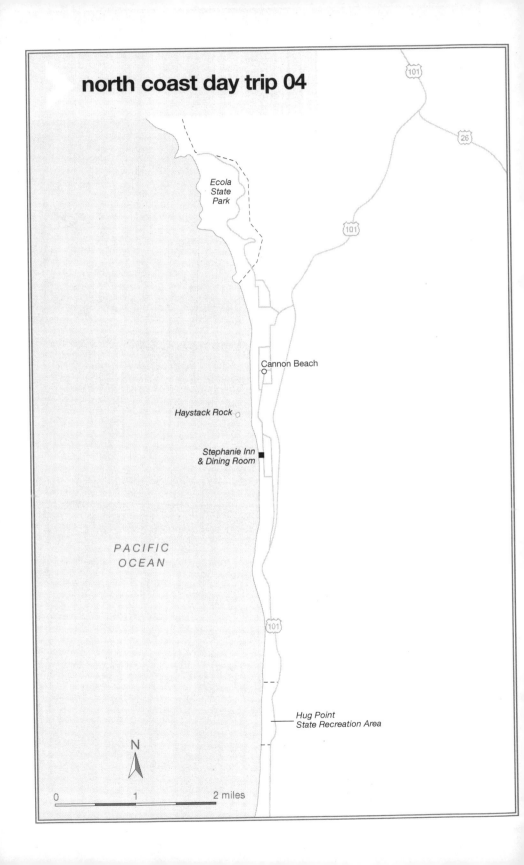

north coast day trip 04

Ecola
State
Park

Cannon Beach

Haystack Rock

Stephanie Inn
& Dining Room

PACIFIC
OCEAN

Hug Point
State Recreation Area

N

0   1   2 miles

getting there

From Portland: Take OR 26 / US 26 W west 73 miles until you reach US 101 S / Oregon Coast Highway. Turn south on US 101 and proceed 4.3 miles to the Cannon Beach exits. Follow signs into town.

where to go

Cannon Beach History Center and Museum. 1387 South Spruce St.; (503) 436-9301; cbhistory.org. Before and after the cannons, Cannon Beach has a very interesting history. This museum features a Native American longhouse, a rotating quilt show, concerts, lectures, and more. There's also information to be found here about the history center's fabulous, well-marked historical walking tour of Cannon Beach, which focuses on buildings in the downtown area. Open every day but Tues. Free admission.

Ecola State Park. Off US 101, 2 miles north of Cannon Beach; oregonstateparks.org/park_188. One of the Oregon Coast's more dramatic headlands, Ecola offers sweeping bird's-eye views of the Pacific Ocean. A paved road leads from Cannon Beach to climb through the thick forest. After winding through Sitka spruce, visitors emerge to a gorgeous view of the Pacific Ocean. Hiking, picnicking, and exploration of the Clatsop Loop Interpretive Trail are all fun things to do at Ecola State Park. Surfers enjoy Indian Beach and tide pool aficionados do too. Migrating whales pass by in winter and spring, and wildlife and birds are here year-round.

Ecola is also the ideal location from which to spot **"Terrible Tilly" Tillamook Rock Lighthouse,** located 1 mile offshore of Tillamook Head Beach. The lighthouse is nicknamed Terrible Tilly because of its location on a rock in the middle of the tumultuous Pacific Ocean. The now-decommissioned lighthouse was built in 1881 by the US Army Corps of Engineers, and lighthouse keepers actually had to be hoisted onto the rock with a derrick. The lighthouse was shut down in 1957 when it had become the most expensive US lighthouse to operate. You can't visit Tilly, but you can enjoy her from safe vantage points, Cannon Beach or Ecola State Park. Ecola State Park daily use $5 permits can be purchased on-site, or display an annual Oregon State Parks permit.

Haystack Rock. Haystack Rock is one of Oregon's iconic symbols, featured on postcards and book covers and in many movies, including *The Goonies*, *Kindergarten Cop*, and *Sometimes a Great Notion*. The 235-foot-tall monolith (or sea stack) rock formation sits just offshore at Cannon Beach and is intertidal, meaning it can be reached by land on foot during low tides. Get a tide table to plan your trip to the popular tourist destination (minus or low tides are optimal). The tide pools here are home to many animals, including starfish, sea anemones, crabs, limpets, and sea slugs. The rock is also home to many seabirds, including terns and puffins. During the summer, volunteer interpreters are on the beach at low tide. Words of warning: The sea life that Haystack shelters is fragile. Treat it with care and do not step on sea life. Stay on sand and bare rocks only. Also pay attention to the tide; people each year become temporarily trapped on Haystack Rock when high tide returns.

Hug Point State Recreation Area. 4 miles south of Cannon Beach on US 101. Before the highway was built, stagecoaches used to run along the beach here, but even at low tide, there wasn't a lot of room, and they had to "hug" the point. North of the parking area at this site you can still walk along the original trail carved into the point. Look for the hidden waterfall around a small headland, and caves carved into cliffs. The view north from Hug Point includes Silver Point Rock and Cannon Beach's famous offshore icon, Haystack Rock. Be careful here—the tide can sneak up on you.

where to shop

Art galleries. A visitor could make an entire day trip out of just Cannon Beach's art galleries. We couldn't list them all here, but this is a start. Bring your favorite art critic and your credit cards. Call for hours—many coastal establishments close up shop for a couple of midweek days in the winter off-season.

Bronze Coast Gallery. 224 N Hemlock St., Ste. 2; (503) 436-1055; bronzecoast gallery.com. Specializing in limited edition bronze sculptures, the Bronze Coast Gallery has been in Cannon Beach for more than 25 years and has become one of the Oregon Coast's premier fine art galleries. The gallery also spotlights original painting, photography, and gicleé reproductions and features more than 30 award-winning regional, national, and international artists.

DragonFire Studio and Gallery. 123 S Hemlock St., Ste. 106; (503) 436-1533; dragonfirestudio.com. DragonFire offers surprisingly affordable original art by local, regional, and national artists in media ranging from paint to fiber to metal. Seasonal 2- and 3-day workshops in everything from portrait composition to watercolors are offered, and live music occasionally accompanies the art.

IceFire Glassworks. 116 E Gower St.; (888) 423-3545; cbgallerygroup.com/ icefire-glassworks. Glass art is a particular favorite of mine. It seems to fit even better at the beach, where the sparkle of the sea complements the beauty of blown and sculpted glassworks, here by artists James Kingwell, Suzanne Kindland, Michelle Kaptur, and Mark Gordon.

Modern Villa Gallery. 224 N Hemlock St., Ste. 6; (503) 436-2428; modernvilla gallery.com. Paintings by Josef Kote, Sarah Goodnough, Anne Packard, and others brighten the walls of this contemporary gallery, and maybe your house next.

White Bird Gallery. 251 N Hemlock St.; (503) 436-2681; whitebirdgallery.com. One of the first galleries to fully incorporate fine art with fine craft, White Bird has been making a mark on the Cannon Beach art scene since 1971.

beach art

For 55 years, Cannon Beach has hosted a sandcastle building contest in June. Everyone is invited to enter, from 6-years-and-under "Sand Fleas" to more experienced "Sand Masters." The weekend also includes a night parade, beach bonfire, live music, and a 5K run and walk. Given that Cannon Beach is repeatedly voted one of the best beaches in the US, it's worth coming on down to the shore and crafting a masterpiece out of sand any old time. See cannonbeach.org for more information.

Center Diamond. 1065 S Hemlock St.; (503) 436-0833; centerdiamond.com. A favorite with quilters and textile artists, Center Diamond offers special contemporary fabrics including a large selection of batiks, Asian, and seashore-related designs. Open daily except holidays.

Dena's Shop on the Corner. 123 S Hemlock St., Ste. 101; (503) 436-1275; denasshop .com. Higher-end contemporary women's clothing in a charming atmosphere. You'll also find jewelry, shoes, and great customer service here. Open 7 days a week.

Found. 1287 S Hemlock St.; (503) 436-1812. A great mix of antiques, repurposed objects, cool artisan jewelry, artwork, stained glass, furniture, and tabletop finds. Found's finds run with a beachy theme—this is the place to find something to decorate your beach house or remind you of your beach vacation once you get back home.

La Luna Loca. 107 N Hemlock St.; (503) 436-0774; lalunaloca.com. The moon may or may not be crazy, but you'd be not to stop in and see La Luna Loca's handcrafts and fair-trade items. Artisan-made clothing, sarongs, jewelry, and decor beat the rhythm of distant lands.

Maggie and Henry. 172 N Hemlock St.; (503) 436-1718; maggieandhenry.com. Henry's used to be a small imprinted sportswear store. Maggie's specialized in casual women's fashion. Then Maggie and Henry got married. Maggie and Henry is a blend of the two original stores, providing casual comfort for both women and men. Open 7 days a week; hours vary seasonally.

where to eat

Cannon Beach Hardware & Public House. 1235 S Hemlock St.; (503) 436-4086; cannon beachhardware.com. Nicknamed "Screw and Brew" by locals, this destination holds the unique distinction of being a place to grab hardware supplies and a pint of beer, simultaneously. The menu features burgers, hot dogs, barbecue pulled pork, an ahi salad, and, most popularly, Cajun-flavored tater tots. A full cocktail bar and wine are also available. The atmosphere is casual, fun, and family-friendly. Sit in a decommissioned airplane or pickup truck seat next to a display of kites or dog leashes for sale, while sipping a local microbrew and eavesdropping on the conversations of the locals that love this place. Open for lunch and dinner Thurs through Tues. $–$$.

Driftwood Inn Restaurant and Lounge. 179 N Hemlock St.; (503) 436-2439; driftwood cannonbeach.com. Locals' favorite for seafood and steaks for over 70 years. The exterior has a Bavarian flavor, and an outdoor patio has become prime real estate for happy diners, especially on sunny summer afternoons. Try the salmon, filet mignon, or steamed clams. Open daily for lunch and dinner. $$–$$$.

EVOO Cooking School. 188 S Hemlock St.; (503) 436-8555; evoo.biz. EVOO is less like your usual evening out and more like purchasing a ticket to a live show—one at which you learn something and are fed a delicious dinner. EVOO is named for a frequently used ingredient, extra virgin olive oil. Chefs Lenore and Bob Neroni took years of culinary experience and a desire to live at the Oregon Coast and opened EVOO in 2004. Their dinner shows in three acts celebrate the local bounty of coastal rivers, oceans, fields, trees, and vines. Guests gather around the chefs' kitchen-bar and watch the preparation of three full-meal courses paired with three wines, followed by a great dessert. Their hope is to entertain and inspire guests to re-create great foods and local flavors in their own lives. A lively discussion about food and wine comes with the experience too. See their website for offerings and availability. $$$.

The Irish Table. 1235 S Hemlock St.; (503) 436 0708; theirishtable.com. Chef and owner Crystal Corbin's daily menus are highlighted by homemade soups, soda bread, and fresh fish. A variety of whiskeys, wine, and Irish beers on tap accompany delicious dishes. Irish classics like shepherd's pie and Irish stew are offered alongside a fresh fish-of-the-day and

a sea-foodie's dream

In recent years, as the foodie culture has blossomed nationwide, the celebration of Oregon Coast foods has grown from a casual given to a devoted ritual. Two events have sprung up in Cannon Beach to celebrate local foods: **Savor Cannon Beach: A Wine and Culinary Festival** *in March and the* **North Coast Culinary Fest** *in May. See chef demonstrations, taste dozens of regional wines, try Dungeness crab and other delights fresh from the sea, and mingle with other seafood-lovers at these multiday events. Miss the festivals? No problem. Year-round, Cannon Beach offers a seat at the table at EVOO Cooking School and many innovative, local-food-inspired restaurants.*

curried mussels at this Pacific Northwest–British Isles fusion spot. (The building is also home to Sleepy Monk Coffee Roasters; see below). Closed Wed and Thurs. $$.

Newman's at 988. 988 S Hemlock St.; (503) 436-1151; newmansat988.com. Newman's at 988 serves classic French/Italian cuisine with a focus on the Piedmont and Genoa areas of Italy. The restaurant serves an à la carte menu as well as a chef's prix fixe menu that changes nightly. Chef Newman uses the finest, freshest ingredients the North Coast has to offer and serves them in an intimate dining atmosphere enhanced by the music of legendary singers such as Frank Sinatra and Tony Bennett. Hours vary seasonally. $$$.

Sleepy Monk Coffee Roasters. 1235 S Hemlock St.; 503-436-2796; sleepymonkcoffee.com. It's not common for two restaurants to occupy one building, but in a coastal town with variable seasonal business, and considering one rent for two different concepts, it might be just plain brilliant. This small, two-room building has two personalities: Sleepy Monk by day, Irish Table by night. At Sleepy Monk, acquire a cup of fresh-roasted organic coffee with names like Monastery Blend and Fiddler's Fusion. You can also take a bag away with you or order it online and have it shipped to your home. Closed Wed. $–$$.

Sweet Basil's Cafe. 271 N Hemlock St.; (503) 436-1539; cafesweetbasils.com. Chef John Sowa conceived Sweet Basil's as a change in his own lifestyle and diet, after cooking Cajun food for years. We all get to benefit from his "fork in the road." Natural, organic, and wild ingredients go into healthy foods that still excite the palate. A nice selection of vegetarian and vegan choices as well as seafood, poultry, and pork dishes by way of salads, cold and hot sandwiches, wraps, panini, and fusion dishes all tickle the taste buds. Open for lunch and dinner Wed through Sun. $–$$.

where to stay

Blue Gull Inn. 632 S Hemlock St.; (800) 559-0893; bluegullinn.net. Cannon Beach's hacienda by the sea, the Blue Gull brings a little Mexico to Cannon Beach. Each cottage has handcrafted wooden furniture made in the Blue Gull's own woodshop, and is located around a central courtyard with a Spanish-style fountain. $–$$.

The Lodges at Cannon Beach. 132 E Surfcrest Ave.; (503) 440-6310; lodgesatcannonbeach.com. The lodges are beautiful, fully furnished Cannon Beach townhomes with state-of-the-art kitchens, great rooms, and open floor plans. Units with 2 or 3 bedrooms accommodate up to 6 adults; furnishings are warm, cozy, and comfortable. $$$.

The Ocean Lodge. 2864 S Pacific St.; (503) 436-2241; theoceanlodge.com. One of the loveliest and most hospitable inns on the whole coast. With hints of a 1940s beach resort, the Ocean Lodge is great place for simple family fun and nostalgic pleasure. Amenities like a library of games and books on-site and a cookie jar aim to please all generations. $$–$$$.

Sea Sprite. 280 Nebesna; (866) 828-1050; seasprite.com. Three great locations—Sea Sprite at Haystack Rock, Sea Sprite on the Estuary, and Sea Sprite Vacation Rentals—with one great sense of beachside charm. Sea Sprite at Haystack Rock offers oceanfront views, while Sea Sprite at the Estuary sits on scenic Ecola Creek with plenty of wildlife viewing. Two additional vacation rental cottages sleep up to 6. $$–$$$.

The Stephanie Inn. 2740 S Pacific St.; (855) 977-2444; stephanieinn.com. The Stephanie Inn is known in Oregon for luxury and romance. With views of majestic Haystack Rock, the Pacific Ocean, and the lovely Oregon Coast Range, the oceanfront Stephanie Inn combines the charm and casual elegance of a New England country inn with the sophistication of a boutique resort hotel. The four-star Stephanie Inn Dining Room serves a complimentary breakfast buffet each morning, and the chef prepares a 5-course dinner nightly, which features the freshest in seasonal Northwest ingredients. $$–$$$.

day trip 05

north coast

down by the bay:
manzanita, nehalem, wheeler

manzanita

Manzanita is a beloved destination for many longtime visitors. Like Cannon Beach, Manzanita is an artsy town with a wide sandy beach, easy walkability, and oodles of charming wood-shake buildings. But Manzanita is just a little bit smaller and a little bit mellower than its cousins to the north. As a destination, it flew under the radar for a while, and while the town has most definitely been discovered now, it holds its quiet past. It's easy to feel relaxed and comfortable wandering around this small, lovely town.

A lot of the appeal has to do with Manzanita's singular charm. Maybe it's the single street that leads from Highway 101 directly to the ocean. Nearly everything shop- and service-wise in Manzanita is located on Laneda Avenue, the town's main business street. It leads to the sea and a large, flat beach just begging for a stroll. Maybe it's the lovely green landscaping around town. You'll see examples of the town's namesake plant on Laneda too—look for the clumps of small, shiny green leaves that indicate manzanita. Maybe it's the welcoming locals selling beach-friendly items and tasty treats to happy coastal visitors. Maybe it's Neah-Kah-Nie Mountain towering protectively over the beach from the north. Maybe it's all of the above. Whatever the source of the charm, Manzanita is an easy place to be and a difficult place to leave.

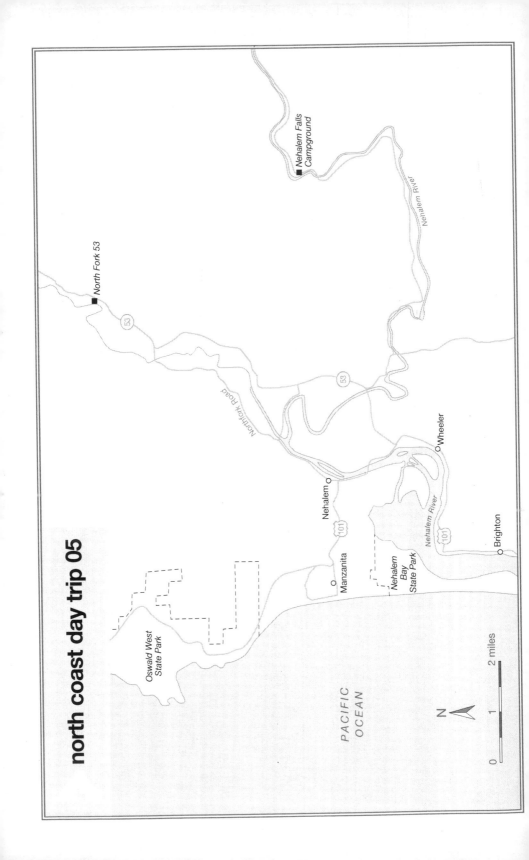

north coast day trip 05

Oswald West State Park

PACIFIC OCEAN

North Fork 53

Nehalem Falls Campground

Nehalem River

Northfork Road

53

53

Manzanita

Nehalem

Nehalem Bay State Park

Nehalem River

Wheeler

Brighton

101

101

N

0   1   2 miles

getting there

From Portland: Take OR 26 / US 26 W west 64 miles until you reach OR 53. Turn south on OR 53 and proceed 18 miles to Manzanita.

where to go

Nehalem Bay State Park. On the south end of Manzanita; oregonstateparks.org. Known for 900 acres of forest trails and awesome vistas, Nehalem State Park offers camping, horseback riding, beachcombing, crabbing, and fishing. RV and tent campgrounds, yurts, a horse camp with corrals, an airstrip with fly-in camping, and a hiker-biker camp provide plenty of overnight options. Take a short walk over the dunes to the beach and watch the sun set over the ocean, in the shadow of Neah-Kah-Nie Mountain.

Oregon Beach Rides. In Nehalem Bay State Park; (971)-237-6653; oregonbeachrides .com. Did you know that horse hooves squeak when they hit the sand? Come and find out with a horseback ride on the beach through this outfitter. One-hour, 2-hour, half-day, and full-day rides are offered right on the beach. Cost per person ranges from $75 to $250.

Oswald West State Park. 5 miles north of Manzanita; oregonstateparks.org. Named for the 14th governor of Oregon, Oswald West State Park is a favorite destination for wildlife viewing, tide-pooling, and surfing. A quarter-mile walk from US 101 through an old-growth forest of spruce and cedar will take you to Short Sands Beach, one of the loveliest beach coves on the Oregon Coast and a very popular surfing spot. Sheltered by high cliffs on both ends and surrounded by well-preserved coastal forest, "Shorty's," as the locals call it, is a beloved beach by many. Several other trails lead to the Cape Falcon overlook or to the Oregon Coast Trail. Oswald West also offers many picnic locations, but no camping.

where to shop

Bahama Mama's Bikes, Boards and Beach Fare. 123 Laneda Ave.; (503) 368-2453; manzanitabike.com. Manzanita's only bike and surfboard rental shop offers fat tire bikes, sit-down cruisers, surfboards, paddleboards, and boogie boards for rent or sale. Cruise the beach in style, or just pick up a hat, towel, sunglasses, or other beach goods.

Cloud and Leaf. 148 Laneda Ave.; (503) 368-2665; cloudandleaf.wordpress.com. This little bookstore is everything a bookstore should be, with nooks, crannies, and books galore. You'll also find plenty of Oregon authors' works here, from memoir to young adult fiction and everything in between.

Manzanita Grocery and Deli. 193 Laneda Ave.; (503) 368-5362; manzanitamarket.com. This is one of those fun groceries where you can buy staple food items, fine wine, or a great deli sandwich and rent a movie all in one stop. A 10 percent senior discount is offered every Tues. Open 7 days a week.

beach rollers

The Manzanita Visitors Center wants everyone to enjoy the beach, no matter their ability or mobility. The center offers three beach wheelchairs at no cost for use seven days a week. Two adult-sized wheelchairs and one kid-sized wheelchair are easy to use and allow for excellent beach mobility. Stop by the visitor center at 31 Laneda Ave. or call (503) 812-5510 to make a reservation.

Manzanita Sweets. 310 Laneda Ave.; (503) 368-3792. Manzanita Sweets offers a breathtaking assortment of old-fashioned candy, handcrafted chocolates, and saltwater taffy from regional sources. A wide array of antiques and novelties round out the offerings.

Unfurl. 447 Laneda Ave.; (503) 368-8316; unfurlclothing.com. High-quality and environmentally sustainable merchandise for men, women, and children. Clothing, shoes, accessories, and the like are all very fashion-forward, with a portion of sales going to support charities. You'll find lots of eco-fiber clothing and planet-friendly accessories for baby and child. Open 7 days a week.

where to eat

Bread and Ocean. 154 Laneda Ave.; (503) 368-5823; breadandocean.com. A fantastic bakery, take-out spot, deli, and restaurant that serves fresh-baked pastries, hot-from-the-oven bread, fresh salads, homemade soups, and creative fresh dinners. Open Wed through Sun for breakfast and lunch, Fri and Sat for dinner. $–$$$.

Left Coast Siesta. 288 Laneda Ave.; (503) 368-7997; leftcoastsiesta.com. This take on fresh Mexican food deserves a hard look—especially when you consider this little burrito shop celebrated 25 years of service in 2019. The big or wet burritos come loaded with organic fillings (try the sunflower seeds) and are available in 5 different tortilla flavors. Inside and outside seating is available at this casual, affordable place with eclectic decor and a beachy vibe. Don't miss the hot sauce bar. Closed Mon and Tues. $.

MacGregor's Whiskey Bar. 387 Laneda Ave.; (503) 368-2447; macgregorswhiskeybar .com. The bartending wizards at MacGregor's can whip up anything you desire, though the focus is on the over 140 bottles of whiskey they keep on hand. Great food, including traditional Scottish favorites and meat and cheese platters, keeps you from getting hungry. Consider visiting on Thurs, which is trivia night. There is also a second location at Cannon Beach. $$.

Neah-Kah-Nie Bistro. 519 Laneda Ave.; (503) 368-2722; nknbistro.com. It's hard to argue with anything labeled "gourmet comfort food." Chef Lynne Hopper brings a background in catering to this little restaurant that quickly made a name for itself with the locals. Lynne's son Eisha runs the bar. Start with "fancy fries," with garlic, parsley, and truffle oil, then move on to the rib eye or stuffed fresh fish. Open Tues through Sat for dinner. $$.

San Dune Pub. 127 Laneda Ave.; (503) 368-5080; sandunepub.com. A locals' favorite voted one of the best bars outside of Portland, this lodge-style pub and restaurant offers sandwiches and seafood alongside a wide selection of domestic and imported beers. Warm your bones next to their big stone fireplace and have your favorite drink from the full-service bar. On the weekends, dance to live music. In the summer, enjoy the patio with bistro tables and market umbrellas. Open 7 days a week. $–$$.

where to stay

Coast Cabins. 635 Laneda Ave.; (503) 368-7113; coastcabins.com. A variety of lodging options include cabins, lofts, and private homes within walking distance of Manzanita's restaurants and services. Special touches include wine service at check-in, fresh fruit and chocolate in rooms, s'mores kits for the fire pit, and a fitness center on-site. $$$.

The Inn at Manzanita. 67 Laneda Ave.; (503) 368-6754; innatmanzanita.com. A tranquil spot for a romantic weekend, this inn is ensconced in coastal pine and spruce in an open coastal garden. Thirteen rooms each have Jacuzzi tubs, fuzzy robes, fireplaces, wet bars, down comforters, and private decks. $$.

Spindrift Inn. 114 Laneda Ave.; (503) 368-1001; spindrift-inn.com. Built in 1946, the Spindrift Inn still retains quaint charm and cozy appeal with beachy, comfortable decor. Affordable rooms open onto a private inner flower garden, where you can relax away from the bustle outside. Quilted bedspreads and kitchenettes make this place cozy and convenient. $–$$.

nehalem

Nehalem is under 3 miles from Manzanita, but it's a very different village. Located inland on the western bank of the Nehalem River, with Nehalem Bay to the southwest, this picturesque town is all about the landscape that surrounds it. The river winds through, creating wetlands and riverfront views in many places. The forest and mountains beckon, and driving upriver takes one to small farms, many of which were once dairies. Wildlife is often in view.

The name *Nehalem* is of Indian origin and means "a place where people live," and if you spend a little time here, you'll see why they do.

getting there

Nehalem is 2.3 miles east of Manzanita.

where to go

Aldercreek Farm. 35955 Underhill Ln.; (503) 368-3203; nehalemtrust.org. A 54-acre historic dairy farm is now a wildlife sanctuary, community garden, ethnobotanical trail, and native plant nursery. Explore on your own on the Nehalem Teaching Trail, to see native wetlands, rocky ecosystems, and many indigenous plants, many of which were used by Native Americans. Once a year, a native plant sale is held.

Nehalem Bay Winery. 34965 OR 53; (503) 368-9463; nehalembaywinery.com. There aren't a whole lot of wineries on the Oregon Coast—most are inland in the Willamette, Umpqua, and Rogue Valleys. Vintner Ray Shackelford has been making wines here at the ocean for four decades. Try his traditional pinot noir or innovative Valley Peach varietals, and enjoy live music in the summer.

North County Recreation District. 36155 9th St.; (855) 444-6273; ncrd.org. A success story of a community coming together to save a treasured location, the North County Recreation District is a pool, a 200-seat performing arts center, a fitness center, and a youth enrichment center. For the visitor, it's a place to find indoor heated swimming year-round, a performance to enjoy on a rainy night, and even an art gallery with works by local artists for sale.

where to shop

Angelina Boutique and Jewelry. 35696 N US 101; (503) 368-7440. This cute little building with high transom windows and lush flowers out front is just begging for a stop-and-see. Venture in here for handmade jewelry, accessories, and unique clothing. Choose from hats, purses, earrings, shoes, and even handmade soap.

the winds of summer

Summer on the Oregon Coast is when the skies are most likely to be clear and the sun shining. But often, that comes with a strong north wind, which is beneficial for blowing those clouds out of the way but not always pleasant to spend a day outdoors in. But Oregon Coasties know a secret. Head inland from practically any coastal location and within 5 miles the wind will have died down and the temperatures may have risen a full 10 degrees. If the winds are powerful in Manzanita and you are in search of warmth and reprieve, drive up the Nehalem River to Nehalem Falls Campground or Cougar Valley State Park. Kick back and relax, wind-free.

Nehalem Food Mart. 35800 N US 101; (503) 368-5639. A small-town grocery store with heart, charm—and fresh oysters. There is a little something for anyone here, alongside staples for everyone. The shop has a sign out front with changeable letters that somehow always manages to make me giggle with its messaging of the day. Look for directives like "milk, worms and beers."

Pete's Antiques. 35990 N US 101; (503) 368-6018. A sweet little antiques shop specializing in glass. Before the era of plastic, the Japanese made fishing net floats out of blown glass, and they would frequently wash ashore on the Oregon Coast. This is the place to find one of these rare antique floats, if you're lucky.

where to eat

Buttercup Ice Creams & Chowders. 35915 N US 101; (503) 368-2469. When it comes to foods to enjoy at the coast, it doesn't get more iconic than chowder and ice cream. The owner of this little shop decided to focus her efforts on just these two treats, and it's working. People flock to Buttercup for a variety of chowders from salmon chowder to provincial fish soup. Ice cream flavors are just as innovative, including lavender lemonade and marshmallow. $.

Pizza Garden. 35815 N US 101; (503) 368-7675. Pizza with a view of the river is what's for lunch and dinner here. Many choices of toppings include seafood and meats as well as all the things vegetarians love. Butterflies and hummingbirds frequently flit by outside, and on a nice day, guests can sit outside too. $–$$.

Wanda's Cafe and Bakery. 12880 H St.; (503) 368-8100. This great breakfast and lunch place has a well-established reputation, evidenced by the fact that there is often a line out the door. Stop in for just coffee and a baked good to go, or stay for a meal and enjoy eggs Benedict, an omelet, tuna melt, homemade meatball sandwich, or more. Wine and beer are available also. $–$$.

where to eat & stay

Bunk House Cabin and Rooms. 36315 N US 101; (503) 368-5424. American diner-style food is served here for breakfast, lunch, and dinner. Stay right on the property in one of 7 rooms, 2 cabins, or an RV parking and camping spot. There's even a little candy shop on-site to satiate your sweet tooth after dinner (or anytime, for that matter). Restaurant closed Mon.

Kendra's River Inn Food & Lodging. 34920 OR 53; (503) 368-7488. At this family-owned inn, stay the night in one of 4 guest rooms for a bed-and-breakfast experience or just come for a meal at the full-service dining room, open 6 days a week (closed Sunday). The small guest rooms each have a private outdoor space, and the menu is large with plenty to choose from. The halibut comes highly recommended. $$.

North Fork 53 Coastal Retreat and Tea Gardens. 77282 OR 53; (503) 368-5382; north fork53.com. This place is several things at once. It's a tea farm and farm store, where you can purchase delicious teas and produce grown on the premises. It's a retreat center, where you can book a peaceful getaway for yourself or a group. It's bed-and-breakfast lodging. And it's just plain beautiful, with views of the river, forest, and gardens at every turn. $$.

wheeler

Just downriver from Nehalem is Wheeler, another sweet little waterfront village full of hidden charms. At Wheeler, the river transitions to bay, providing a wide expanse of water to gaze upon as well as wildlife watching and a jumping-off point for water-based recreation.

In the past, Wheeler and its people made a living primarily on logging and fishing. Today, the quiet town of about 400 people survives on tourism and the sustenance that comes with that expansive view.

getting there

Wheeler is 2.6 miles south of Nehalem.

where to go

Jetty Fishery. 27550 N US 101, Brighton; (503) 368 5746; jettyfishery.com. This family-owned marina has been in business since 1979, offering crabbing, picnicking, hiking, camping, clamming, fishing, birding, and eating some of the best fresh seafood around. Located on the waters of Nehalem Bay less than 10 feet to tide pools, from the Jetty Fishery you can also boat across the bay to Nehalem Bay State Park and enjoy sandy beaches. Rent a cabin or RV spot, learn to dig clams, and more at this fun spot.

Kelly's Brighton Marina. 29200 N US 101, Brighton; (503) 368-5745; kellysbrightonmarina .com. Kelly is the owner, and his passion is teaching people how to catch, cook, and enjoy crab. Choose to crab from the dock or a boat, and select a DIY package or have the Kelly's team clean and cook your catch for you. Crabbing happens year-round, weather permitting. Kelly's also offers bait, tackle, and fishing advice. There is even RV and tent camping on-site. You might not be able to leave without purchasing Kelly's signature bright red crab hat to mark the occasion of your fabulous crabbing experience. Hours vary seasonally; call ahead.

Oregon Coast Railriders. 130 Marine Dr.; (541) 786-6165; ocrailriders.com. With a primary location in Bay City, Oregon Coast Railriders recently expanded to Wheeler. This is a unique opportunity to cycle on a railroad. Four-seated, pedal-powered railroad quadricycles are powered by you and three of your friends along an inactive portion of the Port of Tillamook Bay Railroad. Pass by forests, farms, and waterfronts. The ride from Wheeler goes north along the river for 9 miles round-trip.

Wheeler Marina. 278 Marine Dr.; (503) 368-5780; wheelermarina.com. There's gazing upon the bay from shore, and then there's getting out into the action. Seeing wildlife and scenery up close from a kayak or boat is an amazing experience. Wheeler Marina rents single, double, touring, and touring tandem kayaks; canoes; and stand-up paddleboards. Also available are crabbing gear, motorboats, fishing licenses, bait, and tackle. Get out there! Hours vary seasonally.

where to shop

Wheeler Station Antiques. 425 Nehalem Blvd.; (503) 368-6210. Wind through this laby-rinthian 10,000-square-foot building to find antiques and collectibles from over 100 vendors. Don't worry about getting lost—the staff promises that if you do, they will come and find you. They'll probably even help you carry out what you've found to buy and take home.

Wheeler Treasures. 395 Nehalem Blvd.; (503) 354-4454. Vintage items for sale in this modest shopping mall might include gifts, antiques, items styled in shabby chic, or a wide variety of arts and crafts made by local and Oregon Coast artists. Worth a walk-through—you never know what you might find to take home.

where to eat

Rising Star Cafe. 92 Rorvik St.; (503) 368-3990; risingstarcafe.net. The menu changes fre-quently here based on fresh, organic ingredients and the whims of the owners, who describe themselves as chameleons always willing to reinvent themselves. Rising Star's menu might include steelhead Benedict, cioppino, or an alley omelet crammed with fresh veggies, served in this cute little blue building in the heart of Wheeler. $$.

The Roost. 495 N US 101; (503) 368-2625. Open for breakfast and lunch in a historic build-ing downtown, this little restaurant churns out savory and sweet treats. Homemade bagels, breakfast sandwiches, great coffee, soups, and sandwiches are served by friendly people, with a view of the bay. Open Wed through Sun until 3 p.m. $–$$.

Salmonberry Saloon. 380 Marine Dr.; (503) 714-1423; salmonberrysaloon.com. A view of Nehalem Bay is only part of the charm at this relatively new restaurant, where the food is excellent and there is something for the whole family. Try the smoked seafood chowder, shrimp hushpuppies, risotto, or captain's platter. There is a great kids' menu and a gener-ous happy hour, as well as cocktails, beer, and wine here too. Open Wed through Sun for lunch and dinner. $$–$$$.

where to stay

Old Wheeler Hotel. 495 N US 101; (503) 368-6000; oldwheelerhotel.com. Established in 1920, the Wheeler Hotel housed guests for only a decade or so before the Depression and the fires of the Tillamook Burn closed it down. The building continued to house businesses on its lower level, but it wasn't until the late 1990s that it was brought back to life as a hotel. Today, 8 restored rooms are all a little bit different, some with views of the bay. $$.

Wheeler on the Bay Lodge. 580 Marine Dr.; (503) 368-5858; wheeleronthebay.com. Right on Nehalem Bay with a private dock and outstanding views, Wheeler on the Bay even offers complimentary kayak use to guests who stay 2 nights. Each room is a little bit different; some rooms have a private deck and jetted spa tub. $$.

day trip 06

north coast

>>> **holiday by the shore:**
rockaway beach, garibaldi, bay city

rockaway beach

It's difficult to imagine that there was a time when land on the Oregon Coast was considered nearly worthless. But before a railroad stretched from Portland to Tillamook in 1906, access to the northern coast was extremely difficult. Early visitors came by buckboard and horseback from the Willamette Valley, so excited by the prospect of the beach that they were willing to travel two days over a mountain pass to achieve a glimpse of the sea and hold sand in their own hands. Many of these early travelers had come from the Midwest on the Oregon Trail and had never seen the ocean. Imagine their reaction when they crested that last hill.

Access—and land value—changed, of course, and the community of Rockaway Beach is testament. In 1909, a resort was established, named for the original Rockaway Beach, in New York on Long Island. In 1912, the train reached this area, and visitors became abundant. A natatorium was built, more lodgings emerged, and several separate townships were established along this narrow stretch of the coast.

Rockaway Beach today encompasses many of those original townships. Along the highway, storefronts feel old-fashioned and shops, restaurants, and galleries reflect a leisurely life near the sea. Seven miles of beach stretch along this Rockaway Beach, with more than 20 points of access. The scenic Twin Rocks sit offshore, as props for your sunset photography.

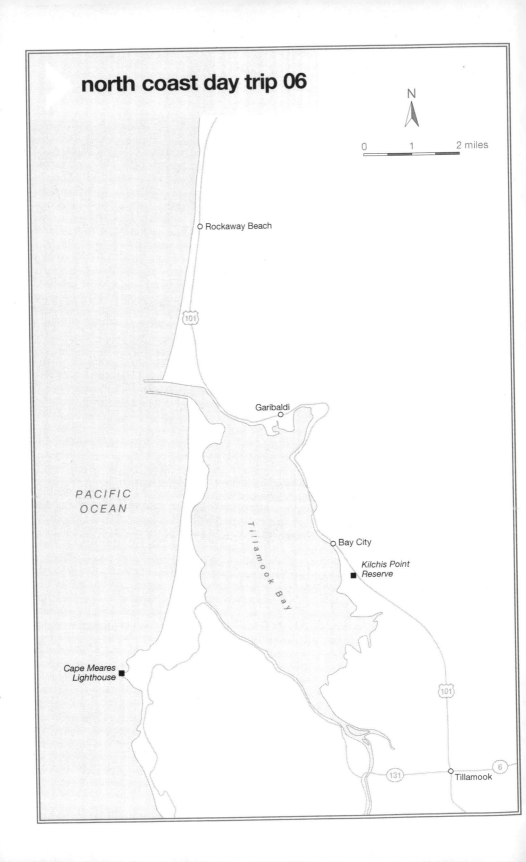

north coast day trip 06

N

0   1   2 miles

○ Rockaway Beach

101

Garibaldi
○

PACIFIC
OCEAN

Tillamook Bay

○ Bay City

*Kilchis Point
Reserve* ■

*Cape Meares
Lighthouse* ■

101

131   ○ Tillamook   6

getting there

From Portland: Take OR 26 / US 26 W west 44 miles until you reach OR 6. Turn southwest on OR 6 and proceed 52 miles to the intersection with US 101. Proceed north on US 101 13 miles to Rockaway Beach.

where to go

International Police Museum. 216 US 101; (503) 457-6056; internationalpolicemuseum .org. Curious about the history of policing? This little museum in the heart of Rockaway Beach is here to inform you. Launched with a collection of ephemera assembled by a retired police chief, the museum displays uniforms, weapons, and tools of the occupation of policing. Methods of communication, collection of evidence, and fingerprinting are explored. Special exhibits feature women and African Americans in policing history. Hours vary seasonally; check the website.

Lake Lytle. US 101 between 6th and 12th Streets. Rockaway Beach's inland lake is a great place to get out of the wind of the oceanfront shoreline and explore a quiet freshwater lake. Carry along your fishing gear to catch bass, trout, and perch from the shore or your own motorized boat. Paddlers, bring your own kayak or schedule a beginner's class with Kayak Tillamook, which chooses this particular lake for learners because of its calm surface.

Old Growth Cedar Preserve Nature Trail. Trailhead begins at the end of Island Street, off of Washington Street. The state-champion western red cedar tree is tucked in the middle of the residential section of town in an ancient cedar bog that somehow escaped logging over decades. The Ascending Giant organization ultimately measured the Rockaway cedar to be 154 feet tall, 49 feet wide. Today, you can hike to this extremely large and old western red cedar, as well as see equally old Sitka spruce. The hike is less than a half mile one-way.

Rockaway Beach Visitors Center. 103 1st Ave.; (503) 355-2291; rockawaybeach.net. Cleverly located in an antique red caboose, you can't miss this visitor center. It's fun to step inside just because it's a train, but there are many worthwhile discoveries here, including brochures on whale watching, the aquarium, attractions, parks, wine tasting, recreation, biking, kayaking, theaters, spas, and tours. Get the big picture before you dive into Rockaway Beach's many pleasures.

Troxel's Rock Garden. 146 S US 101; (541) 418-2842. The Troxels—Jen, a jewelry designer, and Victor, a lapidary who cuts and polishes stones—created this shop and more. Rock-lined pathways allow visitors to stroll past a variety of rocks, minerals, fossils, and petrified wood from around the world. Pick rough examples and choose the price to pay for them. Next door is Troxel's Gem and Jewelry Company. There's even a mini-golf course on-site!

where to shop

Beach Crafters. 116 N US 101; (503) 355-0580. Crafters go on vacation too, and when they do, they love stumbling across a little shop like this one. Full of gifts, cards, jewelry, and plenty of art supplies, Beach Crafters is for scrap-bookers, jewelry makers, and artsy types.

Fishpeople Seafood. 500 Biak Ave.; (503) 360-7899; fishpeopleseafood.com. Buy fresh fish directly from the fisher-people here in this small shop right by the marina. The employees are happy to give you all kinds of information about how to prepare your catch back at home or camp, or check out their website for recipes anytime.

Flamingo Jim's Gifts and Clothing. 234 N US 101; (503) 355-2365; flamingojimsgifts .com. It looks nautical from the outside, and that proves to be true inside. But this shop has plenty to offer beyond ship stuff. Clothing, gifts, rocks, shells, trinkets, and more are all on display. Many coastal visitors name Flamingo Jim's their first and favorite stop each year.

The Little Crow. 104 N US 101; (971) 306-1234. You never know what you'll find at this little shop, which offers an eclectic mix of antiques, collectibles, jewelry, soaps, candles, clothes, gifts, books, and new treasures all of the time. You might discover anything from sterling silver chains to snowshoes to eclectic socks to antique jars and film equipment.

Little White Church Antiques. 344 N US 101; (503) 355-2077. A little bit antiques shop, a little bit gift shop with great finds, Little White Church offers a huge variety of items in several rooms, each with a different theme. Find antique dishes, jewelry made from flatware, or a box covered in shells in this cool store. The building, as advertised, is little, white, and was once a church.

Ringing Anvil Design. 320 N US 101; (971) 306-1043; ringinganvildesign.com. Using tools and equipment handed down from his grandfather, Herman Doty works as a blacksmith in

the rains of december

It doesn't get more Oregon than this. The owners of the shop **Oregon Du Drops** *in Rockaway Beach have been collecting genuine Oregon rain for decades. Cat and Du Bois pour the rain into recycled light bulbs, which are hung from solid brass Indian temple bells. Even better—pick a commemorative day or year from your past and ask them to make a special order for you, filled with the rain from that time. The Du Drops are as unique as they are beautiful and catch the light on even the rainiest day. The Du Drops shop is a colorful, light-and-rainbow-dappled place to behold. See oregondudrops.com* this little studio. Practical metal designs and wonderful works of art alike are the results of his efforts. See him at work, benefit from his vast knowledge, and take home a metal artwork.

Sea Breeze Gifts. 102 N US 101; (503) 355-3335. Tillamook ice cream! Need we say more? Okay—how about saltwater taffy, candy, beach toys, kites, boogie boards, sweatshirts, sweatpants, T-shirts, dresses, flip-flops, hats, wind chimes, and other gifts. The building is painted purple with green and yellow trim—you can't miss it.

where to eat

Beach Bakeshop. 108 N US 101; (971) 306-1245; beachbakeshop.com. Follow your nose to the smells of fresh-baked goods and grab an espresso and a treat here. Buttery biscuits, homemade cinnamon rolls, sandwiches, desserts, fresh bread, and more grace the menu. Don't miss the breakfast handpies—bacon, ham, or sausage with cheese and egg in a flaky crust. $.

The Beach Bite & Dos Rocas. 176 N US 101; (503) 355-2073; thebeachbiteanddosrocas .com. Feel like pizza? Your family wants Mexican food? This place has you covered. From-scratch pizza is served alongside fresh fish tacos and more, with two full bars and a lovely outdoor patio as icing on the cake (and they also have cake and other terrific desserts). $$.

Offshore Grill & Coffee House. 122 N US 101; (503) 355-3005. Open for breakfast, lunch, and dinner 5 days a week, this place is small but worth the wait, should you encounter a line (and you just might). Fresh fish and crab are incorporated into many delectable dishes, but there is also a wide variety of non-seafood dishes to choose from on a frequently changing menu, from cinnamon apple French toast to rib eye steak to a pork belly omelet. Closed Mon and Tues. $.

Old Oregon Smokehouse. 120 N US 101; (503) 355-2817. A tiny beach hut with kitschy coastal appeal, this place has classics like clam chowder, fried halibut, clam strips, and crab cakes. Grab a basket of grub at the counter and sit outdoors at a picnic table. $.

Pronto Pup. 602 S US 101; (971) 306-1164; originalprontopup.com. The corn dog was invented in Rockaway Beach in the late 1930s, and it's all because of the famous Oregon Coast rain. When the hot dog buns at George and Versa Boyington's hot dog stand got wet, George created a "bun" that could be cooked to order. Voila! The Pronto Pup. To this day, this little restaurant serves all kinds of "pups" and sides. Hours vary widely throughout the year, with total closure for a few months in the winter. $.

Sand Dollar Restaurant & Lounge. 210 SW 1st St.; (503) 355-2200; sanddollarrestaurant .com. The usual coastal delights served with style (bacon-wrapped scallops, yum) as well as some pleasant surprises (Grandma's recipe paprikash) appear on this menu. Indoor and outdoor seating, with a view of the ocean, are on hand, as is live music some weekends. $$–$$$.

where to stay

Sea Haven Motel. 520 N US 101; (503) 355-8101; seahavenmotel.net. Each unit at this beachfront location has a full kitchen with dishes, silverware, glassware, and cookware. A wood-fire pit, barbecue, and crab cooker are available in the outdoor picnic area. Pet units are available too. $–$$.

Silver Sands Motel. 215 S Pacific St.; (503) 355-2206; oregonsilversands.com. Several different room types and 39 total rooms make this a great choice for those who need something different than a standard room. Kitchenettes, semi-private decks, and ground-floor rooms that open to the lawn and beach access are all options. There is a heated indoor swimming pool and hot tub too. $–$$.

Tradewinds. 523 N Pacific St.; (503) 355-2112; tradewinds-motel.com. Tradewinds isn't trying to be fancy, and that's okay. This quaint getaway destination is a solid, clean, and well-stocked motel steps from the ocean. Each room has a small kitchen, there are picnic tables outside, and the sound of the ocean waves is free. $–$$.

Twin Rocks Motel. 7925 S Minnehaha St.; (503) 355-2391; twinrocksmotel.net. Each lodging at this oceanfront locale is a sweet little 2-bedroom cottage with a view of the ocean and the Twin Rocks. Private decks and picture windows take in Pacific sunsets, winter storms, and crashing summer waves. Fully equipped kitchens let you dine in or out. $$–$$$.

garibaldi

Highway 101 swings around the bay through Garibaldi in a lazy arc, taking in the sights and sounds of this little city en route. The hillside to the east climbs steeply, displaying a gigantic G to represent the pride of the town. To the west is the northern end of Tillamook Bay, vast and home to many birds and creatures of the sea.

Garibaldi is a small, friendly fishing village with the weight of history behind it. An old railroad and two historical museums anchor the town. The Port of Garibaldi is the community hub, comprising a large area jutting into the bay full of things to explore. Still very much a working port, you might overhear commercial fishermen talking about the record-size ling-cod or rockfish they've netted here. Dungeness crab and even octopus are also plentifully harvested from the port.

Recreation abounds as well, including kayaking and wildlife watching. Kick back for a relaxing day taking in the delights of the bay in this small town.

getting there

Garibaldi is 5 miles south of Rockaway Beach.

where to go

Garibaldi Charters. 607 Garibaldi Ave.; (503) 322-0007; garibaldicharters.com. There are lingcod and rockfish out there just waiting for you to catch them. Deep-sea fishing off the Oregon Coast is an unforgettable experience, and the folks at Garibaldi Charters are happy to help you have it. They'll throw a crab pot or two out as well, and can fillet and clean your catch upon return. Their ultimate offshore fishing experience is for halibut—a 12-hour trip for the hardiest of anglers.

Garibaldi Maritime Museum. 112 Garibaldi Ave.; (503) 322-8411; garibaldimuseum.org. This modest museum preserves the maritime heritage of the Pacific Northwest in displays from the 18th-century sailing world. In particular, the museum depicts the story of Captain Robert Gray and the trade with Native Americans of the Pacific Northwest. Captain Gray's historical vessels, the *Lady Washington* and the *Columbia Rediviva*, are displayed as replicas.

Oregon Coast Scenic Railroad. 306 American Ave.; (503) 842-7972; oregoncoastscenic .org. The railroad truly is a major part of the history of the northern Oregon Coast, and some dedicated residents decided to bring back the train as a recreational opportunity. In operation since 2002, the Oregon Coast Scenic Railroad is a steam train running the original tracks between Garibaldi and Rockaway Beach. The schedule varies but generally runs mid-May through the end of September. Excursions include daily runs, a dinner train, and seasonal events.

gliding over water

One sunny spring day, my husband and I took a guided kayak tour out of the Port of Garibaldi with the tour company **Kayak Tillamook.** *After a safety lesson in the marina, our small group paddled into the bay toward open water in our single-person sea kayaks. As the chop increased, so did the scenery. At the tour's climax, we reached the serene beauty of the Three Graces. Formed between 20 and 30 million years ago of sandstone, when the whole coastline was still underwater, over time erosion whittled the formations to the three towering structures that remain today. These stone outcroppings north of Garibaldi are visible from the highway, but up-close from the water, a paddler can see the small trees and many birds that call these rocks home. We circled the Graces and dug our paddles into the blue water for the return trip, on promises of fresh oysters and craft beer as a post-paddle celebration.*

Port of Garibaldi. 402 S 7th St.; (503) 322-3292; portofgaribaldi.org. One of the larger ports in the area, the Port of Garibaldi has moorage for nearly 300 vessels. Park your car and wander around. The port area is home to an RV park, restaurants, fishing charters, shrimp, crab and fish processing facilities, a lumber mill, and recreational businesses. The marina has a public boat launch for people wishing to fish or crab. At the port's farthest reaches is Pier's End. At over 700 feet in length, this pier is the longest in Oregon. Near its end is a historic building that served as a boathouse for the Coast Guard from 1934 until the early 1960s. The pier itself is open free to the public for a wide range of recreational fishing opportunities, including crabbing, bottom fishing for sturgeon and other species, and salmon fishing. A stairway provides public access to the clam beds below, where diggers with the required shellfish permit will find a good mix of cockle, gaper, and butter clams.

where to shop

Myrtle Wood Factory. 903 Garibaldi Ave.; (503) 322-3224; myrtlewoodfactoryoutlet.com. The Oregon myrtle tree grows along the southern Oregon Coast. It grows very slowly, developing burls which, when polished, have exquisite, intricate markings. Additionally, the dense, fine grain makes it a great material for trays, bowls, and fine items. No two pieces are the same, but each is beautiful. Stop in this shop to learn more about this amazing wood and pick up a functional souvenir to take home.

Vintage by The Bay. 410 Garibaldi Ave.; (503) 322-4335. Classic antique, vintage, and flea market store with plenty to browse and choose from. Find some antique salt and pepper shakers, old toy trains, Christmas teacups, and dozens of other treasures to take home in this little shop by the shore.

where to eat

Fisherman's Korner. 306 Mooring Basin Rd.; (503) 322-2033. On the Port of Garibaldi, Fisherman's Korner looks like a classic old-time diner and serves a range of classic coastal seafood dishes, from coconut shrimp to shrimp-and-chips to clam chowder. Guests rave about the tartar sauce and the friendly service. $–$$.

Garibaldi Portside Bistro. 606 Biak Ave.; (971) 265-1567. Locally lauded as serving delicious food, Garibaldi Portside Bistro also has a beautiful view from its location on the port. The menu is locally sourced and diverse, offering lots of burgers and sandwiches, ribs, and quesadillas, as well as vegetarian items. Typically open for lunch and dinner, but hours vary; call ahead. $–$$.

Source Oyster and Wine Bar. 402 Garibaldi Ave.; (503) 714-1425; sourcenw.com. The small menu revolves around fresh oysters with wine and beer pairings, although there are also a few salads, tacos, and even a hot dog to enjoy here. Wines and beers are all local-regional. Stop in for a bite and a sip. $–$$.

where to stay

Garibaldi House Inn. 502 Garibaldi Ave.; (503) 322-3338; garibaldihouse.com. Nice, newer rooms located on the main highway in Garibaldi can be found here. Choose from a family suite, king suite, or double queen at this hotel, which also offers a complimentary breakfast buffet, pool, hot tub and sauna, fish-cleaning station, and more. $$.

bay city

Bay City is located on the bay front along Highway 101, right in the center of Tillamook Bay. What the city has to offer the visitor is similar to its neighbors to the north and south, with one exception—Kilchis Point. Once the location of the largest Native American village on the north Oregon Coast, the point has been revitalized with trails and offers a close-up view of history and culture. Bay City is also home to a railroad, two golf courses (traditional and disc golf), a skate park, and the world's longest pepperoni stick.

getting there

Bay City is 4.4 miles south of Garibaldi.

where to go

Kilchis Point Nature Trail. 5000 Spruce St.; (503) 842-4553; tcpm.org/kilchis-point -reserve. Covering approximately 200 acres, this land is held in public trust by the Tillamook County Pioneer Museum. This cultural landmark through beautiful forest features interpretive signs on trails to share information about native plants and animals, ecology, flora and fauna, and also history. Native American heritage and early pioneer settlement are well-documented here. Three different trails cover 2 miles total. Much of the trail is ADA accessible, and there is a modified golf cart available for those who need it. If you are traveling with children, make sure you pick up the kids' activity book.

Oregon Coast Railriders. 130 Marine Dr.; (541) 786-6165; ocrailriders.com. With a second location in Wheeler, Oregon Coast Railriders provides a unique opportunity to cycle on a railroad. Four-seated, pedal-powered railroad quadricycles are powered by you and three of your friends along an inactive portion of the Port of Tillamook Bay Railroad. Pass by forests, farms, and waterfronts. The ride from Bay City begins traveling south and is 12 miles round-trip.

where to shop & eat

Pacific Oyster. 5150 Hayes Oyster Dr.; (503) 377-2323; pacificseafood.com. This is a factory and a restaurant at the same time. Enjoy the self-guided tour, which includes interactive kiosks, viewing windows, and videos. Watch oystermen shucking oysters from the bay to your table, then dive into the freshest seafood and shellfish on the Oregon Coast at The Fish Peddler, Pacific Oyster's on-site restaurant. It's not just oysters here (though the oysters are great)—try fresh rockfish or salmon when they have it. $$.

Tillamook County Smoker. 8335 N US 101; (888) 987-4233; tcsjerky.com. If you've ever been in a convenience store, you've seen Tillamook County Smoker jerky, and it all comes from this factory right here. For nearly half a century, from one family's start-up business, this smokehouse has been crafting tasty jerky from meat cuts smoked with fragrant hardwood. Stop in to try samples from spicy and sweet to teriyaki, and buy some to take home, including their famous 2-foot pepperoni stick, often at a price break.

where to stay

Sheltered Nook on Tillamook Bay. 7860 Warren St.; (503) 805-5526; shelterednook .com. Tiny homes have become popular across the nation, but unless you build one yourself, what are the chances you can try one out? Here's your opportunity. Six tiny homes sit on this property, each an example of clever, economical, and welcoming design. Fully furnished with locally made furniture, a TV, and all the cooking utensils you may need during your stay, Sheltered Nook is also nestled in the trees and has a fire pit and community gathering area to enjoy. $$.

day trip 07

north coast

cheese & oysters:
tillamook, oceanside & netarts

tillamook

Hear the word "Tillamook," and Oregonians think of two things—cheese and fire. In 1909, a farmer-owned dairy cooperative was established and laid the groundwork for what would become a nationally recognized dairy products producer. Tillamook cheese is distributed widely, the company's headquarters is a popular tourist destination, and dairy farming continues to be a staple of the Tillamook County economy.

As for the fire, luckily that is a matter of history. Between 1933 and 1951, a series of forest fires swept through the northern Oregon Coast Range near Tillamook, ultimately destroying 355,000 acres of old-growth timber. The fires not only caused huge setbacks to the logging industry (during the Great Depression, no less), but also laid waste to large swaths of forest along the highway from Portland, making the devastation apparent to visitors traveling to the county. The Tillamook Burn, as the fires are collectively known, is still the stuff of legend to Oregonians.

Today, the forest has recovered, and the Tillamook Creamery is thriving. Drivers pass by tall stands of Douglas fir and spruce to descend into the Tillamook Valley, where dairy farms dot the landscape. The working-class city has benefited from the Oregon Coast's general popularity and continues to flourish as a pleasant small town on the upswing. The town is set inland from the sea a few miles, and is bordered by farms, forests, and hundreds of cows.

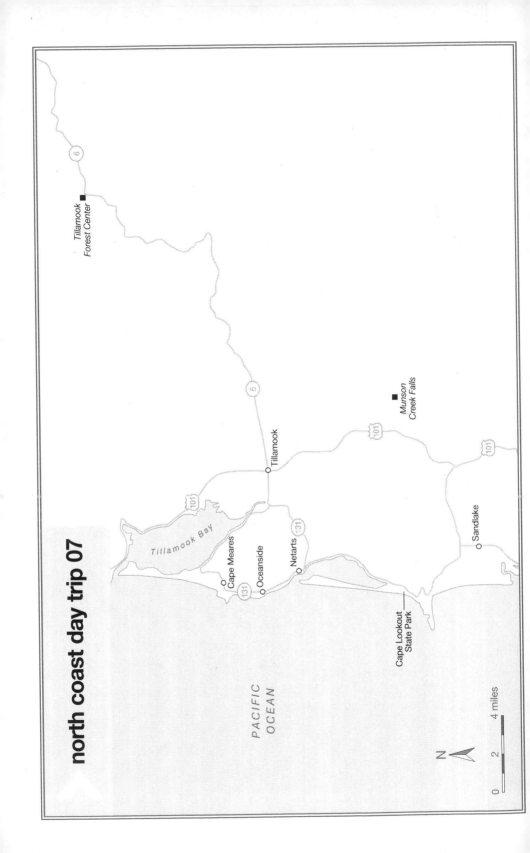

north coast day trip 07

Tillamook Forest Center

6

6

Tillamook

101

101

Munson Creek Falls

Tillamook Bay

101

Cape Meares

131

Oceanside

Netarts

31

Cape Lookout State Park

Sandlake

PACIFIC OCEAN

N

0   2   4 miles

getting there

From Portland: Take US 26 W / OR 26 W west 20 miles to the junction with OR 6 W. Follow OR 6 W for 51 miles, at which point OR 6 W intersects with US 101, and the city of Tillamook.

where to go

Blue Heron French Cheese Company. 2001 Blue Heron Dr.; (503) 842-8281; blueheron oregon.com. Celebrating more than a quarter century on the Oregon Coast, the Blue Heron French Cheese Company is known for their famous brie. The shop includes a deli, unique gifts, and gourmet food. Their cafe is a wonderful stop for homemade soups, salads, sandwiches, and much more. The kids will love the petting farm. Open 7 days a week: 8 a.m. to 8 p.m. in the summer; 8 a.m. to 6 p.m. in the winter.

de Garde Brewing. 114 Ivy Ave.; (503) 815-1635; degardebrewing.com. This small brewery specializes in many diverse styles of ales, but focuses on spontaneous fermentations inspired by the European farmhouse traditions. Drawing on historic traditions and local experimentations, de Garde is making some of the most unique barrel-aged beers in the Northwest and, in turn, has developed an impressive cultlike following. Tasting room open Thurs and Fri 3 to 7 p.m., Sat noon to 7 p.m., and Sun 11 a.m. to 5 p.m.

Munson Creek Falls. 10 miles southeast of Tillamook off US 101 and Munson Creek Road. The tallest waterfall in the Coast Range is accessible by a short hike from a parking lot outside of Tillamook. The 319-foot falls tumbles past a lush old-growth western red cedar and Sitka spruce forest. Munson Creek is an important salmon spawning ground, and in the late fall through winter, keep your eyes open for glimpses of the red backs of spawning salmon.

Tillamook Air Museum. 6030 Hangar Rd.; (503) 842-1130; tillamookair.com. One of the finest collections of World War II war birds, including a P-38 Lightning, F4U Corsair, P51 Mustang, PBY Catalina, and SBD Dauntless dive bomber, is right here in Tillamook. The war planes and an exhibit hall featuring rare historical wartime and aviation artifacts are all housed in a rare World War II blimp hangar, the largest wooden structure in the world. While you're there, take a break for lunch at the Air Base Cafe, open during the summer months. Open to the public daily 10 a.m. to 4 p.m. except for Thanksgiving and Christmas.

Tillamook Creamery. 4165 US 101 N; (503) 815-1300; tillamook.com. Back in 1909, a farmer-owned collective of dairy farms was founded in the Tillamook Valley to ensure that locally produced cheese was the best it could be. The Tillamook County Creamery Association eventually expanded to include all of the small, independent cheese factories in the county, and today the association is made up of approximately 110 dairy families, which collectively own the Tillamook Creamery. In 2018, a brand-new visitor center opened to the public. View the factory floor and see cheesemakers at work, learn about the cheesemaking process, brush up on your understanding of the dairy cow, and, best of all, taste award-winning cheeses and 38 flavors of ice cream. There is a restaurant on-site, serving grilled cheese sandwiches, wood-fired pizza, and burgers—with cheese. A coffee bar and ice cream counter are here too. Open daily 8 a.m. to 6 p.m. the day after Labor Day through mid-June; 8 a.m. to 8 p.m. mid-June through Labor Day. Closed Thanksgiving and Christmas.

Tillamook County Pioneer Museum. 2106 2nd St.; (503) 842-4553; tcpm.org. From the Tillamook Indians to Captain Robert Gray's 1788 voyage into Tillamook Bay, the Tillamook coast has a fascinating history. This is a great destination for all ages. Open Tues through Sun from 10 a.m. to 4 p.m.

Tillamook Forest Center. Located 20 minutes east of Tillamook on OR 6; (503) 815-6800; tillamookforestcenter.org. Located at the heart of the Tillamook State Forest, this interpretive and educational center showcases the legacy of the historic Tillamook Burn through a wealth of innovative exhibits, programs, and interactive displays. Free admission. Open Wed through Sun in spring, summer, and fall; closed Dec through Feb.

where to eat

Alice's Country House. 17345 Wilson River Hwy.; (503) 842-7927. This homey little place is quaint, cozy, and tucked away in the beautiful rural coastal woods. Home-cooked burgers, pie, milkshakes, Philly cheesesteaks, and prime rib please guests. There's nothing fancy here, but the food will fill you up nicely on a rainy day. $.

Pacific Restaurant. 205 Main Ave.; (503) 354-2350; pacificrestaurant.info. A spacious, well-lit interior is the backdrop for Pacific Restaurant, Tillamook's answer to fine dining. Delicious, well-prepared meals incorporate locally sourced foods, as the owners' hope is to preserve the town's rural flavor while emphasizing its assets. Try a New York steak from Tillamook Meats or Alaskan halibut with clams and shrimp. Open daily 11 a.m. until 9 p.m. $$.

Pelican Brewery and Tap Room. 1708 1st St.; (503) 842-7007; pelicanbrewing.com/pubs/tillamook. In 2013, Pacific City's Pelican Brewery moved their main brewing facility to Tillamook. On-site, find brewery tours as well as a 40-seat casual dining area overlooking the brewery floor, which allows for a passive education about the beverage in the glass in front of you. Covered, heated patio seating is good in all seasons. The menu is pub fare, with some unique items like fried cheese curds, an elk burger, and stout ice cream floats, as well as signature clam chowder and fish-and-chips. Open daily 11 a.m. until 9 p.m. $–$$.

Tora Sushi Lounge. 212 Main St.; (503) 354-2645; torasushi.com. The fresh seafood has always been on the Oregon Coast, but strangely, sushi has been slow to arrive. This restaurant in Tillamook is the most recent location for Tora (there is a location in Astoria and another in Seaside). Watch the chefs at work creating your sushi, or be bold and ask for *omakase*, which means "to trust the chef." $$.

oceanside & netarts

Tillamook proper is inland from the sea a few miles, and Oceanside and Netarts to the west are the city's oceanfront communities. The road out of Tillamook tracks due west through agricultural land before winding around a forested headland to emerge in Oceanside, one of the most picturesque small cities on the Oregon Coast. Beach cottages dot the steep hillside, meaning many homes in Oceanside have views of the beach, the Arch Rocks, and Maxwell Mountain, which towers to the north.

Oceanside's charm was the reason two brothers bought the property in 1921, despite the fact that a road had not yet reached the area. Their dream was to create one of the finest resorts on the West Coast. A wooden-plank road was installed from Netarts, a grand dance hall was built, and a tunnel was drilled under Maxwell Point to connect to beaches to the north. Visitors came in droves in the summer, erecting a tent city of vacationing fun. Things are a little quieter now, but the charm and fun remain.

Netarts's roots are all about the bounty of the sea. The bay-front land was the earliest settlement in the county, and in the Native American language of the local Killamook tribe (as they were first known), *Ne ta at* meant "near the water." Native Americans settled here to take advantage of Netarts Bay's prolific oyster beds. Later, European settlers did the same, and the little community flourished. By the 1860s, schooners came in regularly from San Francisco, paying 50 cents per bushel delivered on board. Today, the harvest of oysters and clams is still a big draw, and local restaurants cook them up daily for hungry patrons.

getting there

Oceanside is 9 miles west of Tillamook. Netarts is 3 miles south of Oceanside.

where to go

Cape Lookout State Park. 13000 Cape Lookout Rd. (7.7 miles south of Oceanside); oregonstateparks.org. There isn't a loser in the group of Oregon state parks along the Oregon Coast, and yet, some stand out. Cape Lookout is a personal favorite. A popular campground and day-use area, Cape Lookout is located on a sand spit between Netarts Bay and the ocean, giving visitors a terrific view of the ocean with convenient access to a very walkable beach. Walk the beach or hit the trail through lush old-growth forest. You can even hike to the end of Cape Lookout itself; a trail extends 2 miles along the headland (read the interpretive signs to learn about a bomber airplane that crashed here during WWII). A bench is located at the end of the trail, from which you might catch sight of a whale. Yurts and deluxe cabins are available for rent in addition to tent and RV sites, and a small interpretive center sits in the campground. Along with Cape Kiwanda and Cape Meares, Lookout is part of the Three Capes Scenic Route.

a picnic and a wedding

My husband and I were married at Cape Lookout State Park on the beach on a sunny summer day. Our very small ceremony felt like the perfect testament to Tom McCall's Beach Bill and Oregon's famous public beaches. You don't need a special permit or to pay an exorbitant rental fee to have a wedding with some of this state's most amazing, spectacular places as a backdrop. The guests were even provided, by way of other beachgoers enjoying their picnics and sandcastles and sightseeing, who applauded us at nuptials' end. Should you feel inclined to do the same, I recommend the proprietors of nearby Sandlake Country Inn, who are licensed to wed willing parties, just like us.

Cape Meares Lighthouse and State Scenic Viewpoint. US 101 3 miles north of Oceanside; (800) 551-6949; capemeareslighthouse.org. Cape Meares is the site of the Cape Meares Lighthouse, an informational kiosk, viewpoints, the Three Arch Rocks National Wildlife Refuge, nature trails, and the Oregon Heritage Tree known as the Octopus Tree. From its headland, visitors get an excellent view of one of the largest colonies of nesting common murres on the continent. In winter and spring, the cape can be a great place from which to spot whales. Bald eagles and a peregrine falcon have also been seen here. Cape Meares has more than 3 miles of hiking trails—one trail winds through old-growth spruce trees, including Oregon's largest Sitka spruce. Another trail leads to the Cape Meares Lighthouse, which was constructed in 1889 and is the shortest lighthouse in Oregon. The lighthouse is open daily May through Oct from 11 a.m. to 4 p.m. Mon through Thurs and 11 a.m. to 6 p.m. Fri and Sat. Free admission. The park is open daily, throughout the year, from 7 a.m. to dusk with no day-use fee.

Oceanside Beach State Recreation Site. At Pacific Avenue and Rosenberg Loop, Oceanside; oregonstateparks.org. There is plenty of parking and a nice restroom here, within steps of a truly beautiful small beach. Picnicking, beachcombing, and sandcastle building are on hand, of course, but a few special opportunities are available here too. Agates can be found during the winter season when weather and ocean currents strip the beach of sand. Hang gliders and paragliders come off of Maxwell Mountain, and kite flyers often find favorable winds. At the north end of the beach is a 90-year-old tunnel, which connects in the right conditions to a beach on the other side of the mountain.

Three Arch Rocks National Wildlife Refuge. At Pacific Avenue and Rosenberg Loop, Oceanside; fws.gov. The sea stacks that form offshore of the Oregon Coast have always been a great place for animals to live, and as such, many have been designated wildlife refuges. Three Arch Rocks are clearly visible from the beach at Oceanside. Bring your binoculars to spot common murres, cormorants, oystercatchers, and other seabirds, though there are fewer than there used to be, largely because of bald eagle disturbance. Sea lions and harbor seals still reside here seasonally. Despite the change in habitat and wildlife residency, the Arch Rocks remain an important protected area and part of Oceanside's lovely aesthetic.

where to eat

Blue Agate Cafe. 1610 Pacific Ave., Oceanside; (503) 815-2596. This modest onetime residence, now restaurant, perches in the center of Oceanside with a view of the ocean. The interior is eclectic, featuring historic photos of the area and beach-vibe decor. The Blue Agate serves breakfast, lunch, and sometimes dinner from a large menu virtually packed with goodness. Last time I was there, I devoured crab cakes and eggs with house potatoes and a homemade biscuit for breakfast. It was so delicious, we came back the next morning for another round. Dinner is served weekends in summer; options include crab-stuffed halibut and coconut prawns. $$.

Roseanna's Cafe. 1490 Pacific Ave., Oceanside; (503) 842-7351; roseannascafe.com. Roseanna's, located in an old grocery store, is one of the most delicious restaurants on the coast, in one of the most gorgeous small communities. On the menu you'll find chowder, sandwiches, a variety of fishes, prawns, scallops, oysters, chicken, steak, pastas, quiche, wine, domestic beers, and microbrews. Last but not least, homemade desserts—pies, cakes, puddings, cobblers, ice cream, and more. Open Thurs through Mon for lunch and dinner. $–$$.

The Schooner. 2065 Netarts Basin Boat Rd., Netarts; (503) 815-9900; theschooner.net. The Schooner is one of those almost-perfect destination restaurants: There is something for everyone here, from the atmosphere to the food. This large building on Netarts Bay has a finer-dining room, a separate and expansive bar and lounge, and a huge covered outdoor patio. Each has a completely different vibe. The food is delicious throughout; enjoy fresh seafood like crab cakes or cioppino, or stick with something tamer, like the Schooner's delectable burgers. Oysters directly from the bay in front of the restaurant are almost required eating here—choose Oysters Rockoyaki: Netarts Bay oysters wood-oven-roasted with pork belly, greens, and garlic motoyaki sauce. There is often live music in the lounge. Open for lunch and dinner 7 days a week; brunch is served in the lounge on the weekends. $$.

where to stay

Sandlake Country Inn. 8505 Galloway Rd., Sandlake; (503)-965-6745; sandlakecountry inn.com. This historic farmhouse on the Oregon Historic Registry is a romantic bed-and-breakfast tucked into the forest. Two suites, a room, and a separate cottage are decked out with fireplaces and whirlpool tubs. Breakfast is delivered to your door. Sandlake specializes in elopements and weddings, should the urge overtake you. $$.

Surf Inn. 4951 OR 131, Netarts; (503) 354-2644; pacificviewlodging.com. This old-timey motel is outfitted with retro surfboards along the building. Simple but welcoming, each unit has a kitchen and a view of the massive pampas grass growing out front. Next door is a tiny grocery and across the street a small coffee shop, when the need for provisions hits. $–$$.

The Terimore Lodging by the Sea. 5105 Crab Ave. W, Netarts; (503) 842-4623; terimoremotel.com. Off the beaten path in tiny Netarts is this classic motel with views of the ocean and bay. Cabins and cottages are also on the property, as is the "Airstream by the Sea," a restored vintage trailer for two. Look for postmodern touches and beautiful natural scenery. $–$$.

Thyme & Tide Bed & Breakfast. 5015 Grand Ave., Oceanside; (503) 842-5527; thyme-and-tide.com. Only 2 bedrooms at this tiny bed-and-breakfast, but they are beautiful, and Oceanside is a lovely, small alternative to Tillamook. A hearty breakfast will get you going for your day spent walking the beach or hiking the hills. $$.

day trip 08

north coast

>>> **surf's up:**
pacific city

pacific city

Sometimes history comes full circle. Campgrounds and lodgings to accommodate early Oregon Coast vacationers were some of Pacific City's first business endeavors, and today the destination's largest source of commerce is tourism. The second economic focus back in the early days of this community was fish. Salmon used to swim thick as seaweed in Nestucca Bay. A commercial cannery was built on the east side of the bay in 1886, where it thrived for many years, canning and shipping 12,000 cans of salmon a year. Fishing, logging, and eventually dairy farming became the primary occupations in the Nestucca Valley.

Today, the fishing is still pretty good, at least recreationally, and visitors swarm to this hip, friendly, and highly surfable locale. Pacific City has become known as Oregon's surfing hub, benefiting from the excellent waves created by the point break of Cape Kiwanda. Most days, there's plenty of surf action to leap into, or at least observe from shore. If you're going in, bring a wetsuit—the waves are nice but the water is a frigid 40 to 50 degrees.

Pacific City is also known for its dory boats—small, shallow-draft fishing boats that run right up onto the sand instead of a dock. That means that vehicles are allowed on the beach here, with limits. While ostensibly the vehicles are on the beach to launch boats, many just drive onto the sand because they can. Set up your beach chair on the dune above the beach for all-day entertainment as the cars and boats come and go—and sometimes just get stuck in the sand.

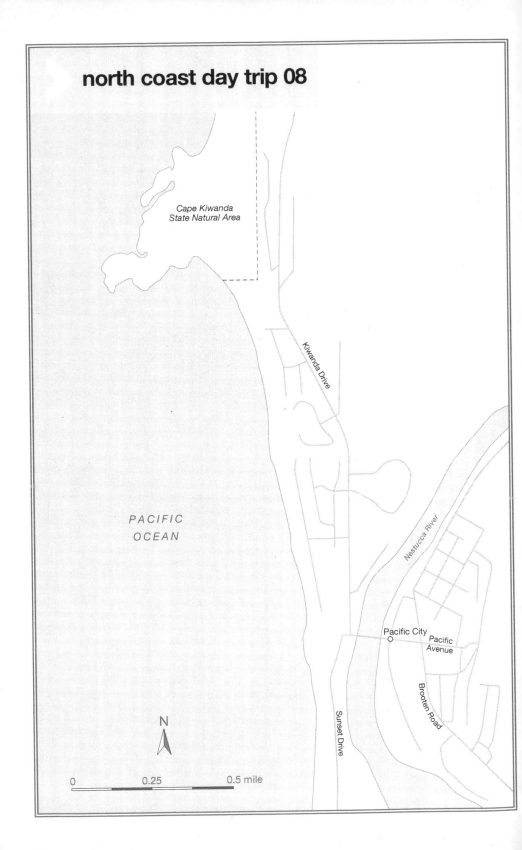

north coast day trip 08

Cape Kiwanda
State Natural Area

PACIFIC
OCEAN

Kiwanda Drive

Nestucca River

Pacific City

Pacific
Avenue

Brooten Road

Sunset Drive

N

| 0 | 0.25 | 0.5 mile |

getting there

From Salem: Travel 44 miles northwest on OR 22. Take a slight left onto OR 130 W and travel 9.4 miles. Take a right on US 101, a left on Brooten Road, and follow the signs into Pacific City (another 4 miles from OR 22).

where to go

Moment Surf Co. 33280 Cape Kiwanda Dr.; (503) 483-1025; momentsurfco.com. Pacific City is one of the best places to surf on the Oregon Coast, and is especially good for beginners (I surfed for the first time there, and was pummeled by the waves in only the gentlest fashion). The break off Cape Kiwanda, on good days, provides a nice rolling surf. On bad days, well, kick back and watch the storm instead. For rentals and lessons, visit Moment Surf Co. This shop offers consistent open hours, fantastic surfing products and equipment, and outstanding service, including lessons. Moment pairs with various local hotels to create packages and has become the place to go around here for purchase, rental, and lessons. Open Sun through Thurs 10 a.m. to 5 p.m., Fri and Sat 10 a.m. to 6 p.m.

Nestucca Adventures. 34650 Brooten Rd.; (503) 965-0060; nestuccaadventures.com. Offering kayak and stand-up paddleboard rentals, this outfitter is located on the Nestucca River with a marina with a dock, making it convenient to launch for all skill levels. The river is nice flatwater, but it's just a short paddle to the mouth of the river and the ocean where the waters get more interesting, should you be feeling brave.

Pacific City Fishing. (503) 351-9019; pacificcityfishing.com. Pacific City is the only place on the Oregon Coast that is home to a large dory fleet. Visitors to Pacific City's beach can't miss the flat-bottomed boats and their trademark manner of taking off and landing—right through the waves onto the sand. Commercial dory fishermen have been fishing for salmon out of Pacific City since the early 1900s, and were the area's primary fishermen in the 1960s and '70s. Today the fleet is more modest but still impressive to watch, the salmon still taste great, and all dory fish are still caught with a hook and line. Pacific City Fishing is a licensed, beach-launched, dory fishing charter that offers ocean fishing for salmon, bottom fish, halibut, and Dungeness crab. Captain Mark Lytle leads the way! Seasonal, depending on ocean conditions, but generally Apr or May through Sept or Oct.

Twist Wine Co. 6424 Pacific Ave., Unit B; (503) 932-1744; twistwine.com. Twist Wine Co. serves Basket Case Wines, created by Chenin and Sean Carlton in 2006 in an effort to radically change the wine business, or at least one tiny corner of it. Here, it's not about exclusivity, arrogance, elitism, or pomposity—it's about having fun. Offering several varieties of wine, all made in the McMinnville area, Twist also is known for great beers on tap.

where to eat

Beach Wok. 6320 Pacific Ave.; (503) 483-1234; pacificcitybeachwok.com. Beach Wok features a menu of Asian-inspired cuisine, which changes frequently to incorporate fresh and local ingredients. Korean meatballs, pork pot stickers, bacon katsu skewers, and Thai curry are popular dishes. Chef/owners Tammy and Timm Lakey are veteran restaurateurs who assure diners that no MSG, peanut oil, or dairy is used, and many dishes are gluten-free. Open Fri through Tues 11:30 a.m. to 9 p.m. $–$$.

Ben & Jeff's Burgers and Tacos. 33260 Cape Kiwanda Dr.; (503) 483-1026; benandjeffs .com. Attached to Moment Surf Co., this delicious destination serves burgers, tacos, burritos, fish-and-chips, beer, wine, soda, and a delicious margarita. Limited seating, or carry your meal out to the beach. On weekends, they open early and sell breakfast burritos and Bloody Marys. Open Mon and Wed through Fri 11 a.m. to 5 p.m., Sat and Sun 9 a.m. to 7 p.m. $.

Grateful Bread Restaurant Bakery. 34805 Brooten Rd.; (503) 965-7337. The stuff of legends. First known for their fresh bread and pastries, Grateful Bread is now long-famous for their great breakfasts, lunches, and pizzas. There might be a wait for a table, but you will leave this lovely, laid-back, well-lit establishment stuffed and happy. This is also a great place to buy a tie-dyed shirt. Open for breakfast and lunch daily. $–$$.

Meridian Restaurant. 33000 Cape Kiwanda Dr., at the Headlands Coastal Lodge and Spa; (503) 483-3000; headlandslodge.com/dining/meridian. This beautiful oceanfront restaurant and bar boasts massive windows with views of the beach and sea, and focuses on locally sourced farm- and ocean-to-table cuisine, prepared by executive chef Andrew Garrison and the culinary team. Mary's Garden is Meridian's own herb garden, named for owner Mary Jones, and grows greens to season the Northwest-inspired menu. The space is modern and fun, with a fireplace at one end and a bar overlooking the open kitchen at the other. Open daily: brunch/lunch 8 a.m. to 3 p.m.; dinner 5 to 9 p.m.; bar opens at 11 a.m. $$–$$$.

Pelican Pub & Brewery. 33180 Cape Kiwanda Dr.; (503) 965-7007; pelicanbrewing.com. Situated practically right on the beach, Pelican Pub & Brewery is a great place to hang out and watch the surf, eat great food, and drink award-winning microbrews. There is an outdoor patio open seasonally, and a large bar to perch at when the wait list for a table gets long. Awarded Champion Small Brewery at the 2014 World Beer Cup, Pelican Pub is often the center of the action in Pacific City. Open Sun through Thurs 10:30 a.m. to 10 p.m., Fri and Sat 10:30 a.m. to 11 p.m. $$.

Stimulus Coffee + Bakery. 33105 Cape Kiwanda Dr.; (503) 965-4661; stimuluscoffee .com. The bakers here start at 4 a.m. and their payoff is that they get to watch the sun rise over Haystack Rock every morning. Come in for a cup of coffee and baked breakfast treats like brioche, scones, muffins, or their signature Beach Buns, accented with hazelnuts and

where all the people are

There was a time when Pacific City was a bit of a secret. The pretty beach town is tucked off of the highway, and to this day, isn't an incorporated city. It took a while for this place to be discovered—but boy, has it ever been, especially in high season. I rolled into town a few years ago on a hot summer day. Temperatures had reached over 100 degrees Fahrenheit inland, and Oregonians were flocking to the shore. We arrived in town only to find one of the largest crowds I'd ever seen, any-where. A line streamed out the door of the **Cape Kiwanda Market** *and a two-hour wait list was on tap at* **Pelican Pub & Brewery.** *The people-watching was amaz-ing, and the cool ocean air and views of the sea still did the trick, but peaceful it was not. If it's no wait times and a beach to yourself that you're after, keep turning these pages—the southern Oregon Coast is the place to go for a delightful dose of privacy and serenity.*

lemon zest salt. There are a few sandwiches and bowls available for lunch. Tip: If you're staying at the Inn at Cape Kiwanda or Headlands Coastal Lodge, Stimulus will deliver room service. $.

where to stay

Cape Kiwanda RV Resort. 33305 Cape Kiwanda Dr.; (503) 965-6230; capekiwandarv resort.com. In keeping with the casual, beachfront, surfer atmosphere, many visitors to Pacific City simply bring their RV, or even a tent. In this case, the Cape Kiwanda RV Resort is the place to be. Right across from the beach and the Pelican Pub, it offers not only easy access to the surf, but also an exercise room, a heated pool and spa, and a full market stocking fresh seafood, clothing, souvenirs, espresso, and fresh-scooped Tillamook ice cream. How many RV parks can say that? The park is also an excellent place to set your kid loose on a bicycle to lap the campground, make new like-minded friends, and pick up some surfing tips. New are a few cottages and cabins to choose from should you wish to camp in luxury. $.

Cottages at Cape Kiwanda. 33000 Cape Kiwanda Dr.; (866) 571-0605; headlandslodge .com/accommodations/oceanfront-cottages. At the base of Cape Kiwanda are these 2- and 3-bedroom luxury oceanfront suites with full kitchens and awesome views overlooking the beach and the cape. Indoor soaking tubs are included, and some units are dog-friendly. These units are available for sale too, should you become so enamored you don't want to leave. $$$.

Hart's Camp Airstreams. 33145 Webb Park Rd.; (503) 965-7006; hartscamp.com. Why camp when you can glamp? Hart's Camp offers vintage and new Airstream trailers equipped with a full kitchen, flat-screen TV, luxury linens, outdoor shower with living plant walls, gas grill, private fenced outdoor space, fire pit, picnic table, and bikes. Many of the Airstreams are pet-friendly too. $$.

Headlands Coastal Lodge and Spa. 33000 Cape Kiwanda Dr.; (503) 483-3000; head landslodge.com. Headlands Coastal Lodge was a long time in the making. Owners Jeff Schons and Mary Jones came to Pacific City for a getaway in 1990 and never left. Since then, they have brought their finesse in property development to the town, founding the Pelican Pub and the Inn at Cape Kiwanda, among a host of other businesses. Headlands was their longtime dream, and since it opened its doors in 2018, stands as their masterpiece. Walk through the grand entry doors and take in the luxurious open room that contains the lobby, restaurant, and bar, with views straight through to the sea and Haystack Rock. Every one of the 33 luxury rooms at this boutique hotel has a private balcony with oceanfront views of the beach and Cape Kiwanda. Rooms are appointed with cast-iron soaking tubs, gas fireplaces, pillow-top mattresses, peekaboo views south and north, and even a bike or surfboard rack to keep your toys tucked easily out of the way.

Jeff and Mary want guests to truly take advantage of the area's natural playground, and Adventure Coaches are on staff and on hand to help you plan your outdoor adventures. Huge maps on each floor also highlight recreation (and are just plain cool to look at). If you prefer, stay in and recharge your batteries at the spa or the workout room, which also has ocean views. Luxury linens, Northwest decor, loaner bikes, and works by regional artists make you feel like a well-tended local. The Meridian Restaurant is on-site (see separate listing in Where to Eat). $$$.

Inn at Cape Kiwanda. 33105 Cape Kiwanda Dr.; (503) 965-7001; innatcapekiwanda.com. Boasting an ocean view from every room and cozy gas fireplaces, the Inn at Cape Kiwanda is a quiet, relaxing, and romantic getaway in Pacific City. Downstairs at this multistoried hotel you'll find restaurants and shops. From your room, views of Haystack Rock, cozy gas fireplaces, and plush pillow-top beds with feather pillows will leave you satisfied. $$–$$$.

Shorepine Vacation Rentals. 33105 Cape Kiwanda Dr.; (877) 549-2632; shorepinerentals .com. A huge variety of fully furnished vacation homes, up to 5 bedrooms in size and located throughout Pacific City, are available through this business. Plenty of choices to accommodate the most discerning beachgoers, from couples seeking solitude to family reunions of grand proportions. $$$.

Surf and Sand Inn. 35215 Brooten Rd.; (503) 965-6366; surfandsandinn.com. This inn was once a Coast Guard headquarters. Today, it is a nice inexpensive alternative to the fancier resorts. The 16-unit motor lodge doesn't have ocean views but is conveniently located within walking distance to shopping and dining. $.

central coast

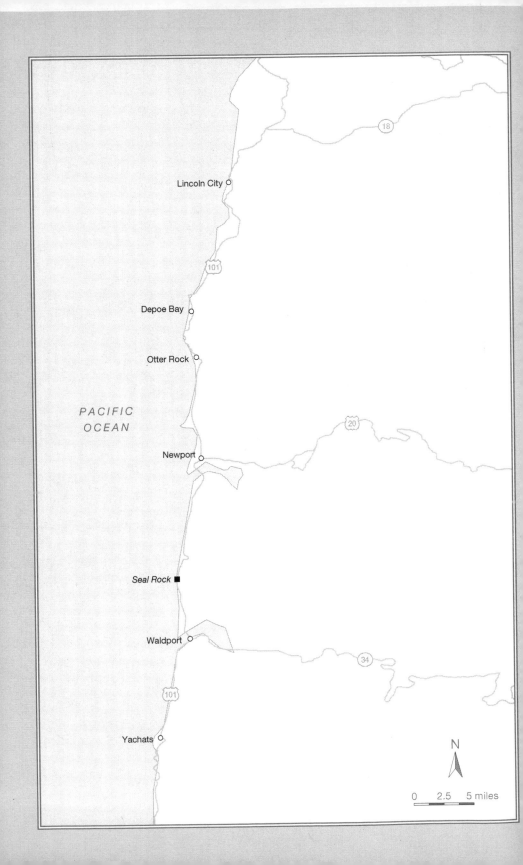

day trip 09

central coast

>>> **sandcastles & glass floats:**
lincoln city

lincoln city

Lincoln City identifies itself by the phrase "7 miles of smiles," referring to the long and lovely sandy beach that stretches from one end of this city to the other. The oceanfront is highly accessible here, which is just one of the draws to this family-friendly city on the central Oregon Coast with a come-one-come-all vibe.

Lincoln City was once five separate towns, and Taft, Delake, Oceanlake, Nelscott, and Cutler City remain as semi-distinct districts strung along Highway 101, with their own unique flavors. Taft, on the south end, is defined by history, art, and clam digging. Oceanlake is the northern of the five, located just to the north of the D River, which divides the town north from south. Like Delake, Oceanlake refers to Lincoln City's frequently overlooked Devils Lake—yes, in addition to the Pacific Ocean at its western flank, Lincoln City claims a 3-mile lake within its city limits.

If your visit to Lincoln City falls between the months of October and May, you're in for a special treasure hunt. The city sponsors artists to create almost 3,000 hand-blown colorful glass floats, a few of which are placed upon the beach daily. If you find one, you get to take it home. The program is a nod to the glass floats historically made by Japanese artisans to keep afloat their fishing nets, and which would occasionally wash up on the shores of the Oregon Coast.

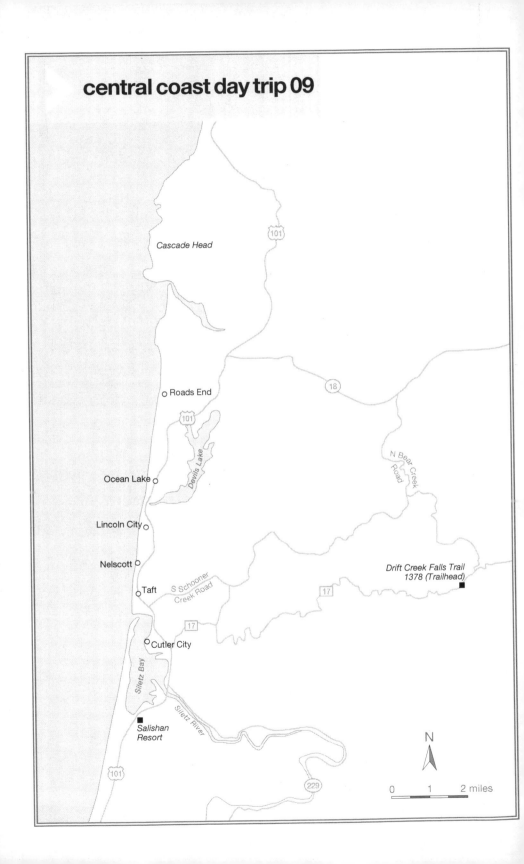

central coast day trip 09

Tons of lodging, a large selection of restaurants, and all the coastal delights one can expect, from taffy to surfing to chowder to kite flying, round out a day trip to Lincoln City.

getting there

From Salem: Travel OR 22 west for 30 miles to the intersection with OR 18. Continue on OR 18 another 30 miles until it intersects with US 101. Continue south on US 101 3 miles into Lincoln City.

where to go

Cascade Head. 9 miles north of Lincoln City off US 101. Cascade Head towers over the north end of Lincoln City and Roads End Beach. A winding dirt road from Highway 101 leads to a network of trails that lead to overlooks offering some of the best views on the Oregon Coast. Explore a 270-acre wonderland full of old-growth forest and rare plant and animal species. Prepare for strong winds on top of the head in any season.

Connie Hansen Gardens. 1931 NW 33rd St.; (541) 994-6338; conniehansengarden.com. This small community garden is run entirely by volunteers. The garden is more than an acre in size, and its many paths reveal blooming shrubs, hundreds of rhododendrons, and flowering trees. Don't miss the marvelous Japanese irises growing on-site. Cultivated in Japan for over 500 years, and once restricted to enjoyment by royalty only, today the flower is still far less common than the bearded iris. Visit the garden in the spring and early summer to see this unique flower in bloom.

Devils Lake. Several access points including East and West Devils Lake Roads. You could visit Lincoln City dozens of times and not notice Devils Lake, which anchors a huge chunk

nelscott reef

*For die-hard, big-time surfers, **Nelscott Reef** offshore of Lincoln City is the stuff of legends. It's one of a handful of waves around the world that rarely are activated, but when they are, they are the biggest of the big guys. The timing is so unpredictable that surfers usually only have a few days' notice to get themselves to Lincoln City to ride waves as high as 40 or 50 feet, in what is annually named the **Nelscott Reef Big Wave Classic.** The wave is too far offshore for visitors to witness the action in the sea, but there is plenty of associated action onshore during the event. Interested in surfing yourself? Nelscott is only for the true experts; for surfing options for mere mortals, stop in at **Lincoln City Surf Shop** for lessons and gear rentals, and try the waves at the spot known as Canyons, south of the D River.*

of the city's northeast acres like a friendly, watery retreat. Sheltered from the coastal winds, visitors ski, boat, fish, and swim in the broad, shallow waters. The 3-mile-long lake is just a quarter of a mile inland. Regatta Grounds Park, located at the central point of the lake, is perfect for BBQs, parties, and swimming. Rent a boat or kayak at Blue Heron Landing. Windsurfing and kitesurfing are also popular.

Drift Creek Falls. 15 miles east of Lincoln City via US 101 and FR 17. The rain-drenched Siuslaw National Forest shelters this amazing waterfall. The 65-foot falls is gorgeous, but another highlight of the hike is the bridge over Drift Creek, which overlooks the waterfall itself. At 240 feet across, the cable suspension bridge is anchored to two bluffs, can hold over 150,000 pounds, and offers a bird's-eye view of the cascading water. The 3-mile round-trip hike is a moderately difficult and family-friendly adventure, descending through a lush forest to the waterfall canyon below. Expect crowds on weekends.

Game Over. 2821 NW US 101; (541) 614-1150; gameover-arcade.com. When the weather keeps you off of the beach, make a visit to this classic arcade in the heart of the city. Over 100 new and classic games and pinball machines keep the whole family entertained. Open 7 days a week.

Jennifer Sears Glass Art Studio. 4821 SW US 101; (541) 996-2569; lincolncityglass center.com. This destination in the Taft District is part art gallery, part studio. Peruse glass art made by local artists and buy some to take home. Or do what I did and sign up to learn to blow a glass float of your own, with the help of an expert instructor. Visitors were lined up out the front door as soon as it opened at the chance for this experience when I was there, and I soon learned why. Making your own float is a blast that results in a very personal and lasting souvenir. It's also educational. Jennifer Sears was an art enthusiast and Lincoln City booster, and this gallery is a fitting tribute to her.

North Lincoln County Historical Museum. 4907 SW US 101; (541) 996-6614; north lincolncountyhistoricalmuseum.org. Lincoln County was once home to a fairy-tale-themed park in Otis (3 miles north of Lincoln City). Pixieland featured a steam locomotive, a log flume ride, and an opera house, but sadly didn't survive 10 years. Learn about Pixieland's history and more at this regional museum. The history of local settlers is on display, as is a large collection of antique Japanese fishing floats, which would wash up on the shores in decades past.

Siletz Bay. South end of Lincoln City, in the Historic Taft District. Home to the mysterious "Four Brothers" rock formations, Siletz Bay is also a great place to catch your dinner. Toss a crab trap right offshore and catch fresh Dungeness crab. Or, at low tide when the bay becomes a mudflat, dig for purple varnish clams. Bring a shovel, a bucket, and the neces- sary shellfish license, available from the Oregon Department of Fish and Wildlife. And wear boots—clam digging is a blast but it's a remarkably muddy experience.

where to shop

Lincoln City Outlets. 1500 SE East Devils Lake Rd.; (541) 996-5000; lincolncityoutlets
.com. Some folks would rather shop than hit the beach. This mall is a destination in itself,
featuring discounts you won't find anywhere else on the Oregon Coast. Lincoln City Outlets
is your one-stop shopping destination in town, featuring the North Face, Nike, and Gap.

Prehistoric. 1425 NW US 101; (541) 614-1294; prehistoricoregon.com. Your destination
for ancient artifacts! Minerals, fossils, and meteorites are on hand in this shop, in the Oceanlake District, that's almost like a mini-museum. The kids will love the break-your-own-geode
machine, gold panning station, and the excavation kits for sale, and there's even a life-size
baby T-Rex to greet you at the front door. There is plenty to look at and more to buy here.

Northwest Winds Kites and Toys. 130 SW US 101; (541) 994-1004; nwwinds.biz. Lincoln
City was once known as the kite capital of the world and still hosts two kite festivals a year,
in the summer and fall. Get your supplies to hit the beach and catch the wind any time of
the year here, where colorful kites of all shapes and sizes are to be found, as well as wind
chimes, wind socks, and much more.

Rock Your World. 3203 SW US 101; (541) 351-8423; rockyourworldgems.com. A couple
of local rockhounds loved beachcombing so much that they decided to make jewelry from
their finds. This quaint shop in the Nelscott district offers necklaces and rings made out of
agates, quartz, labradorite, and jasper, as well as rough rock and loose gemstones.

cascade head and road's end

All of Lincoln City's 7 miles of beach are welcoming and enjoyable for a stroll, but
Road's End, *on the north end of town, is special. The beach here is often littered
with small stones, agates, and shells, making it terrific for beachcombing.* **Cascade
Head** *is at the far north end, a looming and gigantic presence that also creates
tide pools at its base for fun exploration. Watch for surfers off the point break here.
At low tide, continue around the base of the head to a hidden cove beach—but
don't linger too long or you'll be trapped for hours until the tide recedes. For a different perspective, drive Highway 101 to the trail access on top of Cascade Head
and hike out to the overlook to gaze down upon the hidden beach and Road's End
beach. The day we hiked this route, the wind was whipping like mad, and we only
lasted a few minutes taking in that incredible view of the entire stretch of Lincoln
City. Nevertheless, it was worth it.*

where to eat

The Bay House. 5911 SW US 101; (541) 996-3222; thebayhouse.org. There are only four restaurants in Oregon that currently carry a four-diamond AAA rating, and one of them is in Lincoln City. The Bay House features fine dining with a spectacular view of Siletz Bay and eclectic seafood cuisine from award-winning chef Kevin Ryan. Try the sea scallops, the Muscovy duck, or the crab cakes. $$–$$$.

Blackfish Cafe. 2733 NW US 101; (541) 996-1007; blackfishcafe.com. You have to love a place serious enough to deliver elegantly and excellently prepared fresh seafood but casual enough to make their own handmade "ding dong" dessert. Owner and executive chef Rob Pounding brings eclectic influences to the table at this award-wining eatery. Try the grilled Pacific swordfish or the pork brisket. $$–$$$.

Fathoms. 4009 SW US 101; (541) 994-1601; spanishhead.com/fathoms. This restaurant at the top floor of the Inn at Spanish Head has towering, incredible views of the ocean. Have a cocktail, breakfast, lunch, or dinner with the Pacific Ocean and the sandy beach spread out before you. Keep your eye out for whales, seabirds, and mighty storms. The restaurant serves a variety of Pacific Northwest cuisine, while the bar has lighter versions of the same fare. From 4 to 5:30 p.m., an early-bird dinner offers a limited selection of dinner items at a reduced price. $–$$$.

Gallucci's. 2845 NW US 101; (541) 994-3411; galluccispizzaria.com. Gallucci's tastes like my hometown pizza place. This restaurant has been serving quality Italian food for over four decades. A large menu features pizza, pasta, salads, jojos, and delicious broasted chicken. There's a video game room for the kids to keep them occupied while they wait for their pizza meal. $–$$.

Kyllo's. 1110 NW 1st. Ct.; (541) 994-3179; kyllosseafoodandgrill.com. Tide times and sunset times are posted in this restaurant because they matter here. Kyllo's was built on stilts over the D River and the beach near the D River Wayside, and the ocean rolls right up to the restaurant under the right conditions. The restaurant has amazing views of the shore as well as delicious foods. Fresh seafoods from halibut to lingcod, clam chowder, grass-fed beef, and an amazing happy hour are just some of the delights found at this locals' favorite. $–$$$.

Puerto Vallarta. 3001 NW US 101; (541) 994-0300; puertovallartalc.com. Every town needs a locals' favorite Mexican restaurant, with cheerful colorful decor, fun music, and delicious meals to choose from. Burritos, quesadillas, tacos, and the like are fresh-made, as are the house margaritas, in this little white building on the highway. $$.

Rusty Truck Brewing. 4649 SW US 101; (541) 994-7729; rustytruckbrewing.com. Rusty Truck doesn't look like much from the outside, but this brewery and restaurant in the Taft

District is a fun and delicious destination. The old roadhouse-themed brewery is huge inside, with a wraparound bar, stage for live music, and spacious restaurant with booths and tables. Try their award-winning Cherry Chocoholic Baltic Porter, Road Wrecker IPA, or Moonlight Ride Blackberry Ale with a hand-tossed pizza, burger, cioppino, ribs, or mac and cheese. $$.

Wildflower Grill. 4250 NE US 101; (541) 994-9663; thewildflowergrill.com. This little cottage overlooking a wetland is simply an undeniably great place to start your day. Watch birds perch in tall Douglas firs while you nosh on delicious breakfast entrees including crab eggs Benedict or the Northwest omelet, which is stuffed with smoked salmon and cream cheese. The food is downright gourmet, and the view of the forest and water is relaxing and lovely. $–$$.

where to stay

Chinook Winds Casino Resort. 1777 NW 44th St.; (888) 244-6665; chinookwindscasino .com.This large destination hotel and casino offers several restaurants and lounges, a two-story gaming area, and a 300-seat concert room delivering live music both free and ticketed. Affordable child care is available on-site, and the whole place is steps from the beach. $–$$.

Looking Glass Inn. 861 SW 51st St.; (541) 996-3996; lookingglass-inn.com. Located right on the Bayfront next to Mo's (page 18), the Looking Glass Inn is the perfect spot for couples, families, and Fido. *Sunset Magazine* has rated the inn as one of the most pet-friendly hotels in the West. Dog-guests get a complimentary basket full of goodies and treats. All guests enjoy views of Siletz Bay and the Pacific Ocean. $$.

Ocean Terrace Condominiums. 4229 SW Beach Ave.; (541) 996-3623; oceanterrace .com. Families and larger groups will appreciate this oceanfront property for its affordability and location. Just steps from the beach in the Taft District, Ocean Terrace offers suites sleeping up to 6 people with full kitchens and balconies overlooking a staircase to the beach, private to the property. A real hit for the kids are the heated indoor pool and recreation room, with pool table and ping-pong. $–$$.

Salishan Resort. 7760 N US 101; (541) 764-3600; salishan.com. This luxury resort tucked into the forest and near the ocean has been an Oregon Coast icon for 50 years. Locally sourced woods, natural light, and harmony with the natural surroundings were ideals used to construct the lodge and rooms. Some include bay and forest views. A spa, indoor pool, golf course, and tennis courts are on-site. Several restaurants cover the gamut from casual to fine dining. Beach access is via a trail down a hill and across the highway. Look for examples of local and regional art throughout the property. Don't miss the chance to play a round of mini-golf with the kids. $$–$$$.

Surftides Resort. 2945 NW Jetty Ave.; (541) 994-2191; surftideslincolncity.com. A large property with one of the best views in Lincoln City, Surftides features a tennis court, an indoor pool, and an on-property restaurant, Mist Restaurant and Lounge. The resort hosts a fun game—find the hidden mermaid during your stay, and your next visit is complimentary. $$.

day trip 10

central coast

a whale of a good time:
depoe bay

depoe bay

Depoe Bay may be a small town of less than 1,000 people, but it packs a punch when it comes to scenery and action—at least the oceanic kind of action.

A huge sea wall runs the length of the downtown area along Highway 101, providing dramatic ocean views along its length. This sidewalk and overlook are great for a stroll and sightseeing with a bird's-eye view—but be aware of Depoe Bay's famous spouting horns. Waves run beneath lava beds at the base of the sea wall and build pressure to spout water as high as 60 feet into the air. The spouting horns are visible during turbulent seas and stormy weather. On a day when the ocean is tempestuous, the horns can blow seawater all the way across the highway.

Historically, Depoe Bay was a fishing village, and to this day maintains the smallest natural navigable harbor in the world, consisting of a total of 6 square acres. The passageway to and from the bay is notoriously rough, and it takes a great deal of skill on the part of boat captains to maneuver this hazardous, rocky, and narrow passage. But maneuver it they do, going out to sea daily on commercial and recreational fishing tours.

Aside from the spouting horns, Depoe Bay is famous for whales. This small town calls itself the Whale Watching Capital of the World, with good reason. A resident pod of gray whales makes its home off Depoe Bay from March through December, and your chances of

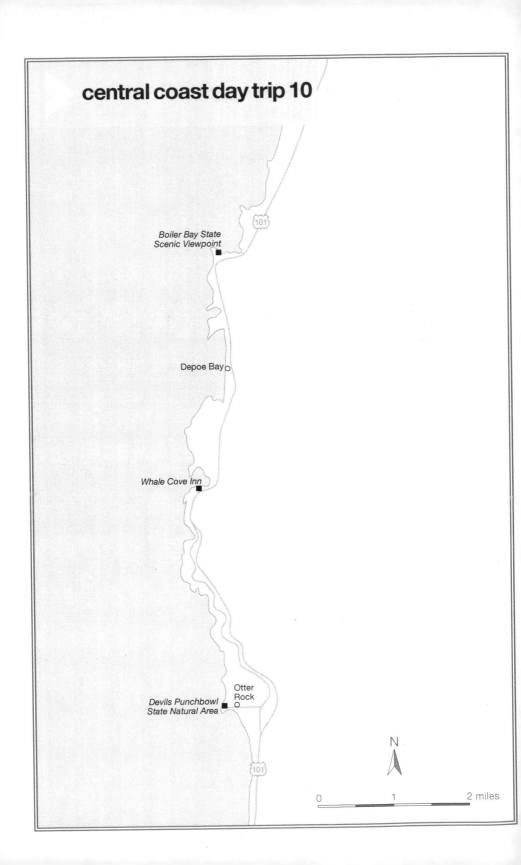

central coast day trip 10

Boiler Bay State
Scenic Viewpoint

Depoe Bay

Whale Cove Inn

Otter
Rock

Devils Punchbowl
State Natural Area

N

0   1   2 miles

spotting a whale here are better than average. Depoe Bay also has terrific restaurants, fun shopping, and a few lodging gems.

getting there

From Salem: Take OR 22 west for 30 miles to the intersection with OR 18. Travel OR 18 west another 30 miles until it intersects with US 101. Continue south through Lincoln City, and continue another 12 miles south along US 101 to Depoe Bay.

where to go

Boiler Bay State Scenic Viewpoint. 1.5 miles north of Depoe Bay on US 101; (800) 551-6949; oregonstateparks.org. Named for a sunken ship's boiler visible at low tide, this rugged, basalt-rimmed bay is a great place to watch wild surf action on the rocky spurs. Watch for migrating and resident gray whales, as well as oceangoing birds like shearwaters, jaegers, albatrosses, grebes, pelicans, loons, oystercatchers, and murrelets.

Depoe Bay Scenic View Area. Park by the fire station at 325 US 101 and walk to Coast Street; look for signs that read Depoe Bay Scenic View Area. A short hike through a magical coastal forest emerges to a clearing with a bench and an incredible view. From here,

whale watching spoken here

*Gray whales have one of the longest annual migrations of any species, swimming more than 10,000 miles round-trip between their feeding grounds in the Bering, Chukchi, and Beaufort Seas of the Arctic to nursery lagoons in the warm waters of Baja California, Mexico. The grays can cover about 100 miles a day, coasting 3 to 6 miles per hour—an impressive speed for an animal that weighs 30 to 40 tons. On each trip, approximately 18,000 gray whales swim by the Oregon Coast, often within 5 miles of the shore. Whale watching is so productive on the West Coast that 30 years ago a unique program was developed called **Whale Watching Spoken Here.** Two weeks a year are specially designated as official Whale Watch Weeks, typically between the Christmas holiday and New Year's Day, and during the last week in March, which coincide with prime whale-watching times. Mid-December through mid-January is when they travel south; spring watching begins in late March and continues until June as they venture north. During official Whale Watch Weeks, hundreds of whales a day pass by and volunteers are on hand at 24 locations on the Oregon Coast to help visitors spot, and appreciate, our offshore friends. See whalespoken.wordpress.com.*

you can see the tip of downtown and turbulent Depoe Bay, and get a glimpse of what the spouting horn is up to.

Devil's Punchbowl State Natural Area. 5.5 miles south of Depoe Bay in Otter Rock. A hollow rock formation shaped like a huge punch bowl sits in the sea just offshore at this roadside pullout, which offers short trails, a picnic area, and terrific views. During winter storms, the ocean slams with a thundering roar into the punch bowl, churning into a swirling frenzy that is a sight to behold. The punch bowl was probably created by the collapse of the roof over two sea caves, then shaped by wave action. This is another spot to watch for whales, as well as just take in a panoramic sea view. On the north side of the area are tide pools to explore. Parking is limited and is only allowed in parking stalls.

Tradewinds Charters Whale Watching and Fishing. 118 US 101; (541) 765-2345; tradewindscharters.com. One- and 2-hour whale-watching excursions are available from this charter, which uses large boats that anchor offshore while whales feed around them. If fishing is your dream vacation trip, there are plenty of options for guided trips here as well, from 5- to 8-hour outings. Catch lingcod, rockfish, and sea bass year-round, and halibut and chinook salmon when in season.

Whale Research EcoExcursions. 234 US 101; (541) 912-6734; oregonwhales.com. Marine biologist Carrie Newell loves whales. She and her team of naturalists have worked with the summer resident gray whale population offshore of Depoe Bay for over 25 years. Unlike many whale-watching excursions, Newell's use Zodiac boats, so that tour-goers are lower to the water and closer to the action (as well as less likely to get seasick). Alongside salty spray and the wind in your face, the trip comes with education, not only on all aspects of the gray whale but also on other marine life including seals, sea lions, and seabirds and unique oceanographic features. There is a small museum at the launch site, with exhibits interpreting whales, wildlife, natural history, and more.

Whale Watching Center. 119 US 101; (800) 551-6949; oregonstateparks.org. Naturally, the Whale Watching Capital of the World needs its own whale-watching center. Visit this destination along the seawall in scenic Depoe Bay and converse with educated and trained park staff, ready to answer your questions and help you spot gray whales. Watch and learn about whales and their behavior, as they blow, dive, spyhop, and breach. Many species including humpback whales, orcas, dolphins, porpoises, and even blue whales have been spotted from these windows.

where to shop

Blue Heron Gallery. 76 US 101; (541) 765-2441; blueheroncollectibles.com. A wide variety of hard-to-find art and collectibles are on hand here including Hummel, Swarovski, Walt Disney Classics, and more. This longtime gallery is also home to jewelry and decorative items made from the Ponderosa Oregon sunstone, a unique and beautiful gemstone mined in south-central Oregon.

Gift shops. The main downtown area of Depoe Bay is great for wandering and shopping, and many gift shops are here for your perusal. What will you take home?

Country Cousins Gift Shop. 38 US 101; (541) 765-2820. T-shirts, figurines, souvenirs, and all manner of beach kitsch for the shopper.

LaVoy's at Depoe Bay. 14 US 101; (541) 764-2251; lavoysatdepoebay.com. Myrtlewood, gems and crystals, scented candles, jewelry, greeting cards, and wood-carved gifts are on hand at LaVoy's.

Pacific Brass and Copper Works. 20 Bay St.; (541) 765-2626. Decorate your home, boat, cabin, or RV with an authentically nautical brass and copper antique collectible by perusing the aisles of this little shop just off the highway.

SeaView Bazaar. 72 US 101; (541) 765-2566. Depoe Bay sweatshirts and T-shirts, souvenirs, sea-life stuffed animals, and more are within the walls of this visitors' favorite bazaar.

Zephyrus. 48 US 101; (541) 764-5483. Find all things that catch the wind here, including whirligigs and both single-string and stunt kites. Also find toys and home, yard, and garden decor.

where to eat

Chowder Bowl. 40 US 101; (541) 765-2300. Lunch and dinner are served here 7 days a week and include burgers, sandwiches, and seafood. Expect large portions, often served with a slice of garlic bread. Feeling brave? Have an oyster shooter. Chase it with an Oregon beer or wine. $–$$.

Gracie's Sea Hag. 58 US 101; (541) 765-2734; theseahag.com. Gracie's has been a Depoe Bay destination since 1963. A maritime theme extends throughout this seafood restaurant, which boasts award-winning clam chowder and live music. Breakfast, lunch, and dinner are served from a huge menu which also includes a light menu and a kids' menu. Try the seafood kabob or the Cannonball Express—a bread bowl full of chowder. Open 7 days a week from 7 a.m. to 9:30 p.m. $$.

The Horn Public House and Depoe Bay Brewing Co. 110 US 101; (541) 764-6886; thehorn.pub. This large restaurant right in the heart of town has two floors as well as a gift shop and a brewery on-site. From the second floor, take in views of the Depoe Bay Harbor and the Pacific Ocean (the Whale Watching Center is just across the street). Brews created on-site include the Sea Witch Porter and the Moby Red. Fish-and-chips, burgers,

fleet of flowers

Since 1945, Depoe Bay has been home to an annual event of remembrance. Those who work on the sea face danger every day. The **Fleet of Flowers** *ceremony, held each Memorial Day weekend, was created to honor two local fishermen, Roy Bower and Jack Chambers, who died while trying to rescue a troller caught in a storm. The event has grown to include the memory of all of those lost at sea. A parade of wreath- and flower-bedecked boats passes under the Highway 101 bridge, which is lined with spectators. Just offshore, the vessels form a circle and place their flowers in the water as a Coast Guard helicopter drops a wreath in their midst. The moving, exhilarating experience is amazing to witness. See depoebaychamber.org.*

sandwiches, and lots of pizza options round out the menu. The dessert menu features a lemon IPA cupcake—a must-try just to say that you did. Closed Tues. $$.

Restaurant Beck. 2345 US 101; (541) 765-3220; restaurantbeck.com. Chef Justin Wills was a James Beard semifinalist for Best Chef Northwest in 2012 and 2013. He and his wife Stormee chose the Oregon Coast as their home, opening this restaurant focused on regionally farmed and locally foraged foods, as well as fresh seafood and local-regional wines. The menu is small, precise, and astonishing, offering foie gras, wagyu beef, and halibut served with fiddlehead ferns. Restaurant Beck is located at the Whale Cove Inn. Open for dinner only, 7 days a week. $$$.

Tidal Raves Seafood Grill. 279 US 101; (541) 765-2995; tidalraves.com. Open daily, with raves coming about the food as well as the views. Wild shrimp sauté, razor clams, cioppino, and many more delectable dishes focused on local seafoods are on the menu, as are specialty cocktails and many incredible desserts. Tidal Raves might be fine dining, but they don't take themselves too seriously, as evidenced by the kids' menu and the fact that the bartender is referred to as the "spiritual leader." Open daily 11 a.m. to close. $$–$$$.

where to stay

Channel House Inn. 35 Ellingson St.; (541) 765-2140; channelhouse.com. Perched on an oceanfront bluff where the bay enters the ocean, this inn has 15 rooms, each a little bit different but with elegance and amenities including whirlpools on oceanfront decks and gas fireplaces. Take in the panoramic views, amazing sunsets, and occasional whales passing by. Breakfast is included. Channel House Inn discourages guests under the age of 16. $$$.

An Ocean Paradise Whales Rendezvous B&B. 147 N US 101; (541) 765-3455; whales rendezvous.com. This romantic getaway allows you to enjoy antiques, elegance, and the comfort of home—if home has an ocean view from every window. This seafront bed-and-breakfast has only two rooms, the Ocean Garden Suite and the Sea Rose Suite. Each offers an outdoor fireplace near a private garden overlooking the sea. Watch for whales, storms, surfers, and more from the comfort of your own deck. $$$.

Whale Cove Inn. 2345 US 101; (541) 765-4300; whalecoveinn.com. This luxury boutique hotel even looks impressive from the highway. Perched on a hillside with stunning sea views, the rooms are finely appointed, and some specialty suites sleep up to 6 and have a kitchen and a Jacuzzi tub on the patio. On-site is Restaurant Beck, where complimentary breakfast is served. Whale Cove Inn discourages guests under the age of 16. $$$.

day trip 11

central coast

poets & fishermen:
newport

newport

Newport's location is about halfway between California and Washington, and that position translates metaphorically too. The city strikes a balance between the artsy coastal towns of the northern Oregon Coast and the working coastal towns of the southern Oregon Coast. Many Newport folks work hard at traditional hands-on jobs in the forest or sea—fishing, logging, or tending to oyster beds—but there's also a big contingent of artistic types residing in Newport, from painters to writers. These diverse communities come together and blend their lives just fine, which is part of why Newport is known as "the friendliest town on the Oregon Coast."

Newport got its start on oysters. A whole batch of them was discovered in Yaquina Bay in 1862, and the delicious sea delicacies began to be exported to San Francisco and beyond. Soon after, the area opened for settlement, and a thriving tourism industry popped up immediately—especially amazing given that there wasn't even a road to Newport until 1927.

From the get-go, development in Newport centered around two distinct areas: the Bayfront and Nye Beach. These remain the city's primary gathering places, each with its own character. Nye Beach is an artsy village, home to dining establishments, bakeries, and shops. It's also the primary access to a long and lovely sandy shoreline. The Bayfront is a traditional coastal vacationer's dream—galleries, saltwater taffy and ice cream vendors,

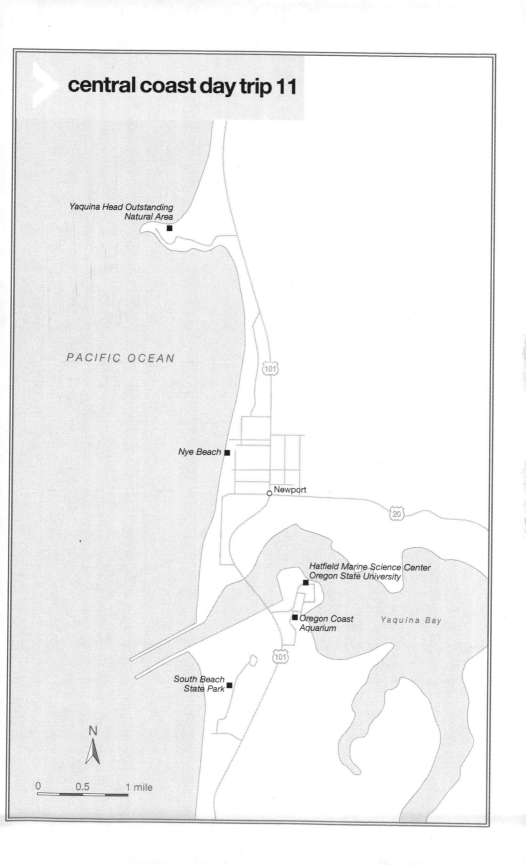

central coast day trip 11

Yaquina Head Outstanding
Natural Area ■

PACIFIC OCEAN

101

Nye Beach ■

○ Newport

20

Hatfield Marine Science Center
Oregon State University ■

■ Oregon Coast
Aquarium   Yaquina Bay

101

South Beach
State Park ■

N

0   0.5   1 mile

beer, fish-and-chips, and attractions abound. Don't overlook South Beach, the location of a terrific state park, the Oregon Coast Aquarium, and Rogue Brewery.

With a population of about 10,000, Newport is the third-largest community on the Oregon Coast, and benefits from a thriving tourism economy and eclectic population.

getting there

From Salem: Take I-5 south for 31 miles to exit 228. Turn west onto OR 34 and travel 10 miles to Corvallis, where OR 34 intersects with OR 20. Continue west on OR 20 for 48 miles until you reach Newport.

where to go

Hatfield Marine Science Center. 2030 S Marine Science Dr.; (541) 867-0126; hmsc.oregon state.edu. The public wing of Oregon State University's Mark O. Hatfield Marine Science Center showcases live marine animals, interactive marine science puzzles and games, and other aspects of our amazing ocean planet. Trained volunteers and a fabulous bookstore are major perks. Visitors might find an octopus in the lobby—science center staff exhibit an octopus for a few months at a time and then return it to the sea, awaiting the next donated animal from a fisherman who accidentally caught one in his net. Open year-round: 7 days a

native son

Rick Bartow was born and raised in Newport, and lived in this coastal town most of his life. The artist was a Vietnam veteran, a lifelong musician and songwriter, and an enrolled member of the Mad River Band of Wiyot Indians. Nationally, Bartow is considered one of the most important contributors to contemporary Native American art. His fine artwork explores dark themes in a riveting, thoughtful manner. The pinnacle of his life's work are two monumental cedar sculptures titled We Were Always Here, *commissioned by the Smithsonian's National Museum of the American Indian. Those sit on the northwest corner of that museum overlooking the National Mall in Washington, DC—but some of Bartow's work remains right here in his hometown. Newport City Hall has four of his works on permanent display, and the Newport Performing Arts Center has two paintings also on display. Local restaurant Arr Place displays a single work. Bartow passed away in 2016, but his life, and work, remain important to the people of his hometown. Once identified, Bartow's unique style will catch your eye again and again as you move around Newport.*

week in summer, Thurs through Mon fall through spring. Free admission, but a suggested donation of $5 per person or $20 per family is gratefully accepted.

Mariner Square. 250 SW Bay Blvd.; (541) 265-2206; marinersquare.com. These two long-time attractions reopened in spring of 2020 after a renovation to make them better than ever. Hours vary seasonally.

> **Ripley's Believe it or Not!** Robert Ripley captured the bizarre, which is definitely what can be found here, from shrunken heads to the magic harp. Don't get lost for all eternity in the deep-space hall of mirrors.

> **Wax Works.** Hundreds of sculptures, each elaborately molded and detailed from wax, in the form of Hollywood legends to sci-fi creatures. Creepy, but cool.

Newport Visual Arts Center. 777 NW Beach Dr.; (541) 265-6540; coastarts.org. The Newport Visual Arts Center, located at the historic Nye Beach Turnaround, is a municipal public art exhibition and programmatic space for art education programs. Two shows every month feature Northwest artists. Open Tues through Sun noon to 4 p.m. Free admission.

Oregon Coast Aquarium. 2820 SE Ferry Slip Rd.; (541) 867-3474; aquarium.org. A truly worthy destination, the Oregon Coast Aquarium is home to more than 15,000 marine animals in a beautiful setting. Resident species include sea otters, sea lions, octopuses, sharks, tufted puffins, and an array of tropical fish, and the grounds are gorgeously, natively landscaped with boxwood, shore pine, and wildflowers. The ocean and bay are both nearby, and exhibits offer a close-up view of what lies at their depths. Don't miss the sea jellies—they are magical. Open every day except Christmas from 10 a.m. to 5 p.m. in winter, 10 a.m. to 6 p.m. in summer.

Rogue Brewery Brewers on the Bay. 2320 OSU Dr.; (541) 867-3664; rogue.com. This big gray warehouse with a red silo out front is where Rogue makes its famous, award-winning microbrews. Visit for brewery tours, lunch or dinner at the upstairs pub, and a taste from—count 'em—50 taps. There is also plenty of logo wear for sale and a panoramic view of Yaquina Bay and the marina. Open daily; hours vary. Brewery tours also daily; call for tour times.

Yaquina Head. 750 NW Lighthouse Dr.; (541) 574-3100; blm.gov/visit/yaquina-head-ona. This 100-acre Outstanding Natural Area is an absolute don't-miss. There's no better view of the ocean, wildlife, and the Yaquina Head Lighthouse than from this natural peninsula just north of Newport. Harbor seals, brown pelicans, auklets, and up to 300,000 common murres inhabit the rocks off the point. Whale watching is a winter and spring seasonal delight. Several trails allow for small hikes with killer views. There is a great interpretive center on-site that sheds light on the natural and human history of Yaquina Head. The wind blows powerfully and storm watching can be excellent. Yaquina Head is open daily; hours vary per season. $7 per vehicle.

where to shop

The Kite Company. 407 SW Coast Hwy.; (541) 265-2004; thekitecompany.com. This enormous retail space houses the largest kite store on the Pacific coast. Every kind of kite you could dream of can be found here, including delta kites, dragon kites, box kites, diamond kites, stunt kites, and parafoil kites. Catch the wind! Open daily; call for hours.

Peerless Puffin. 742 NW Beach Dr.; (541) 265-3153. This cute little shop right by the ocean in Nye Beach with a view of the ocean has been a mainstay for decades. Find fun gifts, cards, bath and body care items, purses, jewelry, and more.

where to eat

Arr Place. 143 SW Cliff St.; (541) 265-4240; arrplace.com. The *A*, *R*, and *R* are the first initials of the first names of the family of three who run this place and live above it. Their motto is "actual food touched by human hands." The menu changes daily and the hours are unpredictable too. You might find teriyaki albacore, mushroom and leek quiche, or bread pudding on a given day's menu—always, there's some sort of scramble/hash option that's a mix of whatever is fresh, available, and yummy. Whatever you choose, it will be cooked and served by the owners, and will taste delicious. Hours vary; check the sign out front. $–$$.

mo's

As an Oregon Coast native, **Mo's Seafood and Chowder** was a mainstay I never gave much thought to. Always there to offer a reliable bowl of chowder and a touch of coastal kitschy ambiance, Mo's was never pretentious. But over the years I've come to see Mo's for much more—a priceless Oregon story. Mohava Marie Niemi founded the first Mo's on the Newport Bayfront in 1946. The "little joint on the waterfront" became a community gathering place with big enough charm to attract outsiders too, including Paul Harvey, Tom McCall, and the entire cast of Sometimes a Great Notion, when it was filmed in Newport in 1970. Director Paul Newman even gave Mo a cameo role in the film. Today, Mo's has eight locations on the Oregon Coast. But the Newport Bayfront remains the flagship restaurant, complete with the garage-door front, added when Mo suggested the idea after a patron accidentally drove her car through the front of the building. 622 SW Bay Blvd.; (541) 265-2979; moschowder.com. Open daily 11 a.m. to 9 p.m.

The Chowder Bowl. 728 NW Beach Dr.; (541) 265-7477; newportchowderbowl.com. This Nye Beach tradition is a simple beach cafe with award-winning clam chowder, seafood, burgers, beer, wine, and lots of other goodies, like bread pudding with hard sauce. You'll often find a line outside. Open 7 days a week for lunch and dinner. $–$$.

Clearwater Restaurant. 325 SW Bay Blvd.; (541) 272-5550; clearwaterrestaurant.com. One of the Bayfront's newer destinations, Clearwater sources fresh seafood, grain-fed meats, and sustainably harvested organic foods from local vendors. The food is great and so are the fresh-made cocktails. The view of the bay includes birds, sea lions, and the lovely arc of the Yaquina Bay Bridge. On weekends, hours expand to include breakfast; in summer, sit on the outdoor patio. Open Mon through Fri 11 a.m. to 9 p.m., Sat 9 a.m. to 10 p.m., Sun 9 a.m. to 9 p.m. $$–$$$.

Kam Meng. 4424 N Coast Hwy.; (541) 574-9450; kammeng.com. Genuine Hong Kong–style cooking in a big green and yellow building on US 101. The exterior is deceiving, but the food speaks for itself. The black bean sauce, seafood hot pot, and green bean chicken are all excellent. Open Tues through Sun for lunch and dinner. $–$$.

Local Ocean. 213 SE Bay Blvd.; (541) 574-7959; localocean.net. A casually sophisticated fish market and grill, and quite possibly the source of the very best seafood on the Oregon Coast. Market-style dining is accented with a central open kitchen where chefs prepare fresh grilled seafood dishes. Diners sit near floor-to-ceiling windows with roll-up glass doors, which overlook fishing boats in the harbor and the Yaquina Bay Bridge in the distance. An upstairs addition offers more seating in a classy space with even more jaw-dropping views. The fish-and-chips are heavenly, and the crab po'boy sandwich is completely refreshing. I never visit Newport without eating at Local Ocean at least once, even if I'm not hungry. Open 7 days a week for lunch and dinner. $$–$$$.

Nana's Irish Pub. 613 NW 3rd St.; (541) 574-8787; nanasirishpub.com. Outdoors it's light and airy, indoors dark and moody. Nana's is the quintessential Irish pub with surprisingly excellent food. Homemade and hearty pot pies, fish-and-chips made with house beer batter, savory Reuben sandwiches, and homemade soups and salad dressings are all freshly prepared and wonderful. Naturally, there's plenty of beer on tap and in the bottle, and, very frequently, live music. Open 7 days a week for lunch and dinner. $–$$.

Ove Northwest. 749 NW 3rd St.; (541) 264-2990. One of Nye Beach's newer additions, Ove Northwest is fine dining served with a view of the ocean. The interior is cheery, with colorful glass lighting fixtures and white linens. The menu is inspired by local foods and changes with the seasons. Depending on the day, try the Tellicherry pepper–crusted beef brisket, fresh Dungeness crab fish stew, and salted caramel panna cotta for dessert. Open for lunch Mon through Sat 11:30 a.m. to 2:30 p.m. and dinner Tues through Sat 5 to 8:30 p.m. $$–$$$.

Panini Bakery. 232 NW Coast St.; (541) 265-5033. Great pizza, excellent scones, pastries that aren't overly sweet, and one of the friendliest, happiest vibes you'll find in Newport. The lunchtime sandwiches change daily, are excellent, and sell out quickly. You'll find very limited seating indoors, along with a couple of outside tables for when it's not raining. $.

Rogue Ales Public House. 748 SW Bay Blvd.; (541) 265-3188; rogue.com. If you don't make it to the brewing facility (above in Where to Go), at least hit the brewpub on the Bay-front. Rogue Ales are made with the finest hops and barley malt, free-range coastal water, and proprietary yeast. The menu is huge and varied—but with all of those beers on tap, who needs food? This is a good place to take the family for pub food and indoor or outdoor seating. Open 7 days a week for lunch and dinner. $–$$.

Sorella. 526 NW Coast St., Ste. C; (541) 265-4055; sorellanyebeach.com. The owners of the award-winning fine-dining destination Restaurant Beck in Depoe Bay created this homey Italian restaurant in Nye Beach to show off their more casual side. Plates of pizza and pasta and other custom rustic Italian fare are crowd pleasers, accompanied by a fabulous cocktail list, local beer, and wine. The 3-course Sunday supper is a locals' favorite. $$.

where to stay

Elizabeth Oceanfront Suites. 232 SW Elizabeth St.; (541) 265-9400; elizabethoceanfront suites.com. The rooms here are fairly standard, but the view and location can't be beat. Located on a bluff overlooking the magnificent Oregon Coast in the heart of Nye Beach, it's the perfect place to stay to take in all of Newport. $$–$$$.

Fairhaven Vacation Rentals. Coast Avenue; (888) 523-4179; fairhavenvacationrentals .com. If you are traveling with a group or extended family, rent one of these classic Victorian and cottage-style homes in Nye Beach. Just a few blocks from the beach, shopping, and great restaurants; several have views, hot tubs, and outfitted kitchens. $$$.

Inn at Nye Beach. 729 NW Coast St.; (800) 480-2477; innatnyebeach.com. One of the newer properties in the area, the Inn at Nye Beach consists of 20 beautiful units, all with ocean views, balconies, and fireplaces. The inn benefits from solar-generated electricity and waste-water heat recycling. Choose from studios or 1- and 2-bedroom units, some with kitchenettes. Many units have sundecks with chairs, and stairs out front lead directly to the beach. $$–$$$.

Sylvia Beach Hotel. 267 NW Cliff St.; (541) 265-5428; sylviabeachhotel.com. Not for everyone, but those who love this place love it with a ravishingly loyal happiness. The funky four-story hotel could be described as old and creaky or full of awesome character, depend-ing on your point of view. It's a hotel with a theme, and the theme is books. Each room is decorated to reflect a single author. Sleep with Mark Twain, Agatha Christie, Dr. Seuss, and many more. There is no TV, no Wi-Fi, no telephones, no radio. Relax, read, or visit quietly in front of the fireplace in the common library with a spectacular ocean view. Come for

cobble beach

The rocky peninsula Yaquina Head holds many charms (see the listing in Where to Go), but the pièce de résistance at this outstanding natural area is **Cobble Beach.** *Over millennia, chunks of basalt have fallen from the hillside, tossed and bashed in the surf, and morphed into hundreds of gorgeous black round rocks known as cobbles. These make up the small beach nestled out of the north wind at the base of the head. As soon as you hear the satisfying crunch of your feet working their way through thousands of lovely spherical stones, as soon as you see the way the black stones illuminate the ocean water in an entirely unique way, you'll know you are someplace special. But the real thrill is to come. Waves arrive on the beach as they do on any beach anywhere—large or small, high or low—but as the waves recede through the basalt cobbles, the most wonderful and unusual sound results: a watery tinkling, a musical waterfall. You've never heard anything like it. See blm .gov/visit/yaquina-head-ona.*

romance, come for solitude, come to make new friends. A fabulous breakfast is served each morning with a view of the ocean. Tip: If you're traveling with family or close friends, and have a solid sense of humor, reserve the Cuckoo's Nest, named after Oregon author Ken Kesey's famous book, *One Flew Over the Cuckoo's Nest*. This top-floor room has 4 single beds and decor reminiscent of the dorms in the state mental hospital featured in the book. $–$$$.

day trip 12

central coast

crab pots & small shops:
waldport

waldport

Waldport is a quiet town surrounded in the beauty of the natural world. Tucked between its bigger sisters Newport to the north and Yachats to the south, Waldport is a residential and vacation rental community that sits on Alsea Bay and along the beachfront, with a lifestyle concentrated on plenty of outdoor recreation and a peaceful aesthetic.

The first settlers on the peninsula floated downriver on the Alsea River in the late 1870s and named the town. The name stems from the German word *wald* for "forest" and *port* for the location on the bay and the sea. Logging was the primary occupation, as well as salmon fishing, and access to the ocean was key.

Today, visitors to Waldport still focus their attentions on the river and the sea. Alsea Bay is one of the most pristine estuaries on the Oregon Coast, and the beach running to the north from the bay is long and sandy. Spend a day in Waldport throwing pots out to catch crabs, digging for clams, observing some of the 400 bird species that live or pass through here, or hitting the beach for shell collecting, wave watching, or just plain relaxing.

getting there

From Salem: Travel I-5 south for 31 miles to exit 228. Turn west onto OR 34 and travel 10 miles to Corvallis, where OR 34 intersects with OR 20. Continue west on OR 20 for 48 miles

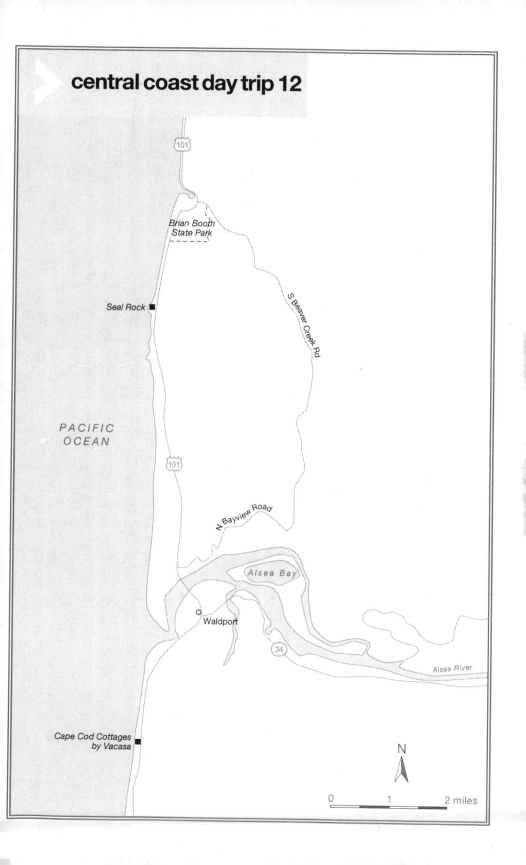

central coast day trip 12

101

Brian Booth
State Park

S Beaver Creek Rd

Seal Rock ■

PACIFIC
OCEAN

101

N Bayview Road

Alsea Bay

O
Waldport

34

Alsea River

Cape Cod Cottages
by Vacasa ■

N

0   1   2 miles

to Newport and the intersection with US 101. From Newport, continue 16 miles south on US 101 to Waldport.

where to go

Brian Booth State Park. 7 miles north of Waldport on US 101. This state park is in two sections—an oceanfront area, also known as Ona Beach, and an inland area, also known as Beaver Creek Natural Area. These beautiful forest and beach areas offer many delights. On the beach, see rounded rock formations, many of which are covered in algae, creating an interesting visual landscape. One mile east of Ona Beach and Highway 101, visit the welcome center to walk, picnic, or take in the views of the marsh from the observation deck. Over 5 miles of easy to moderate hiking trails are also in this upland trail area. Kayaking and canoeing are excellent choices for activities here too. Don't have a kayak? Guided kayak tours on Beaver Creek are offered seasonally, and kayaks, life preservers, and paddles are provided. Preregister and launch with a park guide from Ona Beach to explore the marsh and creek. Tours run from July through Labor Day weekend. The welcome center is open Thurs through Mon.

Dock of the Bay Marina. 1245 Mill St.; (541) 563-2003; portofalsea.com. Pretty much everyone agrees that the best thing to do in Waldport is go crabbing, and that Waldport offers some of the best crabbing on the Oregon Coast. The Dungeness are plentiful here, and Dock of the Bay Marina will rent you a boat and motor to putter out into the bay and drop your (also rented) pots. They'll even clean and cook your crab when you return during weekends and high season. You can also just crab from the dock. Bring your lawn chair, chicken parts from the grocery store for bait, a cooler of drinks and warm clothing, and make a day of it. During fall, chinook salmon make their run; Dock of the Bay can set you up with fishing gear for this annual event too.

where to shop

Caramel Dude. 310 SW US 101; (541) 264-1822; carmeldude.com. Caramel corn, nut brittles, savory popcorn, and kettle corn made in small batches right in Waldport are found at this longstanding locale. Pick up some tasty treats for the road or to take home from this little red hut on the west side of the highway.

The Green Bike Co-op. 115 SW US 101; (541) 563-7328; greenbikeco-op.org. An interesting concept offering helpful service at benefit to others, Green Bike Co-Op began as a community bike-sharing program with a fleet of 100 "green bikes" available at no cost for anyone to ride. The co-op evolved into a multiservice bike shop that offers tune-ups, rentals, repairs, loaners, sales, use of tools, and classes on bike maintenance. Local bike commuters to cyclists passing through on long bike-touring trips along Highway 101 can stop in to use equipment to service their own bikes or let the pros on-site handle repairs. Volunteers work by donation, and proceeds benefit Seashore Family Literacy Center, a local program offering tutoring and education.

Lil' Joes General Store. 250 NW Hemlock St.; (541) 992-1282. An often-changing inventory of merchandise passes through this shop, which is more like an antiques store or thrift shop than a general store. You might leave with a piece of furniture, some jewelry, or a beachy souvenir—or all three.

Waldport Flea Market. 260 SW US 101; (541) 563-6436; waldportfleamarket.com. This classic flea market buys and sells all sorts of vintage and unusual items, including cast-iron pots and pans, Japanese floats, gold and silver, Indian head pennies, collectible books, and much more. Peruse this fun destination, open every day from 10 a.m. to 6 p.m.

where to eat

Flounder Inn. 180 SW US 101; (541) 563-2266. Your classic Oregon Coast tavern, but who doesn't love a little of that from time to time? Not to mention fried halibut, bacon and potato soup, and excellent broasted chicken. There are also pool tables, a dance floor, and karaoke. The people-watching is outstanding too. Open 7 a.m. to midnight 7 days a week. $–$$.

Fresco Family Restaurant. 310 SW US 101; (541) 563-7811. A hidden gem, this place is unassuming from the street, but visitors rave about the portions, the service, and the view of the bay. Fresco serves both traditional Mexican fare and American classics. Come for a classic salty margarita, stay for the sunset. Open for lunch and dinner 7 days a week. $$.

Hilltop Cafe Bistro. 828 SW US 101; (541) 563-2750; hilltopcafebistro.com. Dungeness crab Benedict, anyone? The Hilltop Cafe Bistro is open for breakfast, lunch, and dinner 7 days a week and offers what many say is the best food in town. Try the breakfast crepes, the ahi tuna salad, the Monte Cristo, or the Hilltop clam chowder. Live music Fri and Sat nights. Open every day 7 a.m. to 3 p.m. and 5 to 9 p.m. $$.

Pacific Sourdough Bakery. 740 NE Mill St.; (541) 563-3044; pacificsourdough.com. This small artisan bakery on Alsea Bay offers natural leavened sourdough breads, delicious pastries, and specialty desserts. Locally made butter and organic nuts and fruits in season make everything just a little bit more special. Only open Thurs, Fri, and Sat 10 a.m. to 3 p.m. Get it while it's hot! $.

where to stay

Cape Cod Cottages. 4150 SW US 101; (855) 861-5757; vacasa.com. Twelve units overlook the beach here a few miles south of Waldport. Highlights are fireplaces, kitchens, and lovely decks with views of the sea. Interiors are funky and charming à la the 1950s, but beach access is outstanding and the units are affordable. You can even book the entire lot of them and host a party for 48 people! $$.

worth more time

Just 5 miles north of Waldport is **Seal Rock,** a small unincorporated community of mostly vacation homes, some owned by Oregonians for multiple decades. Families return each year for the quiet and uncrowded beaches, but Seal Rock has a few artsy gallery gems too. Visit **Ocean Beaches Glassblowing and Gallery** (11175 NW US 101; 541-563-8632) to peruse stained glass, blown glass, torched glass, lampshades, vases, floats, and more, all from local glass artists. Nearly every afternoon, glassblowing demonstrations take place on-site here. It's free entertainment, but don't be surprised if you feel inspired to bring home a gorgeous work of art.

Another don't-miss artisan stop is **Brian McEneny Woodcarving Gallery** (10751 NW US 101; 541-563-2452; woodcarvinggallery.com). McEneny has been woodcarving since the 1970s and has had a gallery in Seal Rock nearly as long. His work began with chainsaw art capturing everything from bears to cowboys, but soon marine animals captured his attention. He transforms a log or piece of driftwood into a beautiful whale, otter, seal, dolphin, or other sea animal, with a beautiful wood-grain fine finish and shapes and fluidity that are magnificently lifelike. If you can't take it with you, consider McEneny's coffee-table book *Carving Out a Life*, available at the gallery and showcasing some of his finer work.

After art shopping, grab some sushi at **Yuzen Japanese Restaurant** (10111 NW US 101; 541-563-4766), which boasts a two-story, full-color sushi chef painted on their building.

day trip 13

central coast

storm watcher's dream:
yachats

yachats

In Yachats, the sandy beaches of the northern coast begin to transform to the rugged basaltic cliffs of the southern coast. From here to the California border, the Oregon Coast landscape is for the most part dramatically different than to the north. Waves that might arrive gently in the north enter as crashing spectacles. Pockets of sandy beach are tucked between towering cliffs. Wind whips through thick forests, and you are more likely to see huge groups of birds than huge groups of people.

In the Siletz language, *Yachats* means "dark water at the foot of the mountain." Native Americans settled here long ago, finding the volcanic bench at this oceanfront location to be a convenient, elevated place to make camp. The rocky waterfront was also a limitless provider of shellfish for mealtime, including clams and oysters.

Today, visitors still come for seafood and the view. Many rental houses and hotels are perched along the basalt cliff-front of the small city, providing some of the best views of ocean action available from inside your own lodging on the Oregon Coast. Waves exploding on rocks is dramatic and beautiful, and Yachats has long been a tourist destination and storm-watching mecca. Around this scenery, a community has grown, nurturing some terrific restaurants serving local foods from farms, the forest, and the sea. There are still a couple of sandy beaches to walk too, making Yachats an all-around terrific place to visit, friendly with the kid and dog set as well as romantics seeking a getaway.

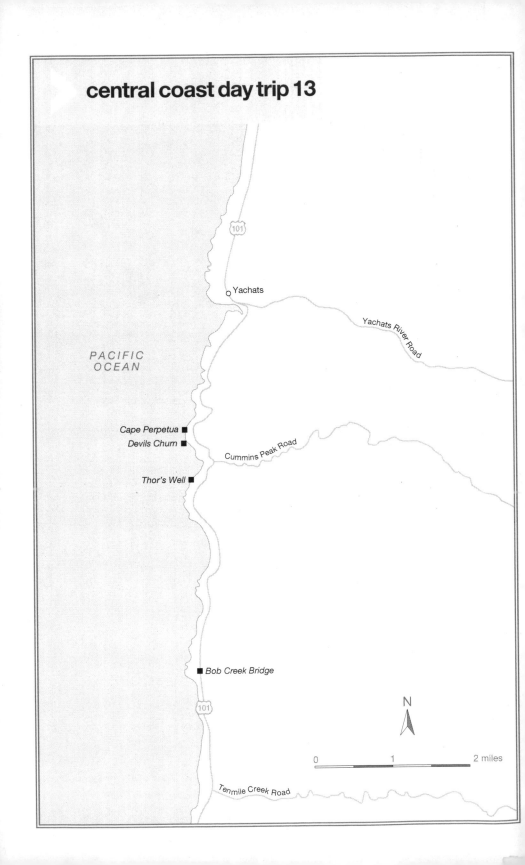

central coast day trip 13

101

○ Yachats

Yachats River Road

PACIFIC
OCEAN

Cape Perpetua ■
Devils Churn ■

Cummins Peak Road

Thor's Well ■

■ Bob Creek Bridge

101

N

0   1   2 miles

Tenmile Creek Road

getting there

From Eugene: Take US 126 to Florence, a distance of 60 miles. Turn north on US 101 and drive 27 miles to Yachats.

where to go

Cape Perpetua. 2.3 miles south of Yachats on US 101. This natural headland and cape was named by Captain James Cook on March 7, 1778, as he searched for the Pacific entrance to a Northwest Passage. Today, it's a terrific place to hike, watch for whales, and gaze out over the Pacific Ocean for miles and miles. Don't miss the interpretive center, where natural and cultural history are on record. See who lived here over time, identify local wildflowers, and learn which whales are swimming by outside, and when. There is also a theater and a children's science area to explore, as well as a bookstore offering guidebooks and narratives of regional interest. Outside, explore many hiking trails, including a 1/8-mile hike uphill from the parking lot to an old stone shelter at the top of the cape. The shelter was built by the Civilian Conservation Corps and was a World War II lookout. It persists as a tremendous place to take in the view, sheltered from the weather. Below are Devil's Churn, Thor's Well, and Spouting Horn—natural phenomena both beautiful and dramatic. Devil's Churn is reached by the Restless Waters Trail and is a narrow inlet that can throw ocean spray hundreds of feet in the air. Spouting Horn and Thor's Well can be reached off of US 101. Spouting Horn is a blowhole, throwing water directly up in a spouting spray. Thor's Well is a hole carved out of the basalt shoreline. It may have initially been a sea cave until the roof collapsed, leaving a hole on the surface level. Waves roll in from underneath and fill the bowl. Depending on the tide, sometimes water bubbles to the top, while other times, it flies out in a wonderful spray.

Gerdemann Gardens Trail. 2222 US 101 N. This beautiful little hidden botanical garden and hiking area is both a labor of love and a natural work of art. In 1981, locals Jim and Janice Gerdemann purchased an acre of property on the edge of the Siuslaw National Forest in Yachats. Find the trailhead behind the art galleries on the highway and pass through a well-worn wooden gate into a lush forested glen, part of the Siuslaw National Forest. The narrow trail winds past trillium, salal, wood sorrel, rhododendron, and other lush native plants. There are many nonnative species here too, planted by the Gerdemanns and others over the years. Look for several varieties of magnolia. The highlight, perhaps, is a 300-year-old spruce tree which has roots that span tiny Mitchell Creek, about halfway up the trail.

Historic 804 Trail. 0.75 mile along the oceanfront in Yachats. Today the 804 Trail is a lovely place to walk and take in the sights of Yachats and the ocean, but its history is more complicated than these simple views reveal. Once a Native American trail used during low tide, eventually the trail became County Road 804, surveyed in the 1890s to carry stage passengers, horse-and-buggies, the US mail, and freight. The road began at Alsea Bay in

Waldport and ran south 8 miles to the rugged shelf of Yachats. Once Highway 101 was created to the east, the 804 was left to disintegrate for a time, and after that, a lengthy battle with property owners ensued to reclaim the historic trail for the public and the greater good. That effort prevailed, and we are so lucky for it. The 0.75-mile footpath provides views of crashing surf, tidal pools, and native vegetation. On the northern end, the paved trail reaches Tillicum Beach and 7 miles of open sandy beach which can be walked all the way to Waldport. On the southern end, the trail passes through Smelt Sands State Recreation Site. Just south of here the 804 officially terminates, although another trail continues on to downtown Yachats, offering restaurants, shops, and views of the Yachats River and Yachats State Recreation Area.

The Little Log Church. 328 W 3rd St.; (541) 547-4547; goyachats.com. Located a block from the ocean in downtown Yachats, the Little Log Church was built in the shape of a cross in 1926, constructed from local timber hauled down the Yachats River. Since 1970, it has been a historical museum displaying many artifacts related to Yachats history, including settler exhibits, an extensive shell collection, and works of local artists and authors. Several times a year, the church plays host to a wedding. The log structure has suffered decay over the years, but community members continually rally to help preserve it, and under consideration at press time was whether the church should be torn down and replaced with a replication. In the meantime, the log church remains open to the public from noon to 3 p.m. every day of the week but Thurs.

not just a pile of shells

For thousands of years before white settlers arrived, Native Americans enjoyed life at the outlet of the Yachats River, where it reached the Pacific Ocean. Their primary food was seafood and shellfish, including a plentiful supply of clams and oysters. After eating their contents, it was customary to cast off shells into large piles, many of which remain today and are still visible along the Oregon Coast, including in and around Yachats. Known as middens, these piles can be 4,000 to 5,000 years old. Some are protected by the government now, but there was a time when these piles were raided for road-building material. In fact, Yachats was virtually constructed on top of many tribal middens. There is more than one street on the coast named "shell," and Yachats has both a Shell Street and a Shellmidden Way. To see a midden, travel south from Yachats 5 miles to Bob Creek Beach. The sloping beach access is part grass and part shell remnants. Walk over it, lean over and inspect it, but don't bring a shovel—disturbing historic middens is illegal.

where to shop

Dark Water Souvenirs. 114 US 101 N; (541) 547-3473. A gift shop and then some with printed T-shirts, etched glassware, embroidered towels, and more—all with a Yachats theme. Bath and soap products, photography, art prints, pottery, and plenty of items representing pirates and mermaids are all on hand.

Fine art galleries. These four galleries are clustered together on the highway, making this an easy and fruitful stop for those in search of something to take home to adorn the wall or the cabinet.

> **Dancing Dogs Pottery and Art.** 2118 US 101 N; (541) 563-3578; dancing dogspottery.com. Find fine hand-thrown porcelain and stoneware pottery in this tiny shop, as well as oil, acrylic, and watercolor paintings, all made by Al Erikson. There is also quirky jewelry for sale by Kelle Bates Erikson, which incorporates recycled metals, sea glass, old and new beads, and even crystals.

> **Earthworks Gallery.** 2222 US 101 N; (541) 547-4300; earthworksgalleries.net. A large, multiroom art gallery with a variety of art on display, including extensive clay works like tiles and sculptures. Wood furniture, fabric art, and glassworks are also available. Each room reveals something more, and there are even clay sculptures outside to study.

> **Touchstone Gallery.** 2118 US 101 N; (541) 547-4121; touchstone-gallery.com. This longstanding gallery is host to fine arts and crafts from many familiar Oregon artists. Wander aisles of vases, fiber arts, glasswork, and jewelry, while in the company of the gallery's three resident cats, who are happy to help you make a decision about what to bring home.

> **Wave Gallery.** 2118 US 101 N; (541) 547-4405; wavegallery.org. Photography by Bob Keller captures the Pacific Northwest, and most especially the Oregon Coast, in all of its glory. Both black-and-white and color captures hang on the walls. From the lush forest to the dramatic and beautiful shoreline, Keller believes in working the local turf—and what an amazing turf it is.

Judith's Kitchen Tools. 261 US 101; (541) 547-3020. A well-curated kitchen store is deeply appreciated by cooking aficionados. Judith's is such a place. Some people come here purposefully, knowing Judith's knack for stocking the shelves with cool and useful kitchen items. Some people wander in, perhaps looking for an item to augment their vacation home's kitchen supplies. Everyone leaves with something.

Planet Yachats. 281 US 101; (541) 547-4410. First of all, how amazing to consider that there might be a "Planet Yachats." Secondly, that such a place would contain planetary items like rocks, stones, crystals, fossils, and minerals. A wonderful shop to wander in,

la de da parade

Fourth of July events are a dime a dozen, but some are more serious than others. If wacky whimsy for the national holiday is your jam, try the popular **la de da Parade** *in Yachats. Patriotism is on hand, but so is plenty of lighthearted fun. Have you ever seen an umbrella drill team? Now's your chance. Prized llamas and wiener dogs are on parade too. The la de da is entirely people-powered, and you won't see one single motorized float. Before and after the parade, celebration abounds, including great food, entertainment, and live music. An afternoon duck race is not to be missed—catch a front-row seat from the beach at the mouth of the Yachats River. From the same beach, or from almost anywhere downtown, enjoy the spectacular fireworks at sundown over Yachats Bay.*

hands tucked cautiously in one's pockets, so as not to disturb the fragile wares. Pull out the wallet and you can take one home, however, to display on your own home planet.

Toad Hall. 237 W 3rd St.; (541) 547-4044. How about some whimsy to take home? This little house surrounded by a pretty garden has gifts of all kinds inside. Cards, books, wind chimes, jewelry, scarves, and more revolve around a theme of playfulness and beachy goodness.

where to eat

The Drift Inn. 124 US 101; (541) 547-4477; the-drift-inn.com. One of my favorite restaurants on the Oregon Coast, the Drift Inn does not disappoint. Start with the atmosphere—a cozy and charming room with booth tables, a bar, colorful walls and glass light fixtures, and umbrellas hanging from the ceiling. Then consider the menu, which is varied, with every item carefully prepared for maximum deliciousness. Finally, revel in the fact that a different local musician plays the small stage in the back corner every evening. The last time we were there, we ate fresh grilled halibut topped with Dungeness crab with a side of mashed red potatoes, sipped a local craft beer, and listened to accordion music. Happiness! The building itself has a colorful history as a dance hall and rough-and-tumble tavern, though during Prohibition, it was an ice cream parlor—publicly, anyway. Read more history on the menu when you come to this iconic spot for a meal. There's a back patio for nice days, from which you can watch the wood-fired pizzas cook in the brick oven. Open 7 days a week: 8 a.m. to 9 p.m. in winter, 8 a.m. to 10 p.m. in summer. $$.

Green Salmon Coffee Company. 220 US 101 N; (541) 547-3077; thegreensalmon .com. Fresh fair-trade organic coffee is served here, alongside distinctive teas and fresh-baked pastries. Light breakfast and lunch items include bagel-and-lox plates, breakfast wraps, and a chicken Caesar salad. Hang out for a while in the spacious room with an awesome casual coffee-shop vibe. Open every day from 7:30 a.m. to 2:30 p.m. $.

Leroy's Blue Whale. 580 US 101 N; (541) 547-3399; leroysbluewhale.com. This large white building on the highway delivers completely satisfying diner-style food and seafood in big portions with great service. It's family-friendly in here, the coffee flows plentifully, and there is a pie case heaped with enormous pastry treats. Open 7 days a week for breakfast, lunch, and dinner. $–$$.

Luna Sea Fish House. 153 US 101 N; (541) 547-4794; lunaseafishhouseyachats.com. It's small, it's not fancy, but the fish-and-chips are outstanding. The building is painted bright blue with a large mural of a fish on the outside, and the sign reads Local Fishmonger. Fresh chinook salmon and albacore tuna are caught daily on hook and line before making their way onto your plate here, and you'll be happy that they did. Burgers, chowder, clams, omelets, and more are on the menu. Open for breakfast, lunch, and dinner 7 days a week. $–$$.

Ona. 131 US 101 N; (541) 547-6627; onarestaurant.com. The motto at this fine-dining destination is "carefully sourced, globally inspired." Oregon Dungeness crab cakes, Yaquina Bay grilled oysters, and rain forest mushroom pâté are served alongside New York steak, meat loaf, and tatay ramen. Desserts and cocktails are handmade and fancy. Open Fri through Tues for dinner only, in season (Ona is closed for a few winter months). $$–$$$.

Yachats Brewery and Farmstore. 348 US 101 N; (541) 547-3884; yachatsbrewing.com. A newer entry on the dining scene, this brewpub is casual hip inside, with lots of wood and light, living plants, and a bookshelf full of reads about gardening, brewing, and local interest. The menu is farm to table, and changes frequently because they only use fresh, seasonal ingredients. Fermentation extends beyond their selection of excellent beer—try sauerkraut, kimchi, and fermented veggies alongside your Thor's Well IPA, Buddha's Head Saison, or 804 Pils. Take one of their bottle selections home with you. Open daily for lunch and dinner. $$.

where to stay

The Drift Inn. 124 US 101; (541) 547-4477; the-drift-inn.com. This collection of unique rooms sits over the restaurant with the same name. Some rooms are spacious with ocean views, others are designed for economy. The Drift Inn caters to the many bicyclists who travel Highway 101 on long-distance tours; five rooms called "Drift In Pedal Out" go for $50 all year long and have a shared bath and bike racks outside. This hotel is charming and funky, friendly and comfortable. $–$$.

The Fireside. 1881 US 101 N; (541) 547-3636; firesidemotel.com. Each room is named for a native bird, some of which you might see fly by your ocean-view room. This property offers both luxury ocean-facing rooms with gas fireplaces and balconies and more economical rooms with north-facing views. Both are steps from the 804 Trail and the crashing waves of the Pacific. The on-site Village Gift Gallery has souvenirs including T-shirts, locally made pottery, guidebooks, jam, chocolate, and more. Pet-friendly rooms available. $–$$.

The Overleaf Lodge and Spa. 280 Overleaf Lodge Ln.; (800) 338-0507; overleaflodge .com. A family-owned business that opened in 1997, the Overleaf Lodge sits on a dramatic cliff overlooking the Pacific Ocean, right near the 804 Trail. Every room has an ocean view. An evening reception includes snacks and sometimes wine tasting; a library offers books and puzzles; and the top-floor spa has a soaking pool with dynamic views of the sea, as well as a full range of spa treatment services. A full and generous breakfast is included in your stay. $$–$$$.

south coast

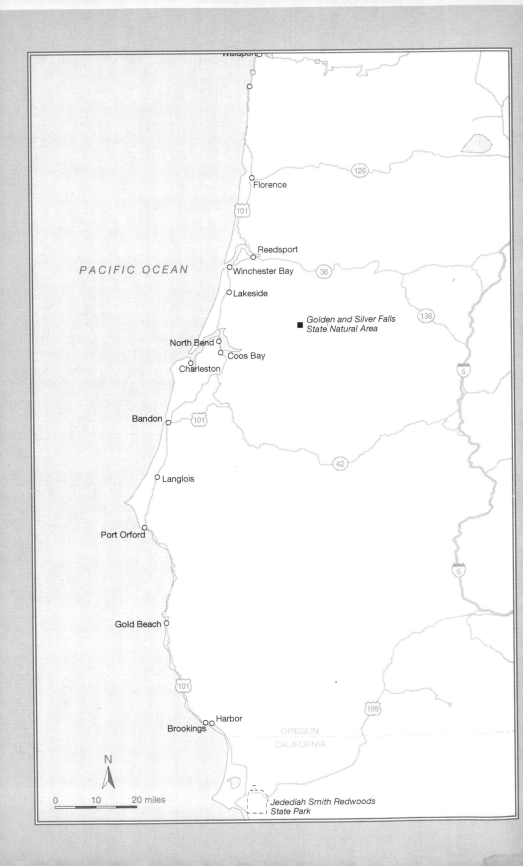

PACIFIC OCEAN

Waldport

Florence

101

126

Reedsport

Winchester Bay

38

Lakeside

Golden and Silver Falls
State Natural Area

138

North Bend

Coos Bay

Charleston

5

Bandon

101

Langlois

42

Port Orford

5

Gold Beach

101

199

Harbor

Brookings

OREGON

CALIFORNIA

N

0   10   20 miles

Jedediah Smith Redwoods
State Park

day trip 14

south coast

>>> **old town charm:**
florence

florence

Like so many other Oregon Coast cities, Florence was born at the mouth of a river. The places where freshwater meets seawater are not only rich and fruitful places to hunt, fish, survive, and thrive, but they were also practical when it came to transportation. Water—and boats—were once the primary means of transportation of getting from here to there without using your own two feet.

A side benefit, of course, is that estuarine environments are also very beautiful. Florence, which sits where the Siuslaw River meets the Pacific Ocean, is no exception. "Siuslaw" is the name of the tribe that first occupied this land, and it's no wonder they made camp here. Explorers and settlers followed, taking advantage of the rich forests and waters themselves.

Today, tourism is the name of the game, and Florence has a little bit of the best of what the Oregon Coast has to offer: sand dunes, a casino, fishing and clamming, shopping, and one of the loveliest old town districts in the Pacific Northwest.

getting there

From Eugene: Travel 61 miles west of Eugene on US 126. Florence sits where US 126 meets US 101.

south coast day trip 14

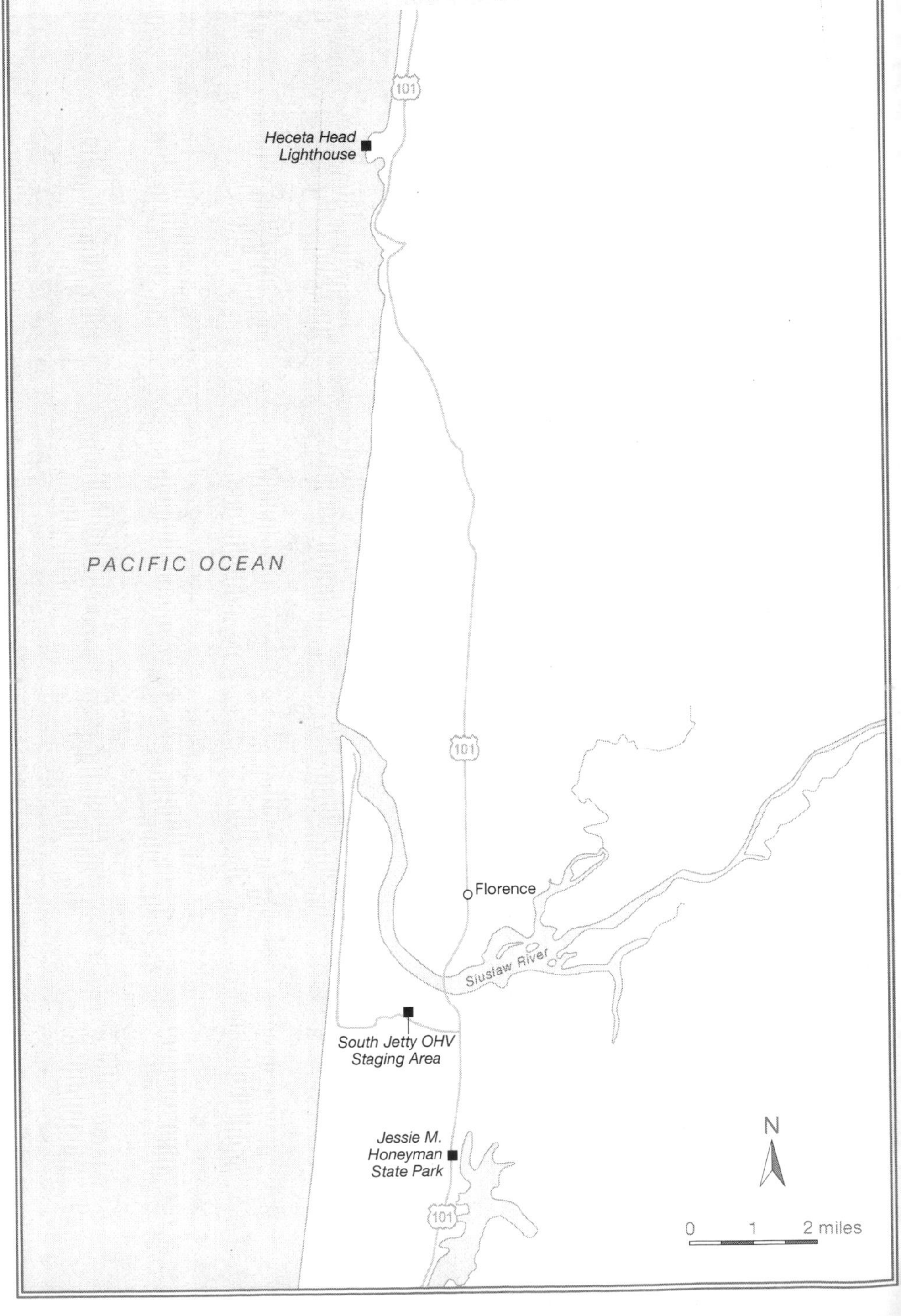

Heceta Head
Lighthouse

{101}

PACIFIC OCEAN

{101}

○ Florence

Siuslaw River

South Jetty OHV
Staging Area

Jessie M.
Honeyman
State Park

{101}

N

0   1   2 miles

where to go

C&M Stables. 90241 US 101; (541) 997-7540; oregonhorsebackriding.com. Even if you've ridden a horse before, there's nothing quite like horseback riding on the beach. The scenery is amazing, of course, but watching the hooves beneath you navigate sand of all consistencies intersected by the occasional wave is quite magical. This stable is one of the few on the Oregon Coast that offers a wide range of rides, including beach rides, sunset rides, dunes trails rides, and more. Children 6 years and up are permitted on some rides. Reservations are suggested, but drop-ins are welcome. Open all year, 7 days a week, 10 a.m. to 5 p.m.

Golf courses. Golf was invented in Scotland, but it thrives on the Oregon Coast—maybe because the two places share terrain and weather, among other things. In the US, golfers seek out classic Scottish-style links courses like these two in Florence.

> **Florence Golf Links.** 1201 35th St.; (541) 997-1940; florencegolflinks.com. Set in a stunning landscape between sand dunes and towering pines, Florence Golf Links was lauded by *Golf Digest*, which gave it a 4.5-star rating in their list of "Places to Play in the USA." The par 72, 6,931-yard, 18-hole course is divided into two nines—the outward nine is in the forest near lakes, and the inward nine is traditional links-style and rolling dunes from tee to green.

> **Ocean Dunes.** 5647 US 126; (877) 374-8377; threeriverscasino.com/golf. This course, part of the Three Rivers Casino Resort, is a favorite for locals and travelers alike. A links course with views of dunes, mountains, and forests, tucked in the heart of town, Ocean Dunes is a great 18 holes, rain or shine. After your round, visit the clubhouse for the 19th hole.

Heceta Head Lighthouse and State Scenic Viewpoint. 13 miles north of Florence on US 101. This white and red beauty is one of the most photographed lighthouses in the world. Perched 205 feet above the ocean on the side of a verdant cliff, this 56-foot-tall working lighthouse casts its beam more than 20 miles out to sea, making it the brightest light on the Oregon Coast. It was built in 1894, as was the adjacent Queen Anne–style light-keeper's home. Both are listed on the National Register of Historic Places, and free tours are available of both. The inn is a quarter-mile from the public parking area at the viewpoint; the lighthouse is a quarter-mile uphill from the inn. Visit the interpretive center and gift shop located between the inn and lighthouse, offering books and souvenirs. The inn is a working bed-and-breakfast (see listing in Where to Stay).

Jesse M. Honeyman State Park. 3 miles south of Florence on US 101. Honeyman State Park is the second-largest Oregon state park campground, offering more than 350 campsites, hiking trails, and miles of sand dunes between the park and the ocean. It's also home to two natural freshwater lakes: Cleawox, which is great for swimming, and Woahink, which has a public boat ramp. Hundreds of families a year visit Honeyman to camp, hike, or ride the dunes; canoe the lake; or picnic.

Oregon Dunes National Recreation Area: South Jetty Area. Sand Dunes Road off US 101, 1 mile south of Florence. The Oregon Dunes stretch 40 miles from the Siuslaw River south nearly to North Bend. This section south of Florence is the northernmost. The dunes are the largest expanse of coastal sand dunes in North America, known for huge hills of sand formed by wind, water, and time. The dunes are also interspersed with islands of trees, marsh-like low points, and access to open beach. While hiking and exploring on foot are an option, most people access the dunes on motorized all-terrain vehicles like dune buggies, dirt bikes, or four-wheelers. Bring your own, rent one, or sign up for a tour from one of these two recreational outfitters.

Sand Dunes Frontier. 83960 US 101 S; (541) 997-3544; sanddunesfrontier .com. This is your destination for sand rail tours, big buggy tours, and ATV rentals. Sand Dunes Frontier also has its own small campground with direct access to the dunes. Open year-round, Tues through Sat in winter and 7 days a week in summer.

Sandland Adventures. 85366 US 101; (541) 997-8087; sandland.com. Sand rail tours and giant dune buggy tours are here, but this place offers more than that in the way of family fun. Try a ride on the half-mile Cloverline Railroad, which tours 9 acres of the scenic property. Follow that with bumper boats, a go-kart round, or 18 holes of miniature golf. Open Mar through Dec 7 days a week.

Sand Master Park. 5351 US 101; (541) 997-6006; sandmasterpark.com. The dunes have inspired more than one sport and the newest is sandboarding—like snowboarding, only on sand. Sculpted dunes offer beginner to advanced slopes at this location right in town. Take a sandboard lesson or rent a sandboard or sled and tackle the slopes yourself. This outfitter also rents surfboards and wetsuits, should you wish to brave the waves as a surfer. Open Mar through Dec.

Siuslaw Pioneer Museum. 278 Maple St.; (541) 997-7884; siuslawpioneermuseum.com. Learn about the people and pastimes of Florence in history, from the first Native Americans to the pioneers who became loggers and fishers. Artifacts on display include historic photos, Mastodon teeth found in the area, and antique toys. You can also pick up a historic tour walking map to explore the old town area on your own. Open Tues through Sun noon to 4 p.m.

where to shop

Blue Heron Gallery. 1385 Bay St.; (541) 997-7993; oregoncoastgalleries.net. The parent gallery to a family-owned business of six galleries on the Oregon Coast, this beauty features

down on main street

*In the 1970s and 1980s, the downtown districts of the Oregon Coast were dying. Shopping malls built on the main thoroughfares or the outskirts of town were the rage, and businesses and people followed, leaving the historical buildings of downtowns abandoned and deteriorating. Eventually, locals realized that much of the character and historical value of their hometowns was right where they'd left it—downtown. Main Street districts entered an era of rebirth, and while the hearts of some coastal cities still struggle, others have reclaimed their rights as the coolest spot in town. This is true of Florence, which jumped on this retro trend earlier than many other places. **Historic Old Town Florence** is thoroughly rejuvenated, and even is home to a few lovely historical buildings relocated from other places. If you go to only one place in the Florence area, make it the historical old town. Park your car and walk around. Don't miss the Old Town Park, site of a former ferry landing (before there was a bridge across the Siuslaw River) as well as a former fishing dock. There is also a lovely gazebo in the park and many botanical plants, flowers, and trees. After your park respite, wander the shops and restaurants of old town, many of which are in the listings in this chapter.*

a variety of jewelry, pottery, glasswork, wood sculptures, and metal art. Most everything is ocean-themed and made by locally, regionally, and nationally acclaimed fine artists.

The River Gallery. 1335 Bay St.; (541) 902-2505; therivergallery.org. Owned by a local artist and her husband, The River Gallery is a nicely appointed gallery featuring prints, oils, glass, photography, and more. The old town location is charming and convenient, and while small, this gallery packs a punch.

Waterlily Studio. 1340 Bay St.; (541) 997-7339; waterlilystudioflorence.com. This gallery is focused on beaded jewelry, though there are many other things on-site too. Sea shells, souvenirs, baskets, pottery, and crystals are here to tempt you. Or stick to theme and buy stone, glass, copper, bronze, and brass beads, and even jewelry-making supplies for the amateur jewelry-maker. If you'd prefer to buy your jewelry finished and ready-to-wear, you will be delighted with the choices.

Wind Drift Gallery. 1395 Bay St.; (541) 997-9182; oregoncoastgalleries.net. A sister gallery to the Blue Heron, Wind Drift offers a large selection of award-winning chocolates, candies, and caramel corn alongside locally themed T-shirts and souvenirs. Toward the back of the shop, enjoy works of many local, regional, and world-renowned craft and jewelry artists.

where to eat

Bay View Bistro. 85625 US 101; (541) 590-3000; bwpierpointinn.com. Located in the Best Western Pier Point Inn, this restaurant is lauded for its views of the Siuslaw River and its bay, and for its surprisingly delectable cuisine. A bar and dining room, early-bird specials, and happy hour make this a popular and versatile dinner destination. Seafood, steaks, pasta, and more are on the menu—try the coconut shrimp and the molten lava cake for a decadent duo of a meal. Open for dinner 7 days a week. $$.

Bridgewater Ocean Fresh Fish House and Zebra Bar. 1297 Bay St.; (541) 997-1133; bridgewaterfishhouse.com. You can't miss this one from the street—the old two-story white wooden building with floor-to-ceiling first-floor windows is enchanting and smacks of history. Inside is equally so, with original rough-hewn floorboards, high ceilings, and plenty of charm. The food is good too. Try the pan-fried Pacific Northwest oysters, the crab melt, or the ocean food linguine marinara accompanied by a bottle of Oregon pinot gris and stay a while. Alternately, hang out in the more-casual Zebra Bar and watch the big game. Closed Tues. $$–$$$.

Hukilau Pacific Fusion. 185 US 101; (541) 991-1071. Hukilau started as a beloved food truck, and the word on the street is that the chefs have only taken things up a notch since they moved into this brick-and-mortar location on the highway not far from old town. Hawaiian pulled pork, sushi, sashimi, pineapple teriyaki chicken, and more delicious Pacific fusion treats are on hand. In case you are wondering, *hukilau* is a method of fishing invented by the ancient Hawaiians. Open 11 a.m. to 8 p.m. Tues through Sat. $$.

River Roasters. 1240 Bay St.; (541) 997-3443; coffeeoregon.com. The purveyors of this fine establishment roast their own coffee, much to the delight of patrons. Small treats and snacks are served here too. If the weather cooperates, sit out back on the small deck overlooking the Siuslaw River and the Siuslaw River Bridge. Open 7 a.m. to 5 p.m. daily. $.

Waterfront Depot Restaurant. 1252 Bay St.; (541) 902-9100; thewaterfrontdepot.com. Located right on the river in old town, the Waterfront is aptly named. Crab-encrusted Alaskan cod, surf and turf, and maple leaf duck breast are on the menu, alongside many other fine-dining and coastal favorites. Or just go for broke and grab a seat at the long, classic bar to sip a cocktail and munch on Oregon berry cake. Open 7 days a week for dinner. $$–$$$.

where to stay

Best Western Pier Point Inn. 85625 US 101; (800) 780-7234; bestwestern.com. It's a national chain hotel, but this location is excellent. The rooms, balconies, swimming pool, and restaurant all have views of the Siuslaw River. A complimentary full hot breakfast is served, and the restaurant—Bay View Bistro—gets rave reviews for their fresh seafood-based menu (see listing in Where to Eat). Another advantage is walking distance to historic old town. $$–$$$.

Driftwood Shores Resort & Conference Center. 88416 1st Ave.; (541) 997-8263; drift woodshores.com. Located on the north end of Florence, Driftwood Shores has long been known as one of the only beachfront hotels for miles. All rooms are oceanfront, and easy access leads to 10 miles of sandy beach. A variety of room types include those with full kitchens or refrigerator and microwave, as well as full condominiums for a crowd. All have private decks or balconies, and there is a heated pool on-site as well. $$–$$$.

Heceta Lighthouse Bed and Breakfast. 92072 US 101 S; (866) 547-3696; hecetalight house.com. This bed-and-breakfast is on some bucket lists. Located in one of the last lighthouse keeper's cottages on the West Coast, the setting is incredible, and the house is remarkably well-maintained considering that it was built in 1894. Antique furnishings, comfy beds, and duvets are accompanied by an amazing view of the ocean. In the morning, enjoy an indulgent 7-course breakfast of locally and regionally sourced delicacies. Sometimes, the inn is the site of a wedding (perhaps yours). $$$.

River House Inn. 1202 Bay St.; (888) 824-2454; riverhouseflorence.com. True to the name, most rooms have a river view of the lovely Siuslaw at this historic hotel located in old town. Watch boat and bird activity on the river pass you by as you relax on your own terrace. A continental breakfast is served in the morning. $$.

Three Rivers Casino Resort. 5647 US 126; (877) 374-8377; threeriverscasino.com. This hotel is located to the east of the highway, nestled in the dunes and forest and tucked out of the wind. A casino operated by the tribes of the Confederated Tribes of the Coos, Lower Umpqua, and Siuslaw Indians is on-site, as are 3 restaurants and a golf course. Entertainment and fun are here for the taking, as well as quality overnight lodging. $$.

day trip 15

south coast

gateway to the dunes:
reedsport, winchester bay

reedsport

The Umpqua River is the second-largest river located between the Columbia and Sacramento Rivers, and has long been a draw to humans. The Umpqua River estuary was first settled by the Siuslaw Native Americans, and later established as a camp for workers building the Southern Pacific Railroad extension south to Coos Bay. In 1912, a city was founded, named for early settler Alfred W. Reed. The Umpqua's easy access and navigability made it a good choice for a port, and the Port of Umpqua was established in 1913.

However, the marshy ground that underlies the small city has presented challenges over the years, most notably during the famous Christmas flood of 1964. Almost every building in downtown Reedsport was destroyed or damaged, but the most interesting outcome had to do with fish. The water level reached the local fish hatchery and breached the troughs, releasing smallmouth bass into the Umpqua River. Smallmouth bass became the most populous fish in the river, much to some anglers' delight.

Visitors still come to Reedsport for the fishing. In addition to the bass, native steelhead and salmon are found in these waters. Access to the Oregon Dunes, sightseeing, and camping also draw folks to this small city. Crabbing is good here, as is harvesting softshell clams. Reedsport isn't the fanciest city on the Oregon Coast, but it's full of good people and outstanding recreation.

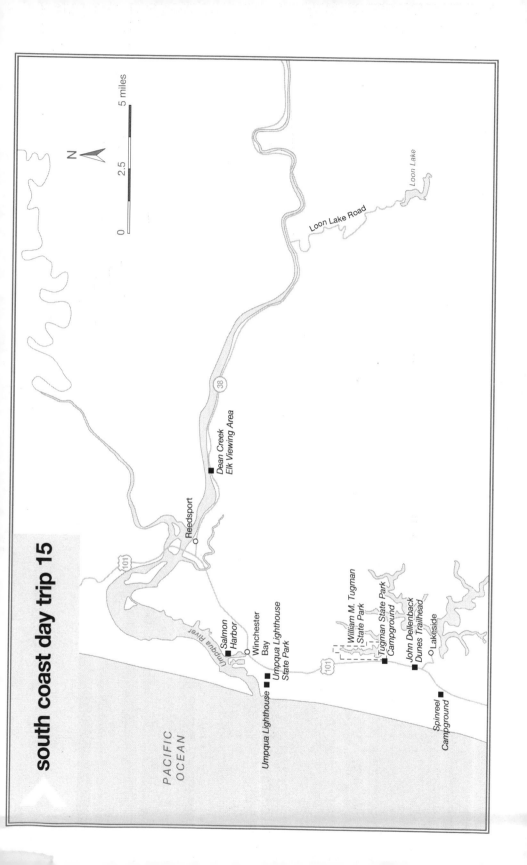

south coast day trip 15

PACIFIC
OCEAN

Umpqua River

Reedsport

Salmon Harbor

Winchester Bay

Umpqua Lighthouse

Umpqua Lighthouse State Park

Dean Creek Elk Viewing Area

38

William M. Tugman State Park

Tugman State Park Campground

John Dellenback Dunes Trailhead

Lakeside

Spinreel Campground

Loon Lake Road

Loon Lake

N

0   2.5   5 miles

getting there

From Eugene: Take I-5 south 32 miles to exit 162, leading to Drain/Elkton. Follow OR 38 for another 56 miles west along the Umpqua River to Reedsport.

where to go

Dean Creek Elk Viewing Area. 48819 OR 38; blm.gov/visit/dean-creek-elk-viewing-area. For decades, a herd of 60 to 100 Roosevelt elk have made home of the pastures alongside Highway 38 east of Reedsport. The Bureau of Land Management protected the land for the elk, and added facilities for the people who stop here every day to view them. There is no camping, but restroom facilities and interpretive viewing areas make for a great pit stop, with the added benefit of wildlife watching. Keep your eyes open for the many birds that make this area home too.

Defeat River Brewery. 473 Fir St.; (541) 808-8862; defeatriverbrewery.com. Reedsport's first craft brewery opened in 2016 as a family operation located in old town. Try the Thor CDA (Cascadian Dark Ale), the Paradox Hazy IPA, or the Pioneer Stout. There isn't any food on-site, but the Defeat team welcomes guests to bring their own food or order out from a nearby restaurant. The copper-top bar is a great place to hang out and sip some creative local brews. Open Wed through Sat 2 to 8 p.m., Sun 2 to 6 p.m. $.

Loon Lake. 9 miles south of OR 38 on Loon Lake Road. This lake perched in the foothills above the Umpqua River offers many delights, from boating to camping to beach lounging and play. A lush forest surrounds the 2-mile-long lake, which warms nicely in the summer and provides much more comfortable swimming than the Pacific Ocean. Damage from treefall during a bad winter shut the BLM-run facilities down in 2019, but renovations were under way at press time to reopen the popular destination for 2020. The Loon Lake Lodge and RV Resort remained open, offering lodging, camping, and a deli and store. The drive to Loon Lake alone is a beauty—the journey along the Umpqua and up into the hills is one of the prettiest in the state.

Oregon Dunes National Recreation Area Visitor Center. 855 Highway Ave.; (541) 271-6000; fs.usda.gov. Learn more about the natural history of the Oregon Dunes and how to navigate them wisely and safely at this visitor center, featuring exhibits, maps, brochures, books, and gifts interpreting the dunes. During the summer, ranger-led talks are available at the Oregon Dunes Day Use Area, 11 miles north of Reedsport. Open Mon through Fri 8 a.m. to 4 p.m. and some summer Saturdays.

Umpqua Discovery Center. 409 Riverfront Way; (541) 271-4816; umpquadiscoverycenter .com. This museum features stories of the past, including the early lives of the Kuuich Indians and the pioneers who settled here later. Learn about logging, fishing, and canning and the other pursuits that kept this tidewater town churning along in the early half of the last

carve it

They come in droves every Father's Day weekend from around the world, wielding chainsaws. They begin with 10-foot sections of tree, and dig in to work until they are satisfied. This is the **Oregon Divisional Chainsaw Carving Championships,** *held mid-June every year since 2000 in downtown Reedsport, next to the Umpqua Discovery Center. Carvers compete in events that include the 90-minute quick carve and the multiday main event. The works that emerge over these few days range in style and subject, from bears to eagles to totems to fish. You might even see some knights and princesses emerge from under the sawblade. While all visitors won't make the event itself, keep your eyes open for examples of the products of the chainsaw carving championship left behind around town. See reedsportcc.org.*

century. A natural history exhibit interprets the beautiful and varied natural world of the area, throughout the seasons. Open 7 days a week year-round except major holidays.

where to shop

Creative Mercantile. 427 Fir Ave.; (541) 808-1900. This shop hosts various artists, artisans, and vendors, ensuring that the variety of merchandise is broad and interesting. You might find antique furniture at one space, handmade earrings at the next, and paintings at a third. Sometimes, classes and events are held here too. Always worth a browse-through when you're in town. Open daily 10 a.m. to 5 p.m.

Myrtlewood Gallery. 1125 US 101; (541) 271-4222; myrtlewoodgallery.com. All of the works of art and practical products in this shop are made by local artists and woodworkers, or made right here in the workshop. The gallery also stocks raw wood, for those who want to take it away and create their own work of art. Wood slabs and lumber in the varietals of myrtlewood, maple burl, and black walnut are all often available. Open Mon through Sat 9 a.m. to 5 p.m., Sun 10 a.m. to 5 p.m.

Reedsport Pharmacy. 1409 US 101 S; (541) 271-3631. This destination is much more than a pharmacy, though you will definitely find aspirin and sunscreen here as well as be able to fill your prescriptions. But Reedsport Pharmacy also stocks toys, women's fashion, and souvenir and place-based clothing like Reedsport logo wear and Oregon Ducks and OSU Beavers gear. Lotions, perfumes, greeting cards, and gifts are on hand too. Friendly local owners don't hurt either. Closed Sun.

where to eat

Harbor Light Restaurant. 930 US 101; (541) 271-3848; harborlightrestaurant.com. For 35 years, this restaurant has been serving burgers, steaks, and seafood to hungry travelers and locals. A huge menu offers something for everyone, from elk shepherd's pie to cedar plank salmon to a bay shrimp melt. A kids' menu offers the usuals, and a dessert menu delivers everything from bread pudding to peanut butter pie. The cute little building on the highway is homey and comfortable. Open 7 days a week for breakfast, lunch, and dinner. $$.

Schooner Inn Cafe. 423 Riverfront Way; (541) 271-3945. Seating indoors and out with views of the Umpqua River are at this little cafe serving lunch and dinner, located next door to the Umpqua Discovery Center. Salads, chowders, hot and cold sandwiches, burgers, and fish-and-chips are on the menu and all known to be delicious. Save room for dessert—the Schooner's signature item is called Criminal Chocolate: a brownie with vanilla ice cream topped with chocolate sauce, mandarin oranges, and whipped cream. $–$$.

Waterfront Restaurant and Lounge. 351 Riverfront Way; (541) 271-1080. This tavern on the riverfront isn't fancy but locals rave about the burgers, pizza, calzones, and Bloody Marys. Separate spaces for the restaurant and lounge make it a family-friendly—or party-friendly—option. Closed Mon and Tues. $–$$.

winchester bay

Winchester Bay is downstream from Reedsport just a couple of miles, and sits at the spot where the Umpqua River terminates into the sea. Salmon Harbor is the name of Winchester Bay's waterfront playground and boat dock. The harbor and the surrounding unincorporated community, set peacefully off of the highway, is a favorite retreat for many.

Established as a fur-trapping outpost long before the economic pursuits of logging, fishing, and canning of the early 1900s took over, Winchester Bay has a quiet but significant history. The Umpqua River Lighthouse was the very first built on the Oregon Coast, lit here in 1857 to help guide boats into the river. Today, the lighthouse serves as a destination more meaningful than practical. Tourism and leisurely days rule this tiny unincorporated town. Come to fish, camp, dine, or gaze at the bay.

getting there

From Reedsport: Take US 101 southwest 5 miles to Winchester Bay.

where to go

John Dellenback Dunes Trail. 5 miles south of Winchester Bay on US 101 at mile marker 222. This trail is a wonderful combination of coastal rain forest, open sand dunes, and oceanfront beach. The trailhead is near the highway, beginning in a lush forest of shore pine, alder, wax myrtle, and Sitka spruce. Choose an easy 1-mile interpretive loop hike on a good trail through rhododendrons and salal, or traverse farther to trek into the loose sand of the Oregon Dunes. It's 2.7 miles to walk all the way through the dunes to the ocean beach, a stunning and rewarding hike, though be advised that hiking in dunes is more tiring than hiking a trail. Also be aware of the possibility of flooding in the wet season. The good news is that there aren't any motorized vehicles allowed in this section of the dunes, so while you may hear ATVs in the distance, you won't see any or, worse, need to dodge them on your hike. John Dellenback was a former state representative who advocated for protection of the Oregon Dunes. Pet-friendly; bring a leash. Don't park in the adjacent Eel Creek Campground unless you have secured a campsite.

Spinreel Dune Buggy and ATV Rental. 67045 Spinreel Rd.; (541) 759-3313; ridetheoregon dunes.com. Ready to get out on the dunes with some speed? Spinreel is your destination for tours or rentals of ATVs, including quads and RZRs. RZRs come with one to four seats; quads seat one. Rent for 1 to 8 hours; prices vary. Tours last 20 minutes and up. Open 7 days a week year-round. A campground next door can be home base.

it's alive!

The **Oregon Dunes** are famous for very large amounts of sand, which is essentially ground-up pieces of the coastal mountain range, eroded by time and weather and washed toward shore. Waves and wind pushed the sand back inland as far as 2.5 miles and as high as 500 feet. Sand is many things, but it isn't always thought of as super-compatible with life. However, there is a lot more going on in the Oregon Dunes than you might think. The Oregon Dunes are home to more than 400 species. Part of that is because the dunes aren't really all sand after all—the open hills of sand are interspersed and bordered with lush forest, small lakes, marshes, and open beaches. Here is where life is nurtured, though you'll also see signs of the animals traversing the open dunes. Look for the tracks of martens, bears, and insects. Also found in the dunes are many birds, including the western snowy plover, which nests in open sand, as well as lots of seabirds, bald eagles, and ospreys. You might even spot a Roosevelt elk, but you probably won't spot a coyote, bear, or cougar, although they too might call the dunes home. The one living thing you can take with you? Wild mushrooms. The forested areas around the dunes offer huge quantities of chanterelle, bolete, matsutake, and lobster mushrooms. You can collect a pound without a permit. As you explore the dunes, remember this: There is really nowhere else on earth quite like the Oregon Dunes.

Tugman State Park. 72549 US 101; (800) 551-6949; oregonstateparks.org. Camp, fish, hike, and play at this wonderful state park just off of the highway. Tugman sits on Eel Lake, which is outstanding for fishing, swimming, canoeing, sailing, and boating. Throw a line in the lake and you might come back with rainbow trout, steelhead, or salmon. Hike around the forests of spruce, cedar, fir, and alder on the south end of the lake to explore, and perhaps you'll see ospreys, cranes, eagles, deer, and other wildlife. Camping includes tent and RV sites as well as yurts.

Umpqua River Lighthouse, Museum and State Park. 1020 Lighthouse Rd.; (541) 271-4631; umpquavalleymuseums.org. The Umpqua River Lighthouse stands out as Oregon's first, but the structure remains distinct in additional ways. It is one of the only remaining lighthouses to which visitors can drive right up to, and at which visitors can enter and ascend stairs to the top. There is also a small museum associated with the lighthouse, next door. The original Umpqua River lighthouse, visible only as ships approached the river, was lit in 1857, but its engineers had little understanding of how dynamic and ever-changing the river mouth was. A storm and flood led to erosion that collapsed the lighthouse in 1863. In 1892, the new tower, a virtual twin to the Heceta Head Lighthouse being built simultaneously to the north between Florence and Yachats, was built 100 feet above the river, and lit in December. The volunteer-run museum interprets both the lighthouse and the adjacent operational US Coast Guard Station, and is broken into three sections: early history including Fort Umpqua; shipwrecks and transportation; and the lighthouse buildings, way of life, and the historic lens.

where to shop

Dockside Gifts. 120 Coho Point Loop; (541) 271-1210. What is it about being near the sea that makes us crave sweet treats? At this shop, they get your cravings, and provide accordingly. Fresh-made fudge is the specialty, but saltwater taffy and more are on hand too. Also peruse gifts, novelties, souvenirs, and home decor items to remind you of your days by the ocean.

where to eat

La Herradura Mexican Restaurant. 208 Bayfront Loop; (541) 361-6544. Terrific service is just the beginning here at this little local Mexican restaurant that gets a whole lot of love from guests. Large portions, fresh and tasty flavors, and delicious cocktails are also on the raves list. Try the fish tacos, the seafood chimichanga, or the chile relleno. $$.

Sourdough Bakery. 75318 US 101; (541) 234-4989. All of the breads here are sourdough, from the baguettes to the bagels. Sourdough Bakery's signature item is the cinnamon roll, large enough to feed at least two people. They also make breakfast sandwiches, lunch sandwiches, and garlic bread. Pick up a bottle of wine, locally made jam, and other items in this shop too. $$.

where to stay

Harbor View Motel. 540 Beach Blvd.; (541) 271-3352; harborviewmotel.org. This small, friendly, and affordable motel is in the heart of Winchester Bay, with great views of the harbor (as promised). New owners took charge a few years ago and began improving each room for comfort and style. $.

Salmon Harbor RV Park & Cabins. 75325 US 101; (541) 271-2791. This RV park on the highway is just far enough away from the ocean to be out of the wind, but close enough for a stroll to the sea or lighthouse. An on-site recreation room offers a pool table, woodstove, big-screen TV, comfy seating, small library, videos, and exercise equipment. Cabins are here too; rates are affordable. $.

Winchester Bay RV Resort. 120 Marina Way; (541) 271-0287; winchesterbayresort.com. Sandwiched between the Umpqua River as it meets the sea and Salmon Harbor, the Winchester Bay RV Resort offers water views at every turn. Full-hookup sites for RVs are available, as are 2 cabins, also with views. $–$$.

worth more time

Lakeside is a small community that rests just to the east of Highway 101, about 11 miles south of Winchester Bay. About 1,500 people call Lakeside home, drawn to the lush forested area surrounding Tenmile Lake, with easy access to the dunes but out of the often-windy weather of the beach. Life in Lakeside is mostly about sand-duning, fishing, and camping. Tenmile Lake has 42 miles of shoreline and 3,000 surface acres for fishing and water sports. Looking for a pro bass tournament? This is your destination. Recreational anglers can fish for bass, steelhead, crappie, perch, and rainbow trout.

Set up camp at **Osprey Point RV Resort** (1505 N Lake Rd.; 541-759-2801; osprey pointrvresort.com) or **North Lake RV Resort and Marina** (2090 N Lake Rd.; 541-759-3515; northlakeresort.com). Grab a bite to eat at **Osprey Point Pub and Pizza and More** (1505 N Lake Rd.; 541-759-2801; ospreypointrvresort.com) or **8th Street Grill** (235 S 8th St.; 541-510-3690; 8thstreetgrill.business.site). Stay a minute or stay a while; it's slow-going living here.

day trip 16

south coast

>>>

ships & bridges:
north bend, coos bay

north bend

The name of the town of North Bend is a literal geographical descriptor—the city is located on the north bend of the Coos River as it nears the sea. South of North Bend is Coos Bay, and the adjacent cities function as one community in many ways. The greater area has the largest population on the Oregon Coast. North Bend is home to one of the Oregon Coast's two regional airports—the Southwest Oregon Regional Airport offers daily direct flights to San Francisco and Denver.

During the last ice age, sea level in this area dropped about 300 feet, as water froze into thick sheets. About 10,000 years ago, when the ice melted, it flooded the mouth of the Millicoma River and created Coos Bay. Once a region rich in timber and fish, North Bend suffered more than one economic slump in the last decades. But today tourism is steadily increasing, and no wonder, as it's stunningly beautiful here with tons of recreational opportunities around every turn. Access to the Oregon Dunes, some of Oregon's most scenic state parks, rivers, beaches, waterfalls, lakes, forests, and estuaries are all part of the draw. Nature does not disappoint here, and there is plenty to explore from wildflowers to wildlife.

As the economy improves, so do dining, cultural, and entertainment options. The region's rich Native American tradition is on display at local museums and at the more-modern casinos run by the tribes of the Coos, Lower Umpqua, and Siuslaw. From gambling to beachcombing to dune-buggying, there's something for everyone in this town.

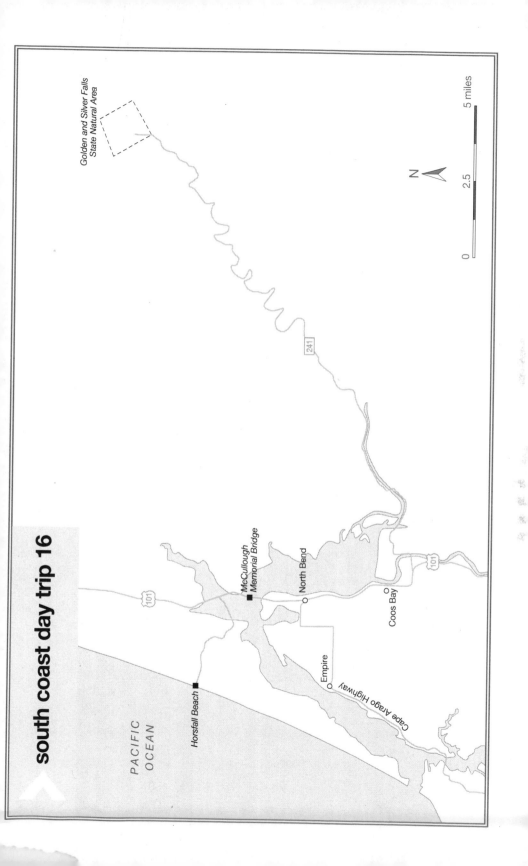

south coast day trip 16

Golden and Silver Falls State Natural Area

PACIFIC OCEAN

Horsfall Beach

McCullough Memorial Bridge

North Bend

Empire

Cape Arago Highway

Coos Bay

101

241

N

0   2.5   5 miles

getting there

From Eugene: Travel I-5 south 32 miles to exit 162, leading to Drain/Elkton. Follow OR 38 for another 56 miles west to Reedsport. From Reedsport, travel 24 miles south on US 101 to North Bend.

where to go

Horsfall Beach. Horsfall Road, 1 mile east of US 101 via Trans Pacific Lane. A wide variety of opportunities await at this large area northwest of town, including access to the Oregon Dunes, wide open sandy beaches facing the Pacific Ocean, inland lakes, camping, and hiking through forest. The Bluebill Trail circles a small seasonal lake, offering glimpses of wildlife, including a wide variety of birds. There is a campground at Bluebill Lake, and another closer to the highway called Horsfall Campground. Horsfall is the southernmost access to the Oregon Dunes National Recreation Area, and access to ATV recreation comes from several points, most notably the parking lot at the end of the road near the ocean. The beach,

a most elegant span

Legendary engineer Conde McCullough designed hundreds of bridges in his time, over 20 of them in Oregon, primarily along the Oregon Coast on Highway 101. McCullough's bridges are known for their stunning architectural beauty. He advocated that bridges be built economically, efficiently, and with beauty. The native of South Dakota worked for the Oregon Department of Transportation for 25 years.

Keep your eyes open for his elegant structures spanning rivers, bays, and inlets as you drive Highway 101. Many of McCullough's bridges are in the art deco style, with architectural details such as Gothic spires, obelisks, and Romanesque arches. The bridge of his design here in North Bend, which spans Coos Bay, not only is widely considered McCullough's masterpiece, but also was also his personal favorite. Completed in 1934 and named the Coos Bay Bridge, after McCullough's death in 1946 the bridge was named the **Conde McCullough Memorial Bridge.** *Motorists driving south into North Bend on Highway 101 see the bridge appear in the distance over the bay as a gorgeous green beacon. As a North Bend native, to me, the sight of the McCullough Bridge means I'm home. See other McCullough bridges in Newport, Waldport, Florence, Reedsport, and more. Once you learn to spot his style, McCullough's beautiful bridges are hard to miss.*

however, remains free of motor vehicles and is terrific for beach walking, sandcastle building, and the like. The area is also great for kite flying, beachcombing, and horseback riding.

Liberty Theatre. 2100 Sherman Ave.; (541) 756-4336; thelibertytheatre.org. Home of the Little Theatre on the Bay, named as a nod to the theater's long-running Little Ole Opry performances, the Liberty also produces musicals, dramas, comedies, and variety shows of all kinds. The renovated 1939 theater has been operated by the same group since 1957—one of the longest-running theater groups in the state. See what's running on stage while you're in town.

Steve's ATV Rentals. 68512 US 101; (844) 278-3837; stevesatvrentals.com. The southernmost part of the Oregon Dunes National Recreation Area extends almost to North Bend. Rent an ATV or take a tour with the operators at Steve's ATV Rentals. Here you'll find a wide selection of quads, dune buggies, ATVs, UTVs, and Side by Sides (RZRs) to choose from for your day of adventure on the sandy slopes.

where to eat

Ciccarelli's Restaurant. 2072 Sherman Ave.; (541) 751-1999; www.ciccarellisrestaurant .com. This family-owned business in North Bend specializes in Italian food, fresh-baked bread, hand-cut steaks, pasta, brick-oven pizza, homemade desserts, and coffee roasted on-site. Patio dining is available during the summer months. Visit the adjoining Coffee Shop and Roastery, where you can enjoy fresh-roasted coffee and espresso. A variety of pastries, sweet treats, quiches, wraps, salads, and pizza and a full espresso bar are available daily. Restaurant open Tues through Sat 11 a.m. to 2:30 p.m. and 5 to 9 p.m. Coffee Shop and Roastery open Tues through Sat 8 a.m. to 9 p.m. $–$$.

The Liberty Pub. 2047 Sherman Ave.; (541) 756-2550; thelibpub.com. Located downtown in a 1908 building that originally held one of North Bend's earliest saloons, The Liberty Pub is a locals' favorite known for excellent pizza. On offer are 11 taps of craft beer, fresh handmade pizza, some Irish favorites like shepherd's pie, and tons of appetizers including the "Amaizeballs"—deep-fried creamed corn. Visit for traditional Celtic music every Wed from 7 to 9 p.m. Open Wed through Sun at 4 p.m. 21 and over only. $–$$.

Mom's Kitchen. 1603 Sherman Ave.; (541) 756-2710. This tiny, family-owned, and very quaint restaurant has just a few tables and an old-fashioned counter with spinning stools for seats. The service is excellent, and the food is even better. Huge platters of fresh-to-order eggs, waffles, potatoes, and more might take a little longer than some places, but the wait is totally worth it. Don't miss out on the hash browns—you'll want seconds. $–$$.

Pancake Mill. 2390 Tremont Ave.; (541) 756-2751; pancakemill.com. A longtime locals' favorite, often with a wait on the weekends, the Pancake Mill is right on Highway 101 near the original location of the lumber mill. A large menu offers delicious portions of a wide variety of meals from blintzes and potato pancakes to omelets and crepes. The pie menu alone will blow your mind, with two dozen kinds as well as cakes and cheesecakes. Still hungry? Cinnamon rolls and muffins are homemade and fresh. And we haven't even gotten to lunch yet. Open 6 a.m. to 3 p.m. daily. $–$$.

Tin Thistle Cafe. 1972 Sherman Ave.; (541) 267-0267. The Tin Thistle is a Celtic-themed whole-foods vegan cafe featuring pasties, village bowls, vegetarian burgers, soups, pies, and smoothies in downtown North Bend. The menu changes but you might find gyros, a chili dog, or Indian pasties on it (yes, all vegan). Open Tues through Sat 11 a.m. to 4 p.m. $–$$.

Wildflour Cafe & Catering. 1989 Sherman Ave.; (541) 808-3633; wildflour-catering.com. Wildflour Cafe & Catering believes in fresh, simple, and delicious ingredients and is passionate about food, to include where it comes from, how it tastes, how it is prepared, and how it is presented. Enjoy sandwiches, salads, comfort foods, pastries, and vegetarian options. Open Mon through Fri from 8 a.m. to 3 p.m. You can also find Wildflour Cafe at the downtown Coos Bay Farmers' Market every Wed from May to Oct. $–$$.

Yeong's Place. 1120 Virginia Ave.; (541) 756-1914. This burger joint has been described by more than one happy diner as "burger heaven." From Yeong's very unassuming building emerges an excellent array of diner food including a wide variety of burgers, milkshakes, tater tots, and more. Get crazy and try the lamb, bison, or elk burgers. $–$$.

where to stay

Itty Bitty Inn. 1504 Sherman Ave.; (541) 756-6398, ittybittyinn.com. One of the oldest lodgings in town, the Itty Bitty Inn has provided refuge for travelers along Highway 101 since 1950. Five rooms are eclectic, fun, and affordable. Each room includes Oregon-made soaps and locally roasted coffee. Borrow a loaner cruiser bike to head into town for dinner or coffee. $.

The Mill Casino Hotel & RV Park. 3201 Tremont Ave.; (541) 756-8800, (800) 953-4800; themillcasino.com. A variety of lodging options are here at this casino hotel overlooking Coos Bay, on the site of the former lumber mills. Choose a well-appointed room with an elevated view of the water in the tower section of the hotel, another of the more than 200 rooms and suites, or one of the 100 pet-friendly RV sites. Enjoy free airport shuttle, parking, and valet services, as well as the pool and spas, fitness room, arcade, and business center. All rooms feature complimentary Wi-Fi, an in-room refreshment center complete with a coffeemaker and Red Wagon Organic Coffee, luxurious pillow-top beds, and more. Several restaurants and bars are on-site, including the signature Plank House Restaurant, featuring fine dining with views, and Whitecaps, a smoke-free adult-only lounge. Entertainment galore is here as well, including over 700 slots and card and table games. $$–$$$.

coos bay

Adjacent to North Bend is the somewhat bigger city Coos Bay—the largest town on the Oregon Coast, fronted by the largest bay between Seattle and San Francisco. Originally named Marshfield, Coos Bay was founded upon its excellent commercial access to the sea. Shipping, shipbuilding, and wood products were prominent economy-building activities, as were fishing and coal mining.

Long before such industry, of course, the Native Americans had made this place home. The word *Coos* comes from one of the Native tribes and carries two meanings: "place of pines" and "lake." Several Native American tribes called the Coos Bay region their ancestral homeland, including the Confederated Tribes of Coos, Lower Umpqua, and Siuslaw Indians and the Coquille Indians.

The expansive geography of the hilly city includes a variety of landscapes, including vistas that overlook the Coos River and Coos Bay. Downtown Coos Bay has been revital-ized, and includes an excellent art museum, interpretive signs on the waterfront telling of the area's history, a renovated historic theater, and plenty of dining options.

getting there

Coos Bay is adjacent to North Bend, directly south on US 101.

where to go

Coos Art Museum. 235 Anderson Ave.; (541) 267-3901; coosart.org. The third-oldest art museum in Oregon was founded by local artists in 1966. The 1936 art deco former post office building downtown features 7 galleries with up to 24 changing exhibitions annually, from sculpture to watercolors to ceramics. The Steve Prefontaine Memorial Room features photographs, trophies, and memorabilia honoring the great American runner Steve Prefon-taine, who was a Coos Bay native. The museum's permanent collection highlights contem-porary fine art printmaking and artworks in all media by Pacific Northwest artists. Open Tues through Fri 10 a.m. to 4 p.m. and Sat 1 to 4 p.m.

Coos Bay Boardwalk. Downtown Coos Bay waterfront. This short stretch of wood-plank pier is a relatively new improvement to the waterfront, and a worthy stroll. Sweeping views of Coos Bay are here, as well as a fish market, a number of informative displays, and a few picnic tables for sunny day dining. Interpretive exhibits cover history, including the region's coal and lumber industries. Check out the *Koos #2*, a retired tugboat docked here. Nearby, in downtown, extend your walk by taking in a variety of antiques and boutique shops, cof-feehouses, and restaurants.

Coos History Museum. 1210 N Front St.; (541) 756-6320; cooshistory.org. This impressive building on the waterfront stands out as you drive through town on Highway 101. A community-built facility that opened in its current location in 2015, the Coos History Museum is run by Oregon's oldest continuously operated historical society. Inside, take in multiple delights including more than 250,000 historic photographs, exhibits, event and rental space, a unique museum shop, and a developing bay-front plaza. Gain a historic overview of the Coos and Coquille Indian tribes, as well as the coal miners, loggers, and shipbuilders that helped to shape the area. Read about local shipwrecks and a wide variety of topics from prehistory to the present. Open 10 a.m. to 5 p.m. every day but Mon.

Egyptian Theatre. 229 S Broadway; (541) 269-8650; egyptiantheatreoregon.com. This gorgeous historic theater is listed on the National Register of Historic Places and boasts one of the only remaining operable Wurlitzer organs in the state of Oregon. Built in 1925, the Egyptian Theatre struggled to stay open over the years, like so many treasured performing arts centers of its era. The community rallied around its preservation more than once, including raising funds for a million-dollar structural overhaul in the early 2000s, and today the Egyptian is a community center and point of pride. Movie events and fund-raisers are the weekly fare, but the theater is also available for private events and screenings. Live music is featured on occasion, and beer and movie nights are common. Original, ornate design elements in the Egyptian theme remain, including hieroglyphics, antique Egyptianesque characters, two 8-foot-tall bronze pharaoh statues seated on thrones, and a King Tut bench. With a new projection system and top-notch surround sound, visitors today experience a beloved community theater with modern amenities backed by nearly a century of experiences.

Marshfield Sun Printing Museum. 1049 Front St.; (541) 269-1565; marshfieldsunprinting museum.org. The *Sun* newspaper was published from 1891 to 1944, at this specific location beginning in 1911. Original equipment including printing presses, type cases, imposing tables, and other tools of the printing trade is on display here at this site listed on the National Register of Historic Places. Exhibits on printing and local history are here too. Open from Memorial Day to Labor Day, Tues through Sat 1 to 4 p.m.

Oregon Coast Historical Railway Museum. 766 S 1st St.; (541) 297-6130; orcorail.org. It's hard to fully appreciate what an incredible impact the railroad had on early Oregon Coast history. This museum, a must-stop for railroad enthusiasts, interprets this important past with railroad and logging equipment in an outdoor exhibit, as well as a mini-museum with photos and railroad memorabilia indoors. Ring the bell of the signature 1922 Baldwin steam locomotive, check out a 1942-era steel caboose, and see vintage conductor's uniforms. The museum is run by the Oregon Coast Historical Railway, an organization that works to provide a place to restore and display vintage railroad and logging equipment. Open Wed and Sat. 9 a.m. to 3 p.m.

the land of waters

One of the meanings of the word Coos is "lake," and whether lake or bay or ocean or river, the Coos Bay area is defined by water. The early Native Americans knew this better than anyone—their primary method of transportation was by canoe. Over time, the traditional wooden "dugout" canoes that had once been prolific were replaced by more-modern transportation, and the remaining canoes of the early era deteriorated and disappeared. But a dedicated group of tribal members from around Oregon sought out traditional designs and began re-creating the canoes. Then came celebrations, events, and even competitions to honor the historic canoes. Every September, a traditional Native canoe race occurs on Coos Bay, sponsored by the Mill Casino as part of the Mill-Luck Salmon Celebration. Also at the Mill Casino, in the Plank House Restaurant, see replicas of traditional paddles made by Native American artist Shirod Younker, a native of Coos Bay, on display year-round. Other re-creations of traditional tribal canoes can be seen on the Oregon Coast at Fort Clatsop and the Columbia Maritime Museum, both in Astoria. See themillcasino.com for more information on the September canoe races.

Surfing. For the bold and unafraid of the cold, Coos Bay has some great surfing options. Check out one of these stores for advice, rentals, lessons, and gear.

Bahama Boards. 650 Ivy St.; (541) 808-3535; bahamastyles.com. Boards for sale or rent are on hand here. Check out their website for a surf forecast and advice on where to surf on the Oregon Coast, whether in Coos Bay or elsewhere.

Waxers. 242 S Broadway; (541) 266-9020; surfwaxers.com. Rent a surfboard, buy one, or hire the pros to take you out for a lesson from this shop on the Coos Bay-front, attached to Shark Bites restaurant. Wetsuit included in lessons; group rates available. Waxers is also an official dealer of Hobie kayaks and rents stand-up paddleboards too.

Three Rivers Casino. 1297 Ocean Blvd.; (877) 374-8377; threeriverscasino.com. A newer outpost to the Three Rivers Casino main location in Florence, this location in the historic neighborhood of Empire features over 250 electronic gaming machines. Check out their weekly tournaments on Tues and bingo nights offered every Thurs. Open 24 hours.

where to shop

Coos Bay Farmers' Market. On Central Avenue between US 101 and 4th Street. Operating seasonally between May and Oct on Wed from 9 a.m. to 2 p.m., this farmers' market is one of the largest on the Oregon Coast. An average of 80 vendors per week sell produce and much more, including art, baked goods, coffee, and a variety of lunch options.

Cranberry Sweets & More. 1005 Newmark Ave.; (541) 888-9824; cranberrysweets.com. This longtime establishment dates back to 1962, when Bandon resident Dorothy Johnson captured the taste of the local cranberry in a candy. This candy-maker continues to make hundreds of unique fruit candies and chocolates with traditional methods and time-honored recipes. At this shop, watch candy being made and try samples too. Don't leave without a bag or two for the road.

Leaf's Treehouse Antiques & Collectibles. 311 S Broadway; (541) 266-7348. This collective features several small individual stores within a big space, each exhibiting their own individuality, craftsmanship, and artistry. Wander through and peruse an interesting mix of vintage, repurposed, antique, eclectic, and just plain fun merchandise. Don't forget to go upstairs where even more discoveries await.

Organic Glass Art & Gifts. 201 S Broadway; (541) 808-0577. This large shop carries a wide variety of traditional crafts and contemporary art. Choose from a collection of pendants, beads, marbles, ornaments, purses, pottery, pipes, and apparel, many created by local artists and artisans. A great stop to shop for a gift for yourself or someone else.

Painted Zebra Boutique. 1997 Sherman Ave.; (541) 808-2500. This boutique carries clothing for women and juniors. Check out their eclectic mix of the latest fashions, plus jewelry, handbags, and more. Specialty items include formal gowns for homecoming, prom, and bridal events; seasonal items like Halloween costumes and Christmas stockings; and greeting cards and organic lotions. In need of a corset? This is where to find one.

where to eat

The Boat. 102 Hall Ave.; (541) 808-9500. This restaurant isn't ironically named—it is indeed located in a retired boat that has been dry-docked on the bay. Fish-and-chips are their specialty and come in cod or halibut, or try an oyster sandwich, shrimp basket, or clam strips. Sit inside in a small dining area or choose the large outdoor deck on sunny days. Open for lunch and dinner 7 days a week. $$.

Front Street Provisioners. 737 N Front St.; (541) 808-3420; frontstreetprovisioners.com. This old warehouse on Front Street has put some time in on a rugged working bay front, and presents all of the charm to prove it. Original wide-plank wood floors, high ceilings, and steel beams are just part of what make this space interesting. The owners transformed the warehouse into a cafe and wine shop, with the intention of creating community and enhancing regional identity. The menu features wood-fired Neapolitan-style pizza, seasonal salads, and house-made gelato and sorbetto. Local beers and regional wines are on hand, as are cocktails and specialty bottles. Front Street Provisions is also an event hall, hosting community gatherings regularly. During summer months, enjoy dining on the outdoor patio. Open Mon through Thurs 11 a.m. to 9 p.m., Fri and Sat 11 a.m. to 11 p.m. $$.

7 Devils Brewing Company. 247 S 2nd St.; (541) 808-3738; 7devilsbrewery.com. A great vibe is just the beginning of the appeal at this wonderful craft brewpub in downtown. A warm, eclectic interior is accompanied by a variety of terrific beers made on-site using locally sourced ingredients. Try the Groundswell IPA, the Lighthouse Session Pale, or the McCullough Mocha Stout. They also brew nonalcoholic kombucha and ginger beer. The menu is small but includes delicious items, also with locally sourced ingredients. The albacore tuna melt is divine, or try the roasted veggie sandwich or a platter of fried Coos Bay oysters. 7 Devils has a special interest in green practices and promotion of the local Coos Bay community. From the outside patio, don't forget to look up—an amazing mural painted on the wall depicts the greater Coos Bay area. Open for lunch and dinner every day except Tues. $$.

Shake N' Burger. 63023 US 101; (541) 808-9013. Burgers and all kinds of fries—including curly fries, waffle fries, and classic fries—are on the menu here. Not in the mood for a burger? The menu at this dine-in/take-out/drive-thru joint even includes a few seafood items and a handful of meals from south of the border, including a burrito and nachos. Sides include onion rings, coleslaw, garlic bread, and mashed potatoes. $–$$.

SharkBites Cafe. 240 S Broadway; (541) 269-7475; sharkbites.cafe. The seafood is fresh and delicious here. Don't miss an order of their famous fish tacos, which come in many varieties, or try award-winning fish-and-chips or clam chowder. Burgers and baskets are great too. Burlap sacks, surfboards, and driftwood decorate the walls, invoking the casual Oregon Coast aesthetic. Wine, beer, and a full bar and creative cocktail list round out every meal. Open for lunch and dinner every day but Sun. $$–$$$.

Stockpot Restaurant. 63097 Barry St.; (541) 266-7070. This American-diner-themed destination in a former A&W is raved about for breakfast, especially if you like your first meal of the day to be ample and delicious. Corned beef hash, country skillet breakfasts, fresh biscuits, and more light up the morning menu. For lunch, fish tacos, a bacon cheeseburger, or a chicken salad are just some of the options. $–$$.

Tokyo Bistro. 525 Newmark Ave.; (541) 808-0808; tokyocoosbay.com. Located in the historic Empire neighborhood, this sushi restaurant takes the freshest seafood and produce and turns it into delectable sushi and more. All of the delicious usuals are here, from octopus to soft-shell crab to ahi tuna, in both rolls and sashimi. There is a dining room and a small bar; bring the family or make it date night. Open Tues through Sun for lunch and dinner. $$–$$$.

where to stay

Coos Bay Manor. 955 S 5th St.; (541) 269-1224; coosbaymanor.com. This historic Colonial-style home was built in 1912 and is today listed on the National Register of Historic Places. Six rooms boast historical, comfortable flair, and all have private baths and include fireplaces. Enjoy a full breakfast in the morning. Ask about the airport shuttle and pet policy. $$.

Edgewater Inn. 275 E Johnson Ave.; (541) 267-0423; edgewaterinns.com. Comfortable rooms are here on the bay front. Choose a room or suite, each with a refrigerator, microwave, and free Wi-Fi. Fish from the small deck that overlooks the water, and take a dip in the indoor pool. $–$$.

worth more time

Just 26 miles east of Coos Bay on OR 241 is **Golden and Silver Falls State Natural Area,** the location of two beautiful waterfalls. The road along the Coos and Millicoma Rivers is winding and narrow, so take your time and take in the scenery. Once you're there, the hike to the falls is an easy one. Choose the 1.4-mile trail that leads through dense coastal forest and scenic canyons to the midpoint of Silver Falls and to the top of Golden Falls, where the views of the water plunging over sheer rock cliffs to moss-covered boulders 100 feet below are not to be missed. There is a picnic area along the banks of Glenn and Silver Creeks—bring a lunch and enjoy a peaceful reprieve under the maple, alder, and Oregon myrtle trees.

day trip 17

south coast

>>> **scenic capes & working harbors:**
charleston

charleston

Charleston is an unincorporated community of less than 1,000 that sits just inside the mouth of the Coos River, and at the entrance to Coos Bay. This working harbor with a large commercial fishing fleet has a bustling marina, with recreational and commercial fishing endeavors under way year-round. Oyster beds and clam-digging flats are nearby too, and the copious harvest of these shellfish is evidenced by large piles of shells visible as you drive through town. The overarching theme in Charleston is seafood—catch or dig your own, buy it fresh to cook yourself, or choose from a variety of vendors and restaurants to provide you with a taste of the fruits of the sea.

Charleston is gateway to some of the most breathtaking scenery on the Oregon Coast. South of the community are several beaches and the renowned Shore Acres State Park, which boasts cliffs, trails, and vistas to die for. Charleston is also a place of science and study, as the site of both the University of Oregon's Oregon Institute of Marine Biology and the South Slough National Estuarine Research Reserve. Both offer interpretive sites and the opportunity to learn more about this uniquely beautiful place.

getting there

From Eugene: Take I-5 south 32 miles to exit 162, which leads to Drain/Elkton. Follow OR 38 for 56 miles west to Reedsport. From Reedsport, travel 24 miles south on US 101 to

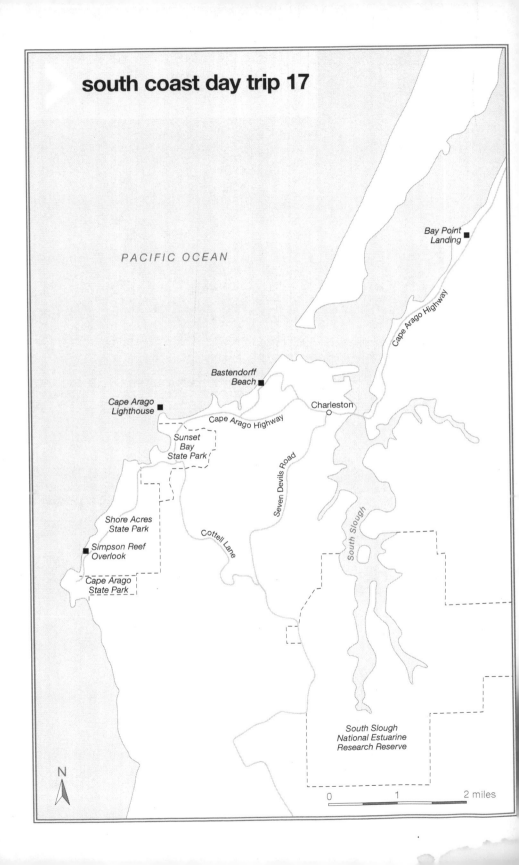

south coast day trip 17

PACIFIC OCEAN

Bay Point Landing

Cape Arago Highway

Bastendorff Beach

Cape Arago Lighthouse

Charleston

Cape Arago Highway

Sunset Bay State Park

Seven Devils Road

South Slough

Shore Acres State Park

Simpson Reef Overlook

Cottell Lane

Cape Arago State Park

South Slough National Estuarine Research Reserve

N

0   1   2 miles

North Bend. In North Bend, follow signs to OR 540 / Cape Arago Highway, which leads into Charleston. Charleston is 9 miles southwest of North Bend on OR 540 / Cape Arago Highway.

where to go

Bastendorff Beach. 2 miles south of Charleston on Cape Arago Highway. Bastendorff is a mile-long stretch of beach tucked between the jetty and bar into Coos Bay and a small cove that is accessible when the tide is out. The sandy beach is popular with surfers, kiters, sand-castle builders, and beachgoers of all kinds. On-site is a 74-site campground, open year-round. The day-use area has covered picnic areas with electricity, sinks and running water, and charcoal grills. A playground is here too, with rustic wooden forts the kids will love.

Cape Arago Loop. A scenic drive and natural and historical exploration not to be missed, the Cape Arago Loop is about 10 miles round-trip south from Charleston. Here are some of the loop's highlights, listed in the order in which travelers will encounter them.

Sunset Bay State Park. Sunset Bay is first and foremost a lovely little beach ensconced in a concave bay surrounded by tall sea cliffs. But there is more here, including tide-pooling, hiking, and a campground for tents, RVs, and featuring some yurts for rent. Rent a kayak or SUP from South Coast Tours (southcoast tours.net) and spend a morning, an afternoon, or the whole day paddling around this mostly calm, peaceful ocean bay. Tide-pool on either end of the beach under towering cliffs. Feeling ambitious? Leave your car and hike the trail that extends south to the other scenic outposts on this tour.

Shore Acres State Park. Five acres of formal gardens are here, including a Japanese-style lily pond, rose test garden, and plots where a wide variety of flowers and evergreen shrubs grow year-round. The gardens are the legacy of the estate of Louis Simpson (see sidebar below). From the overlook, take in expansive views of the ocean as it crashes into steep, jagged cliffs. Storm watching is marvelous in the winter from here, as waves collide into sea stacks to fly toward the sky in marvelous sprays. Hike down a well-marked, short but steep trail behind the gardens to Simpson Beach, a lovely little cove surrounding turquoise waters that roll dramatically in to a deep sandy beach. Hang out here, do some tide-pooling, and relax out of the wind. During the holidays, the botanical gardens are adorned with thousands of holiday lights, and nighttime visitors soak up the gorgeous sights of illuminated trees.

Simpson Reef Overlook / Shell Island Interpretive Stop. From this overlook and small parking lot, see Shell Island and the surrounding reefs, which provide breeding and rest areas for seabirds and marine mammals. A sharp eye might reveal gray whales, northern elephant seals, harbor seals, sea lions, stellar sea lions, black oystercatchers, great blue herons, and pelagic cormorants from this spot. Bring binoculars for a spectacular view.

Cape Arago State Park. At the end of the road is this state park, with many scenic vistas and several trails to explore. Take in views of the seals and sea lions from the north trail, or descend a steep trail to a secluded beach on the south side of the cape, with more tide-pooling, beachcombing, and surfing opportunities. Follow the road as it loops around, carrying you back to the north the way you came to return to Charleston.

Charleston Marine Life Center. 63466 Boat Basin Rd.; (541) 888-2581; charlestonmarine lifecenter.com. This small gem of an interpretive center, part of the University of Oregon's Oregon Institute of Marine Biology campus, is not to be missed. Step inside and pay a small

louis, louis

Louis Simpson came to the south coast in the early 1900s from California, sent by his wealthy father to learn the family shipping and lumber business. He did that and more, eventually buying a huge property south of Charleston and building his wife a marvelous summer estate on a spectacular site, offering amazing views of the powerful sea from the cliff. The three-story mansion, completed in 1910, had a swimming pool, ballroom, its own power plant, and marvelous botanical gardens. Simpson and his wife Lela dubbed the estate "Shore Acres."

As with far too many mansions of its era, the first Simpson home burned down in 1921. The Simpsons rebuilt a home even grander, with 17 rooms, but the Great Depression took its toll, and in 1942 the Simpsons sold their property to the state of Oregon. Before the state could enact plans to make the site a public park, the US Army stepped in and took control of the grounds and mansion as a World War II outpost. By the time the army left, the mansion and gardens were in disrepair. The state persisted, much to all of our benefit today. **Shore Acres State Park** *is one of Oregon's most popular and finest destinations. Simpson's legacy extends further than these gorgeous grounds—he also purchased the entire townsite of Yarrow (now North Bend), becoming its first mayor and booster.*

Over the years, Simpson donated land for churches, hospitals, and businesses. He also worked tirelessly to bring a railroad to the area, and encouraged the construction of Highway 101. Louis Simpson died in Barview in 1949, but his imprint on the region lingers for us all.

fee to discover aquaria representing different coastal ecosystems, a tide pool touch tank, whale and sea lion skeletons, underwater video from deep reefs and undersea volcanoes, and a variety of specimens. You'll leave with a deeper appreciation of the hidden and remarkable diversity of life off the coast of Oregon, from the coastline to the deep sea. Open Wed through Sat 11 a.m. to 5 p.m.

Clamming and crabbing. Dungeness crab are plentiful here, and tasty too. You can toss a crab ring right into the bay from the dock in the Charleston Harbor if you wish. Clam digging can be pursued in multiple locations around the bay. Clams come in many species, including razor, gaper, butter, cockle, littleneck, soft-shell, and purple varnish. You'll need a shellfish license, and can benefit from information, gear, bait, and/or a tour from one of these outfitters.

Basin Tackle. 63510 Kingfisher Rd.; (541) 888-3474; basintackle.net. Become a clamming expert here! Rent a bucket and clam pump, as well as rubber boots. Or, sign up for a clamming class. Bring your own shellfish license.

Davey Jones' Locker. 91139 Cape Arago Hwy.; (541) 888-3941. Rent a crab ring or a clam gun here, but Davey Jones' Locker is much more than a gear outfitter. Sometimes called the "cultural mecca of Charleston," this place sells grocery items, hot foods like pizza and burritos, beer, soda, saltwater taffy, lottery tickets . . . need we go on?

Pacific Charter Services. 63480 Crossline Rd.; (541) 378-3040; pacificcharter services.com. Prefer to hire a boat and a guide for your search for the Dungeness? Pacific Charter Services offers an ocean crabbing tour, and also takes guests out on chinook salmon and deep-water lingcod and rockfish adventures.

South Slough National Estuarine Research Reserve and Interpretive Center. 61907 Seven Devils Rd.; (541) 888-5558; oregon.gov/dsl/SS/Pages/About.aspx. Today, South Slough is known for its designation in 1974 as the first unit of the National Estuarine Research Reserve System (NERRS). Nearly 6,000 acres of the Coos estuary is a protected natural area, encompassing a mixture of open-water channels, tidal and freshwater wetlands, riparian areas, and forested uplands, safeguarded and managed for the purposes of long-term research, education, and coastal stewardship. But for much longer, and without so much science-speak, the slough has been a treasured and beloved destination for residents of the greater area. Native Americans lived and thrived here, feeding on abundant fish and shellfish. In more recent times, visitors have come here to paddle the waters, watch the wildlife, hike the trails, and take in the peace and beauty of this natural network of estuary habitats. Visit to take a hike on one of the trails, many which are great for all ability levels. Here on Oregon's second-largest estuary, fresh and salt water meet, and the plants and wildlife of both intermingle to create a natural wonderland.

where to shop

Chuck's Seafood. 91135 Cape Arago Hwy.; (541) 888-5525; chucksseafood.com. Step into this tidy shop for fresh, prepared, and canned seafood caught and gathered from local waters. Chuck's Seafood also runs Coos Bay Oyster Company, and you'll find fresh oysters here as well as whatever fishes are fresh and available. Premium salmon, tuna, sturgeon, and shrimp are available in cans to take with you back home to enjoy whenever you wish— and they also make a great gift.

Kinnee's Gifts N Shells. 91134 Cape Arago Hwy.; (541) 888-5924. Take home a souvenir from your visit to Oregon's Bay Area from this fun little shop. Here you'll find T-shirts and hoodies for those windy beach days as well as a variety of shells, gifts, and jewelry to take home for yourself or a friend.

where to eat

High Tide Cafe. 1124 Cape Arago Hwy.; (541) 888-3664; hightidecafeoregon.com. Eat indoors or out on the patio overlooking the bay and South Slough at this terrific restaurant in the heart of town. Try the grilled shrimp and cheese, pesto or cheese garlic bread, award-winning clam chowder, or the seafood special of the day. Cocktails come out of the "Sand Bar," a small on-site lounge, which also offers regional beers or wines to sip with your daily catch. $$–$$$.

Miller's at the Cove. 63346 Boat Basin Rd.; (541) 808-2404; millersatthecove.rocks. A casual eatery located in an old church, Miller's is a locals' favorite for burgers, fish-and-chips, fish tacos, chili, and more. Count on a menu and atmosphere that pleases all ages— Miller's is family-friendly, with junior and senior portions. In the winter, cozy up around the fireplace. Open daily at 11 a.m. $–$$.

Portside Restaurant & Lounge. 63383 Kingfisher Rd.; (541) 888-5544; portsidebythebay .com. Overlooking the slough feeding into the Charleston Marina, Portside offers local sea-food caught daily, steak, and a Friday-night seafood buffet. Choose your own live Dunge-ness crab or lobster from the tanks. Live easy-listening music and karaoke happens in the lounge. The full bar features cocktails, wine, and beer, including microbrews. Open daily 11:30 a.m. to 11 p.m. $$–$$$.

where to stay

Bay Point Landing. 92443 Cape Arago Hwy., Coos Bay; (541) 351-9160; baypointlanding .com. A new concept and lodging destination is here along the wetlands of Coos Bay en route to Charleston. Bay Point Landing creates high-end camping options with a combi-nation of 17 furnished cabins, Airstream trailers, and 161 RV sites to choose from. A few well-designed and attractive buildings serve as event centers, common gathering areas, restrooms, and showers. Doggie care stations, outdoor games, and other amenities are found throughout the scenic, waterfront location. It isn't the cheapest camping you'll find, but it might be the fanciest. $$–$$$.

Charleston Harbor Inn. 63361 Kingfisher Rd.; (541) 888-1178; charlestonharborinn.com. Private patios and balconies from each room overlook the harbor at this small but comfortable motel. Several suite sizes are available, and the largest have kitchenettes, dining tables, washing machines and dryers, and dishwashers. Daily, weekly, and monthly rates available. $–$$.

Oceanside RV Resort and Campground. 90281 Cape Arago Hwy.; (541) 888-2598; This campground and resort with an ocean view and beach access is a great option for staying in the Charleston area. Lodging includes tent and RV sites, as well as vacation cottages with full kitchens and more-rustic "beach shanties." On-site is a crab cooking and cleaning station, a community outdoor fire pit, and showers. Visit the Oceanside Snack Shack for light meals from clam chowder to burgers. Oceanside Resort is pet-friendly. $$–$$$.

day trip 18

south coast

> **golf & lighthouses:**
> bandon

bandon

Bandon is renowned for several things—fire, cheese, cranberries, and golf among them. The small town is also known for breathtaking scenery, a beautiful lighthouse, and, according to some residents, a powerful and mystical spherical field of force called the Bandon Vortex.

But before the force, there was fire. The commercial downtown of Bandon burned nearly to the ground in 1936, and the blame fell largely on a plant. The town founder, Irish peer George Bennett, introduced the plant gorse from his native Ireland to the town and surrounds. Gorse makes a decent hedgerow, but the spiny, oily plant is also (it turns out) highly flammable. When a forest fire alit east of town in 1936, it moved quickly, born on gorse, directly into downtown, destroying a majority of the buildings.

Bandon rebuilt and continued to churn its economic engine along on the basis of cranberry bogs and cheesemaking, both introduced in the 1880s. Golf came later—much later. The first golf course here, designed in the Scottish links style, was installed in 1999. No one could have predicted the popularity such challenging courses on the wild Oregon Coast would engender. Now there are five golf courses, and guests travel to Bandon from all over the world for a chance to hit a ball here.

Bandon is named for Bandon, Ireland, and there remain a few Irish touches here and there throughout the town. It's a lovely destination to wander shops, grab a bite to eat, and gaze at spectacular offshore scenery.

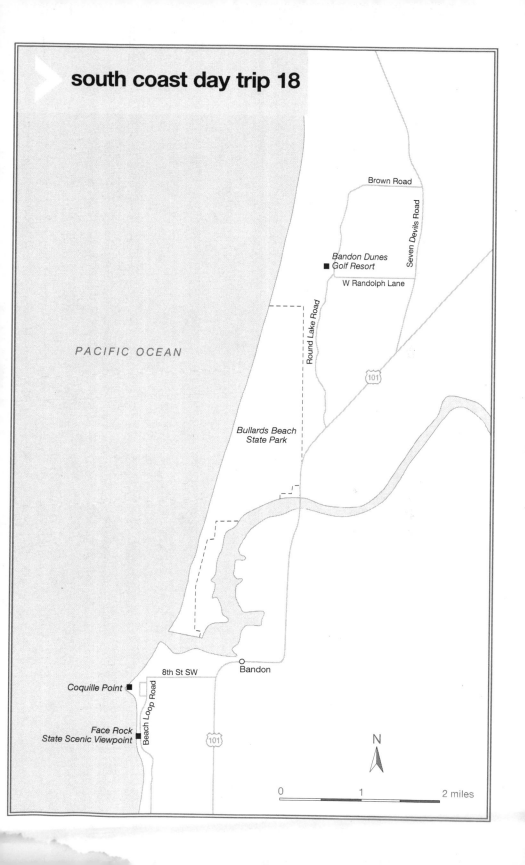

south coast day trip 18

PACIFIC OCEAN

Brown Road

Seven Devils Road

Bandon Dunes
Golf Resort ■

W Randolph Lane

Round Lake Road

[101]

Bullards Beach
State Park

Coquille Point ■

8th St SW

Bandon ○

Beach Loop Road

Face Rock
State Scenic Viewpoint ■

[101]

N

0   1   2 miles

getting there

From Eugene: Travel I-5 south 32 miles to exit 162, which leads to Drain/Elkton. Follow OR 38 56 miles west to Reedsport. From Reedsport, travel 50 miles south on US 101 to Bandon.

where to go

Bullards Beach State Park. US 101 just north of Bandon. This large park includes a beach and campground and is a lovely family-oriented destination for day or overnight use. A campground is tucked into the trees out of the wind and has tent and RV sites as well as many yurts for rent. Explore 4.5 miles of beach, mountain bike the hard-packed sand along the surf, or stroll the ocean shore with views of the Coquille River. The historic Coquille River Lighthouse is located at the end of Bullards Beach Road, and is seasonally open to the public. The lighthouse, built in the late 1890s, is staffed from mid-May through Sept with volunteers who interpret the history of the area. Across the river is Bandon Marsh National Wildlife Refuge, home to a large variety of wildlife. Bullards Beach also offers a horse camp, biker/hiker camp, and boat launch.

Coos Boat Tours. (541) 999-6575; coosboattours.com. Hop aboard and take a 2-hour tour of the Coquille River to delve deeper into local history and scenery. The pocket tug *O'Flynn* can carry up to 6 passengers to tour past remnants of lumber mills and fish canneries, getting a sense of a time when boat builders and river ferries lined the banks. Tour-goers also spy many bird species, forests of spruce and myrtle, and stunning landscapes around every turn.

Coquille Point National Wildlife Refuge. West of Bandon off Portland Avenue SW. This destination is a unit of Oregon Islands National Wildlife Refuge, which comprises more than 1,800 rocks, reefs, and islands spanning the entire Oregon Coast. Locally, this section is known as Coquille Point, or Kronenberg County Park, and recognized as a very scenic outpost on the Oregon Coast. Sea stacks offshore provide homes to seabirds and marine mammals, including common murres, pigeon guillemots, tufted puffins, Brandt's and pelagic cormorants, black oystercatchers, and western gulls, many of which can be seen from shore (bring binoculars). Gray whales are often seen from this point from Dec to Jan and Mar to May, and harbor seals are present year-round during calmer surf conditions. Stairs lead down to the beach for beachcombing and walking.

Face Rock Creamery. 680 2nd St.; (541) 347-3223; facerockcreamery.com. Founded in 2013, Face Rock Creamery has won a number of cheesemaking awards in its short history. This shop on the highway is more like a visitor center, with walls lined with media articles about Face Rock's rise, awards, and displays about the founder, the cheesemaker, and the family that runs the dairy that supplies milk to the creamery. In this attractive, welcoming space, buy fresh curds as well as cheeses in varieties ranging from Vampire Slayer garlic

it's cheesy

*Cheesemaking is in Bandon's blood. The high humidity and cool evenings of the Oregon coastline make an ideal climate for supporting the lush green pastures that dairy cows feast upon. Over the past century-plus, the fertile valley of the Coquille River has been recognized as some of the richest dairy land in the country. By the late 1800s, over 10 dairy farms were making local cheeses. Bandon had nearly become synonymous with cheese, but a string of fires, including the devastating 1936 fire that destroyed much of the city, drove many cheesemakers out of business. One rebuilt and remained on the north end of town—the **Bandon Cheese Factory.** The factory became a Bandon icon, serving as a productive creamery and tourist destination until 2000, when it was purchased by a larger corporation, suddenly shuttered, and torn down. Locals and visitors were dismayed, but no one forgot Bandon's cheesy legacy, and in the early 2010s, a creamery was reborn. Bandon local Brad Sinko, who grew up learning the ropes at the Bandon Cheese Factory, which was once owned by his father, returned to town to become cheesemaker for the upstart **Face Rock Creamery.** Today, Face Rock is known for cheesemaking excellence, and a new "factory" is open for business, and visitors, daily. Long live the cheese!*

cheddar to smoky cheddar, horseradish cheese, and cranberry walnut cheddar. The creamery also serves light meals, ice cream, beer, and wine. Souvenirs and gifts are on hand too.

Face Rock State Scenic Viewpoint. Beach Loop Road at Face Rock Drive. Face Rock is a sea stack that rises from the sea offshore of Bandon. The image of the profile of a face gazing up to the sky is visible on the north side of the rock; from the cliff overlooking the ocean, you can easily pick out the face. This small waterfront park boasts picnic tables, restrooms, easy beach access, and views of many gorgeous landmark sea stacks, including Face Rock. There is a well-kept trail to the beach, and several rocky intertidal areas to explore at low tide.

where to shop

Misty Meadows Jams. 48053 US 101; (541) 347-2575; oregonjam.com. Some say Misty Meadows is the source of the best jams and jellies in Oregon. It is certain that this spot is a great place to find jams made using local cranberries, blueberries, and so much more, from Oregon cherry butter to loganberry jam to blackberry honey. No-sugar-added spreads, BBQ sauces, and a variety of syrups are also on hand.

about that vortex

As a child growing up on the Oregon Coast in the 1970s, I recall hearing discussion of the strange energy field called the **Bandon Vortex.** *My mother and her friends took me on a pilgrimage to a museum and gallery celebrating the unique energy field occurring in Bandon. That museum is gone, but the legend remains. According to believers, the Bandon Vortex is a spherical field of force, half above the ground and half below sea level, caused by the intersection of two ley lines. Points of power cross here, creating a special kind of energy. Reports over the years of lights rising from the sea along these lines keep the Bandon Vortex theory alive, and some call Bandon a "city of light." Creative energy, illumination, and knowledge are said to thrive here. Believe it or not, but it's hard to deny that Bandon has a special appeal and great vibe.*

Mother's Natural Grocery and Deli. 975 2nd St. SE; (541) 347-4086; bandonbythesea .com/mothers. A natural food store and more, offering a variety of natural grocery items, organic produce, bulk foods, whole-grain breads, herbs, vitamins, beauty aids, gifts, books, and more. There's also a gourmet vegetarian deli—grab some soups, salads, sandwiches, baked goodies, fresh juices, or one of their daily specials to go for your beach or bay-front picnic.

South Coast Bicycles. 805 2nd St. SE; (541) 347-1995; southcoastbicycles.com. For some, bike touring the Oregon Coast is the only way to go, and this bike shop has all the skills and tools to keep you pedaling along. New bikes, repairs, clothing, and accessories are on hand. South Coast Bikes is also an outlet for the rental of fat tire bikes, so you can partake in the latest beach-biking phenomenon.

WinterRiver Books & Gallery. 170 2nd St. SE; (541) 347-4111; winterriverbooks.com. There is more to discover here than books, although plenty of beach reads and terrific books can be found on the bookshelves. You'll also find a unique selection of cards, jewelry, music, games, and more. Local-interest books are a specialty—look in the nonfiction section for books about Bandon's history and natural history.

where to eat

Alloro Wine Bar. 375 2nd St. SE; (541) 347-1850; allorowinebar.com. This small but beloved wine bar is known for upscale but comfortable dining in a lovely, white-tablecloth atmosphere. Come in for award-winning Italian-inspired coastal cuisine, an extensive wine cellar, and seasonal menus including locally farmed and imported Italian specialty ingredients. Dishes range from sea scallops to duck breast to lamb osso buco. A full bar and specialty beers and wines from around the region to around the globe are on the menu, and all pastas are made in-house. Open for dinner Thurs through Mon. $$–$$$.

Bandon Brewing. 395 2nd St. SE; (541) 347-3911; bandonbrewingco.com. Located right under the entrance sign spanning the road to Old Town Bandon, Bandon Brewing is your destination for wood-fired pizza and craft beer made on the premises. Choose from a seat at the bar, an indoor table, or a spot outside on the patio where you can take in the bustle of downtown Bandon. Soups, salads, and a few sandwiches round out the menu. $$.

Tony's Crab Shack. 155 1st St. SE; (541) 347-2875; tonyscrabshack.com. For 30 years, Tony's Crab Shack has been serving the freshest seafood from this bright blue building near the waterfront. Crab sandwiches, grilled halibut, smoked salmon alfredo, fish tacos, and more are on the menu. Tony's also rents tackle, rents and sells crab rings, and sells bait, and will even cook your catch for you when you return! Open for lunch and dinner 7 days a week. $$.

Wilsons Market. 90 June Ave. SE; (541) 347-3083. Looks like an ordinary market, and it is—but step inside and discover what the locals rave about as the "secret burrito place." The deli sells all kinds of things from smoked mac and cheese to chicken sliders, but specializes in "BBQ Mexican," including to-die-for tacos and burritos. Don't miss the Smoky Pig. $.

where to stay

Bandon Dunes Golf Resort. 57744 Round Lake Rd.; (877) 652-2122; bandondunesgolf .com. There are golf resorts, and then there's Bandon Dunes. Lauded as the "#1 golf resort in the country," "on every golfer's bucket list," and "the greatest pure golf experience in the world," it's safe to say that golfers love Bandon Dunes. Guests come from around the planet to these traditional Scottish links courses that boast challenging designs and impressive views. Golfers walk (no golf carts allowed), which means they earn their fine dining and cocktailing (which is top-notch) for later. Six golf courses, 5 restaurants, a golf shop, and 5 different kinds of overnight accommodations are available at this grand luxury resort. $$$.

Bandon Inn. 355 US 101; (541) 347-4417; bandoninn.com. Located on a bluff, this inn has sweeping views of the greater Bandon area, including historic Old Town, the Coquille River, the marina, and the Pacific Ocean. Rooms are recently updated and include a complimentary shuttle service, an on-site espresso stand, and more. $$–$$$.

Bandon Wayside Motel and RV. 1175 2nd St. SE; (541) 347-3421; bandonwaysidemotel rv.com. This unique property is three things at once: small retro motel, micro RV park, and tiny campground. The owners fixed up a neglected 1949 roadside motel into this small but powerful destination, welcoming and full of fun amenities like benches, hammocks, and outdoor cabanas for gathering, smoking, and the like. Rooms are clean and thrifty, spotted with thrift store treasures. It's likely you'll make at least one new friend here. $–$$.

Inn at Old Town Bandon. 370 US 101; (541) 347-5900; innatoldtown.com. This modest motel is located right near Old Town and within convenient walking distance to restaurants, shops, and coffeehouses. The Inn at Old Town Bandon has just 8 rooms, each clean and comfortable. This affordable option has partial views of the harbor from the upstairs deck. $.

day trip 19

south coast

>>> **sea stacks & battle rocks:**
port orford

port orford

Port Orford is the oldest platted town on the Oregon Coast and the westernmost city in the lower 48 United States. The small town of 1,100 people is very quiet and dramatically beautiful, with plenty of outdoor recreation to be enjoyed. Creative people are drawn to this gorgeous, peaceful place, and an artsy vibe emanates throughout the town.

While the Oregon Coast is infamous for wet and wild weather, there exists a "banana belt"—a region of the southern section of the coast with relatively warmer weather. Port Orford is known as the northernmost point of this region. While "hot" may still be a stretch in defining the weather, temperatures here can be downright balmy, and sunny warm days appear almost any time of year.

Small, friendly, and quirky, Port Orford is a welcoming, relaxing place to day-trip. Residents like to boast that their town has no stoplight, no crowds, and no fast food. Slow down here, take your time, and soak up the beauty.

getting there

From Roseburg: Travel west 83 miles on OR 42 to the junction with US 101 at Bandon. Continue south 78 miles on US 101 to Port Orford.

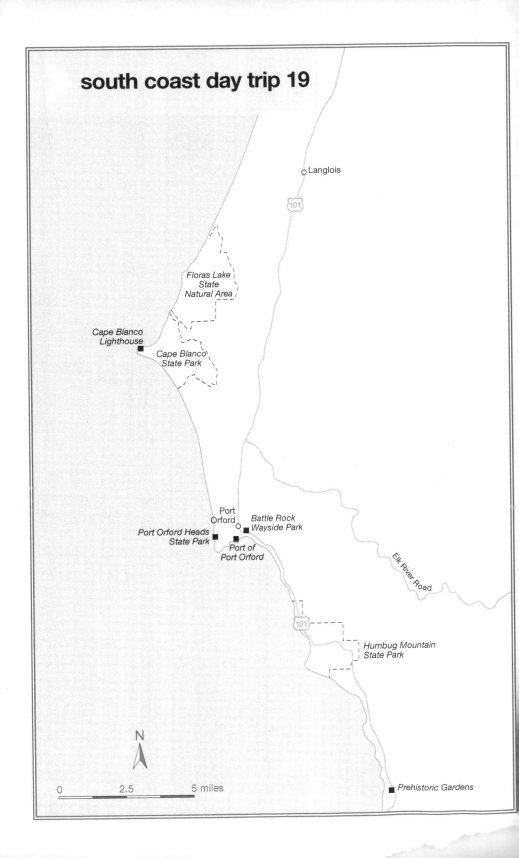

south coast day trip 19

Langlois

101

Floras Lake
State
Natural Area

Cape Blanco
Lighthouse

Cape Blanco
State Park

Port
Orford

Battle Rock
Wayside Park

Port Orford Heads
State Park

Port of
Port Orford

Elk River Road

101

Humbug Mountain
State Park

N

0   2.5   5 miles

Prehistoric Gardens

where to go

Battle Rock Wayside Park. US 101 in the center of Port Orford; (541) 332-4106; enjoy portorford.com. A historic battle is behind this rock's name. In 1851, a skirmish took place between the native Qua-to-mah people and a group of nine men who were left ashore by the steamship *Sea Gull*, with instructions to attempt to establish a settlement. The Natives attacked, and the men set up camp on the naturally fortified rock. The men eventually fled, pursued by the Natives. Today, Battle Rock is simply a peaceful place to visit. The rock itself is a rugged narrow spine, rising from the beach below the viewpoint and extending over 400 feet into the ocean waters. During accessible tides, hikers can walk to the top of the rock for a dramatic view. There's a visitor information center at the park too. From the beach or the rock, views offshore take in a grouping of sea stacks that collectively make up the Redfish Rocks Marine Reserve. This highly productive habitat for fish and marine life is one of five marine reserves in Oregon dedicated to conservation and scientific research, and therefore is off-limits to fishing. Gray whales are often spotted here too.

Cape Blanco State Park and Lighthouse. Cape Blanco Road from US 101 at Sixes; (800) 551-6949; oregonstateparks.org. Built in 1870, Cape Blanco Lighthouse is the oldest standing lighthouse in Oregon as well as the most westerly lighthouse on the Oregon Coast. On-site at this state park also sits the Historic Hughes House, a Victorian-style farmhouse built in 1898 for ranchers Patrick and Jane Hughes. The charming 3,000-square-foot home is open seasonally for tours. More than 8 miles of hiking trails within the state park lead to the beach, viewpoints of ocean vistas, fishing spots along the Sixes River, and the lighthouse. A campground with 52 sites is first-come, first-served. Cape Blanco is horse-friendly; a 7-mile trail leads from the horse camp and there is a 150-acre open riding area nearby. The lighthouse and the Hughes House are open for tours Apr through Oct, Wed through Mon from 10 a.m. to 3 p.m.

Humbug Mountain State Park. 6 miles south of Port Orford on US 101; (541) 332-6774; oregonstateparks.org. This massive natural feature rises nearly 1,800 feet above sea level, and its western flank drops dramatically into the Pacific Ocean. From a distance, it's a sight to behold; up close, it's a wonderful place to picnic, camp, and hike. Surrounded by forested hills and protected from ocean breezes, a campground features 39 sites. The trail to the top of the mountain is a strenuous 5-mile round-trip hike. Views of the ocean and coastal mountains are on hand, and native flora and fauna abound. Many visitors to the park also enjoy windsurfing and scuba diving.

Pineapple Express Adventure Rides. 832 US 101, Ste. 1; (772) 633-7385; pineapple express.bike. Rent fat tire or mountain bikes here and explore the area on two wheels. Fat tires are the latest craze, allowing cyclists to traverse the sandy beaches easily on bike. Mountain bike trails galore are found in the area, from the rugged to the benign. Guided

wild rivers coast

*The region from Bandon to Brookings is sometimes called the **Wild Rivers Coast.** For Oregon Coast visitors, the great and wondrous Pacific Ocean earns most of the glory, but there are marvelous rivers to explore along the coastline as well, especially in this remote, rugged southern coast region. The Elk River is Port Orford's own riverine waterway, known for fishing, camping, hiking, and wildlife viewing. Whitewater boating, camping at three state campgrounds, and dipping in swimming holes are also popular activities. But there are more riches like the Elk—Bandon has the Coquille River, and the Sixes River flows into the tiny community of Sixes just to the north of Port Orford. South of here, the Rogue River flows into Gold Beach and the Pistol River enters the sea just to the south of Gold Beach. At Brookings, meet the gorgeous waters of the Chetco River. Each river offers its own charms, but they share this: The farther you get from the ocean, the warmer the air and the weaker the wind. Almost always, anywhere along the coast, it's a nicer day upriver.*

tours are also available on mixed terrain, singletrack, and fat tire routes. There's a little bit of something for everyone here.

Port of Port Orford. 300 Dock Rd.; (541) 332-7121; portofportorford.org. The Port of Port Orford is one of only four dolly docks in the world. What's a dolly dock, you ask? It's a crane that lifts boats into the water from an elevated port. No boats are moored in the water here at the Port of Port Orford—each rests on a dolly or trailer on land until ready to head to sea, when they are wheeled over to the crane and lowered into the water. Visit the dock in the morning to catch the action as the boats are setting off, or in the afternoon when they return with their catch. The port is also home to a tour company, a restaurant, and public restrooms.

Port Orford Heads State Park and Life Boat Station. 92331 Coast Guard Hill Rd.; (800) 551-6949; oregonstateparks.org. This rugged headland juts into the Pacific, protecting small coves and Port Orford's natural harbor. The Port Orford Lifeboat Station, constructed here in 1934 by the Coast Guard to provide lifesaving service to the southern Oregon Coast, is now a museum that features shipwreck memorabilia and artifacts from years of service to ships. The museum is free to the public and open May through Oct, Wed through Mon from 10 a.m. to 3:30 p.m. If the museum is closed, you can still observe the 36-foot motor lifeboat on the premises, and hike several short trails through a thick Sitka spruce forest to outstanding views of the sea. A viewpoint on the south side of the headlands overlooks many miles of coastline; the trail to the northwest delivers 180-degree panoramic vistas of the sea-stack-studded coastline. Choose a quick and easy 0.75-mile trail out to the headland and back or do the entire perimeter loop, totaling about 1.25 miles. Keep your eyes peeled for blacktail deer.

Prehistoric Gardens. 36848 US 101; (541) 332-4463; prehistoricgardens.com. You have to see it to believe it! The Prehistoric Gardens experience begins with a glimpse of a brontosaurus peeking from the foliage along Highway 101 south of Port Orford. The story of a roadside attraction devoted to dinosaurs goes back to the 1950s and the late E. V. "Ernie" Nelson—artist, sculptor, entrepreneur, and dinosaur enthusiast. Nelson opened Prehistoric Gardens on January 1, 1955, ultimately completing 23 dinosaurs in total over the next 30 years. Visitors today wind through the forest on a short self-guided tour, crossing bridges and taking in the natural rain forest—and dinos galore.

South Coast Tours. 300 Dock Rd.; (541) 373-0487; southcoasttours.net. This company is your destination for tours on and off the water, in Port Orford and throughout the south coast region. South Coast Tours specializes in kayak tours on local rivers and in the sea, as well as stand-up paddleboarding, rafting, fishing, and more. Van tours range from a beach and breweries tour to a 3-day adventure tour.

Surfing. Port Orford is home to two of the best surf breaks on the southern Oregon Coast. Bring your own board and give one of these two spots a try. If you're experienced, dabble in the waters south of Battle Rock Park. The Hubbard Creek area, a sandy beach about a mile to the south, is good for all levels of surfing abilities. Catch a wave—but bring a wetsuit!

where to shop

Hawthorne Art Gallery. 517 Jefferson St.; (541) 366-2266; hawthornegallery.com. This gallery represents the works of many members of the multitalented Hawthorne family of Big Sur, California, the location of the first art gallery of this name. Other regional artists are here as well in this top-notch gallery featuring world-class art. The Hawthorne family also owns Redfish Restaurant, next door in the same building, with views of the ocean and Battle Rock (see separate listing in Where to Eat).

Port Orford Co-op. 812 Oregon St.; (541) 366-2067; portorfordcoop.com. If you think food co-ops are a thing of the 1970s, stop in this store to see how modern and relevant one can be. Fresh organic produce is just the beginning—check out the great bulk section and the daily-made lunch items. The co-op is member and volunteer powered, but anyone is welcome to shop here.

Quilters Corner. 335 7th St.; (541) 332-0502; quilterscorneroregon.com. Do you dream of colorful fabric sewn together into gorgeous quilts? This shop is a must-stop while you're in town. Offering quilting supplies, patterns, books, quality quilting fabric, a large selection of wide backing fabric, and a beautiful array of batiks, you won't leave empty-handed.

South Coast Gourmet. 832 Oregon St.; (541) 366-2074; south-coast-gourmet.business
.site. This friendly deli offers all sorts of specialty and gourmet lunch and picnic items from
salamis and cheeses to fresh delicious breads and quiches. Baked goods like cookies and
coffee cake are on hand, as is a selection of beer and wine. Open Wed through Sat 10 a.m.
to 4 p.m. and Sun 10 a.m. to 3 p.m.

where to eat

The Crazy Norwegian's Fish and Chips. 259 6th St.; (541) 332-8601; the-crazy
-norwegians-fish-and-chips.business.site. Crazy is debatable, but delicious is a fact. This
place has been pleasing day-trippers and vacationers with fresh, well-prepared seafood for
decades. Homemade soups, sauces, coleslaw, and—of course—freshly fried fish-and-chips
are on the menu. Save room for pie! Open for lunch and dinner Tues through Sun. $$.

Golden Harvest Herban Farm and Bakery. 620 9th St.; (541) 366-2193. This gem is
welcoming and friendly with great service and fresh home-cooked food. A hybrid restaurant,
deli, and produce vendor, Golden Harvest offers a hot buffet, paninis, vegan options, baked
goods, and more. Take your selections to go or stay and dine at their indoor or outdoor
seating. Don't forget the ice cream! Open Thurs through Mon 9 a.m. to 5 p.m. $–$$.

Griff's on the Dock. 210 Dock Rd.; (541) 332-8985. It's not fancy, but Griff's is a local
institution with a terrific location. As advertised, this small diner is right on the dock at the
Port of Port Orford, which means access to the freshest fish in town. Prawn cocktails, clam
chowder, fried shrimp, fried oysters, crab and cheese sandwiches, and more are on the
menu. But make sure at least one person in your party orders the fish-and-chips—it's divine!
Open daily 10:30 a.m. to 8 p.m. $$.

Mr. Ed's Espresso & Juice & Underground Pub. 1320 Oregon St.; (541) 366-2042.
Breakfast burritos, breakfast pizzas, wraps, and traditional pizza are on the menu at this
breakfast and lunch restaurant. All kinds of espresso as well as juices and smoothies hydrate
and rejuvenate. The Underground Pub part of this destination is in the back—occasional
evenings, catch live music here. Open 6:30 a.m. to 9 p.m. daily. $–$$.

Redfish Restaurant. 517 Jefferson St.; (541) 366-2200; redfishportorford.com. Hands-
down the best restaurant view in town, as well as the classiest atmosphere. The food is
excellent too. Redfish overlooks a sweeping, spectacular view of Battle Rock, the ocean,
Humbug Mountain, and the Redfish Rocks—sea stacks offshore that shelter amazing sea
life. The dining room features huge floor-to-ceiling windows as well as a variety of bright and
cheery art. The menu showcases the freshest ingredients from the area, sourced from local
farmers and fishermen, artfully presented. In good weather, sit outside on the deck. Open
daily for lunch and dinner. $$–$$$.

Tasty Kate's Cafe and Bakery. 917 US 101; (541) 290-4999. This bakery offers freshly made baked goods as well as espresso, coffee, and tea, of course. But Kate's is hiding a few surprises here too, like fresh pho on Fridays, occasional Chinese food or tacos, and a wine shop on-site. This small cottage with an artist's touch is colorful inside and out. Call for hours. $.

TJ's Cafe and Diner/Pub and Grill. 831 Oregon St.; (541) 366-2073. A classic diner on one side, pub on the other, TJ's has a little bit of something for everyone. A large menu offers a variety of breakfast, lunch, and family-style dinner items. The pub side has a dance floor as well as wine, beer, and spirits. Open daily 6 a.m. to 8 p.m. $$.

where to stay

Castaway by the Sea. 545 5th St.; (541) 332-4502; castawaybythesea.com. A variety of accommodation types here include standard king rooms, condominiums, and townhomes with kitchenettes. Pet-friendly with ocean views from every room, sun porches, and beach access, Castaway by the Sea's best feature is sweeping views. $$.

The Loft at Redfish. 517 Jefferson St.; (541) 366-2266; airbnb.com. Above Redfish Restaurant and Hawthorne Gallery is this unique 1-bedroom, 1-bath lodging, owned by the same family. The amazing views from the private balcony, comfortable and attractive space, and easy access to the beach make this place appealing. Plus it's the only apartment on the premises, meaning privacy for you. $$$.

Wild Spring Guest Habitat. 92978 Cemetery Loop Rd.; (541) 332-0977; wildspring.com. There is really no place else quite like Wild Spring Guest Habitat. Five cabin suites are nestled into the lush woods, each with radiant floor heating, unique homey decor, and plenty of comfortable amenities, but no phones, TVs, or other distractions. Windows reveal the rain forest outside. Walk up the hill past totems and various works of art interspersed in the forest to the guest hall, a communal gathering place with games, music, and views of the ocean in the near distance. In the morning, a delicious breakfast is laid out with more food than you can possibly eat. Don't miss a soak in the open-air, slate, jetted hot tub overlooking the ocean. Wild Spring has won awards for their eco-friendly approach. This is the place to truly escape the real world and live like a well-fed and nurtured wood sprite for a few days. $$$.

worth more time

The little town of **Langlois** is 13 miles north of Port Orford and home to a few surprising delights. Start with a detour off of Highway 101 to Floras Lake, a sandy-bottomed, freshwater lake tucked just over the dune from the ocean. Proximity to steady northwest coastal winds on such a moderate-size lake has drawn windsurfers and kiteboarders for years. Camp at one of 31 sites at **Boice-Cope Park** (541-247-3386; co.curry.or.us/departments/parks/boice_cope_park.php), or secure a room at **Floras Lake House Bed and Breakfast**

(92870 Boice Cope Ln.; 541-348-2573; floraslake.com). The innkeepers also run **Floras Lake Kite & Windsurf** (541-348-9912; floraslakekiting.com) and will rent windsurf or kite-surf gear, stand-up paddleboards, or kayaks during the summer season. Qualified guides also provide lessons and classes for the uninitiated.

When you're done playing on the water or just watching the action, journey into Langlois for a meal at the **Langlois Market** (48444 US 101; 541-348-2476; langloismarket .com), home of the world-famous hot dog, as well as soups and salads, deli sandwiches, and ice cream. Or try **The Spoon** (48396 US 101; 541-348-1015), a tucked-away classic diner beloved by locals and travelers alike.

day trip 20

south coast

> **a wild rogue:**
> gold beach

gold beach

There was once gold in Gold Beach. Hundreds of placer mines were set up in the late 1800s at a beach near the mouth of the Rogue River, and the region filled with hopeful miners. As is true of the gold rush everywhere, the gold came and went, as did the miners. But the name Gold Beach remained, more people arrived, and metaphorically, many locals and visitors alike still feel like they find gold here today.

Gold Beach extends between the outlets of the Rogue River on the north end of town and Turner Creek on the south end, and the town has plenty of sandy beaches and viewpoints in between. Access to the wild and scenic Rogue River is part of the appeal, along with terrific recreation opportunities. The small town boasts great salmon fishing in the widely loved Wild and Scenic Rogue River, hiking and biking in the mountains and near the sea, windsurfing, and more.

Gold Beach is in Curry County, and there's a saying that locals have: "There's no hurry in Curry." Come to this little town to slow down and take in the breezy beaches and roiling sea.

getting there

From Roseburg: Travel west 83 miles on OR 42 to the junction with US 101 at Bandon. Continue south 55 miles on US 101 to Gold Beach.

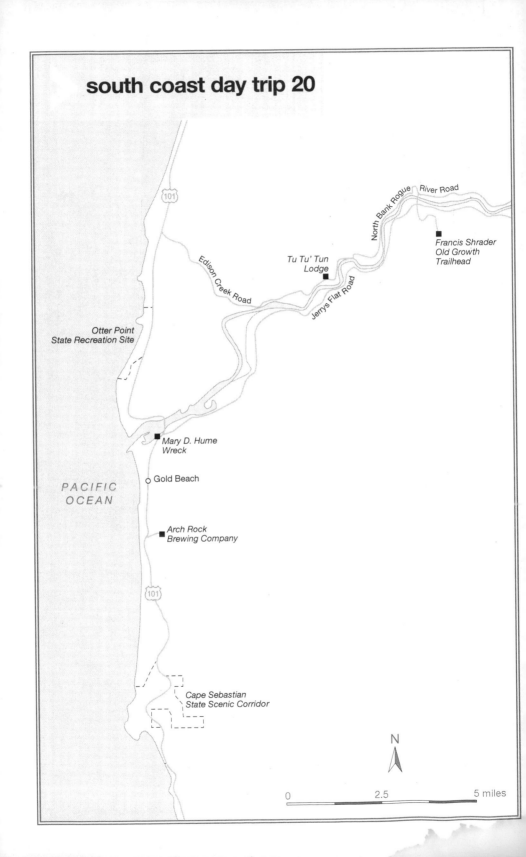

south coast day trip 20

101

North Bank Rogue River Road

Francis Shrader
Old Growth
Trailhead

Edison Creek Road

Tu Tu' Tun
Lodge

Jerrys Flat Road

Otter Point
State Recreation Site

Mary D. Hume
Wreck

PACIFIC
OCEAN

○ Gold Beach

■ Arch Rock
Brewing Company

101

Cape Sebastian
State Scenic Corridor

N

0   2.5   5 miles

where to go

Arch Rock Brewing Co. 28779 Hunter Creek Rd.; (541) 247-0555; archrockbeer.com. Visiting this brewery is like having a beer in a friend's garage. Located up Turner Creek on the south end of town in a small industrial park, Arch Rock Brewing Co. crafts fresh beer in what is not exactly a garage but in fact a former cabinet shop. Those beers have been voted the best on the Oregon Coast. Sip a few tasters and chat with the owner or brewer right where the magic happens. Try the State of Jefferson Porter or the Pistol River Pale, fill a growler to go, and be on your way.

Cape Sebastian State Scenic Corridor. 6 miles south of Gold Beach on US 101; oregon stateparks.org. Two elevated parking lots on this cape deliver views of the sea and shoreline north to Humbug Mountain and south to California. Hike a 1.5-mile trail through a forest of Sitka spruce to explore the lower levels of the cape. Keep an eye out for migrating gray whales as they pass by.

Curry County Historical Museum. 29419 Ellensburg Ave.; (541) 247-9396; curryhistory .com. This small but well-done museum located in the Alice Wakeman Memorial Building interprets the people and history of the area, including Native Americans, the shipping indus-try, the Salmon King of Oregon, the Wedderburn Quilt pioneers, the 1964 flood, and more. Open Tues through Fri 10 a.m. to 4 p.m.

Francis Shrader Old Growth Trail. 13 miles northwest of Gold Beach via Jerry Flat Road / OR 595 and FR 050. This 0.8-mile lightly trafficked loop trail located near Wedderburn (about a 30-minute drive from Gold Beach on a narrow, winding road) is good for all skill levels. The trail is primarily used for hiking, strolling, and nature trips and is best from June until Nov. See a beautiful forest of old-growth Port Orford cedar and Douglas fir. Dogs are allowed but must be kept on leash.

Jerry's Jet Boats and Jerry's Jets Museum. 29985 Harbor Way; (541) 247-4571; rogue jets.com. Jerry's Jet Boats is a Gold Beach institution, dating back to the 1950s, when three brothers installed hydro-jets in boats and became the first commercial jet boat tour company in the nation. Today, Jerry's tours 35,000 people annually on the magnificent Rogue River. Choose from a 64-, 80-, or 104-mile trip. The longer trips venture into deep canyons and whitewater. Even if you have no intention of zooming upriver on a powerful boat, Jerry's is worth a stop for the small but extensive museum exhibit in the back. Covering local history dating back to the time of the Native Americans, fur trappers, gold miners, and the early mail boats on the Rogue, the displays are simple but informative (and the museum is free to enter). Jerry's also has a huge gift shop selling just about every kind of tourist souvenir you might think of.

Otter Point State Park. 4.5 miles north of Gold Beach on US 101. There are so many beautiful headlands and viewpoints along the southern stretch of the Oregon Coast, and

the magnificent rogue

The **Rogue River** *lives large in the minds of many. The river begins on the slopes of Crater Lake and flows through steep canyons and rugged mountains to emerge 215 miles later on the shores of Gold Beach. Named one of the original eight rivers in the Wild and Scenic Rivers Act in 1968, and renowned for white-water rafting, fishing, hiking, and wild adventure, a visit to the Rogue has made it onto more than one bucket list. When I was a child, my father and I did a yearly backpack trip on a portion of the 40-mile Rogue River Trail, which travels from Grave Creek to Big Bend. Those days made amazing memories. We wandered in the wild and remote woods, gazed upon a frothy whitewater river, and slept under the stars. Whether you backpack, observe the Rogue from a roadside overlook, take a half-day whitewater float through Class II water, or venture out on a multiday rafting trip, an experience on the Rogue lingers in the heart. Some say it's the very definition of a wild river: magnificent, majestic, untamed, and a little bit rowdy.*

Otter Point is one of them. Marked by unusual sandstone formations sculpted by wind and waves, Otter Point has terrific walking trails and a quiet, pretty beach to offer the outdoor aficionado. The overlook trail is short and easy at a third of a mile, and great for all ages. Look for wildflowers in the spring and swallows nesting in the rocks.

Rogue Playhouse and Ellensburg Theater Company. 94196 Moore St.; (541) 247-4382. A variety of performing arts shows are staged at this theater over the course of a year. Visit for improv nights, radio plays, musical concerts, dramatic plays, and more. The local company pours their hearts and souls into entertaining guests at this restored theater.

Wreck of the *Mary D. Hume*. 29980 Harbor Way. This historic whaling vessel slowly rots in place near the Patterson Bridge over the Rogue River, just a few hundred feet from where she was originally constructed. Built in 1881 by R. D. Hume of Astoria, Oregon, the vessel was named after his wife. The boat went on to 97 years of active service, still holding the record for longest-serving vessel of the Pacific coast. In 1978, the *Mary D. Hume* was retired to Gold Beach, and in 1979 the ship was placed on the National Register of Historic Places. A few signs interpret her history near where she now sits, slowly sinking into the mud.

where to shop

Gold Beach Books. 29707 Ellensburg Ave.; (541) 247-2495; goldbeachbooks.com. A gigantic and delightful bookstore to explore, Gold Beach Books has both new and used books in all the genres. Peruse rare books and first editions as well as local art and forgotten lore. The small on-site cafe called Biscuit CoffeeHouse sells baked goods and coffee drinks. Open 7 days a week.

Rogue Resale. 29527 Ellensburg Ave.; (541) 425-5412. Who doesn't love a good thrift store, especially one with upscale castoffs? Spend some time browsing the used clothing, shoes, and accessories for men, women, and children in this shop. From dresses to swimsuits, boots to vests, great finds await and all at a good price.

Rogue River Myrtlewood Gallery. 29750 Ellensburg Ave.; (541) 247-2332; rogueriver myrtlewood.com. The myrtlewood tree is only found on the southern Oregon / northern California coast. This hardwood with a brilliant wood grain in a variety of shades makes for beautiful carved, crafted, and polished items. From bowls to spoons to decorative items, you'll find something you just need to take home. Many of the objects for sale at this gallery—including their signature lighthouses—are made right here on the premises. Open Mon through Sat 9 a.m. to 5 p.m., Sun 10 a.m. to 4 p.m.

where to eat

Barnacle Bistro. 29805 Ellensburg Ave.; (541) 247-7799; barnaclebistro.com. This fun and friendly location has terrific food and great service. Located in a round building on the highway, the small space inside is packed with goodness. Grilled sandwiches are served with fresh-made ginger slaw, garlic fries, or couscous on the side. Tacos of three kinds, crab cakes, and coconut lime mussels also grace the menu. Regional beers and wines are on tap. Open Mon through Sat 11:30 a.m. to 8 p.m. $$.

Spinners Steak and Seafood. 29430 Ellensburg Ave.; (541) 247-5160; spinnersrestaurant .com. Gold Beach's fine-dining destination, Spinners serves fresh seafood and choice meat cuts. Daily specials come alongside a menu featuring salads and chowders, seafood, steak, pasta, and classic American fare. Historic photographs line the walls, white tablecloths are on tables, and a bar and lounge bring back memories of years past. Open 7 days a week 4:30 to 9 p.m. $$–$$$.

where to stay

Bluebird House B+B. Bellview Lane off US 101; airbnb.com. Ever wanted to sleep in a treehouse? This is your chance. This small cabin perched on a hillside with ocean views is built around a tree. One double bed and two single beds are inside the lovely open-room wooden cabin, which has a sink and bath, a loft, and a private deck outside overlooking the ocean. $$.

Gold Beach Inn. 29346 Ellensburg Ave.; (541) 247-7091; goldbeachinn.com. A variety of lodgings are available at this oceanfront property on the south end of town. Select a standard room, ocean-view room, beach-view room, or a 2- or 3-bedroom beach home with a full kitchen and patio. Three hot tubs with ocean views, continental breakfast, and beach access all come with an overnight here too. $–$$.

Ireland's Rustic Lodges. 29330 Ellensburg Ave.; (541) 247-7091; goldbeachinn.com. A variety of lodgings here range in decor from vintage knotty pine to a sleek and modern style. All are situated on the oceanfront with easy beach access. Wood-burning fireplaces, some rooms with ocean views, complimentary breakfast, mini-kitchens, and 3 oceanfront hot tubs round out the offerings. $–$$.

Pacific Reef Hotel and Light Show. 29362 Ellensburg Ave.; (541) 247-6658; pacificreef hotel.com. Both ocean-view and economy rooms are available at this comfortable hotel on the beach. Newly added is the Adventure Theater, an entertaining light show designed to introduce guests to the many wonders of the coast with nightly shows in season. The Chowder House provides casual breakfast, lunch, and dinner dining on-site. A short trail leads to the beach. $$.

Tu Tu' Tun Lodge. 96550 N Bank Rogue River Rd.; (541) 247-6664; tututun.com. The Tu Tu' Tun is one of those magical lodgings that lives in your dreams long after you've left the premises. Tucked along the Rogue River in a lush forest, upriver from Gold Beach and away from any distractions, this marvelous lodge is the epitome of luxury and peace. The main lodge is a grand structure with a massive rock fireplace and river views, where wine is sipped in the late afternoon and morning and evening meals are served communally. Rooms have ultra-comfortable beds, private patios, wood-burning fireplaces with a supply of seasoned Oregon wood, and coffee and chocolate on hand. Wander the expansive lawn to the riverfront to skip a few rocks, watch the boats go by, or simply kick back in a chair and relax. Stay as long as you can at this Oregon icon. Dining: May through Oct, full dining; Nov through Apr, breakfast only. $$–$$$.

day trip 21

south coast

>>> **redwoods by the sea:**
brookings

brookings

The farthest city south on the Oregon Coast is known for redwood trees, Easter lilies, and a terrific climate. Brookings is one of the northernmost North American locations to boast a subtropical climate, and the small city can reach temperatures of 70 to 100 degrees Fahrenheit throughout the year. In the last four decades, the population has grown extensively, largely because of retirees moving to the area to enjoy the mild weather, beautiful coastline, terrific scenery, and outdoor adventures.

As with most of the coast, timber and fish were the founding industries in Brookings and its unincorporated neighbor, Harbor. But Brookings has a twist in its economic past by way of fields and fields of beautiful white Easter lilies. Over a century ago, an American soldier returned to the southern Oregon Coast from a tour in the Pacific with native Japanese lily bulbs in his suitcase. By 1920, commercial production of the bulbs in the rich coastal soil between Brookings and the Smith River in California, 12 miles to the south, was under way. To this day, the area produces about 90 percent of the world's Easter lily bulb crop.

Brookings is also the northernmost location of the growing range of the remarkable redwood tree—the largest tree in the world, which can live for thousands of years. Sunny days, amazing flora, scenic beaches, and a thriving economy make Brookings a great place to spend a day or a weekend.

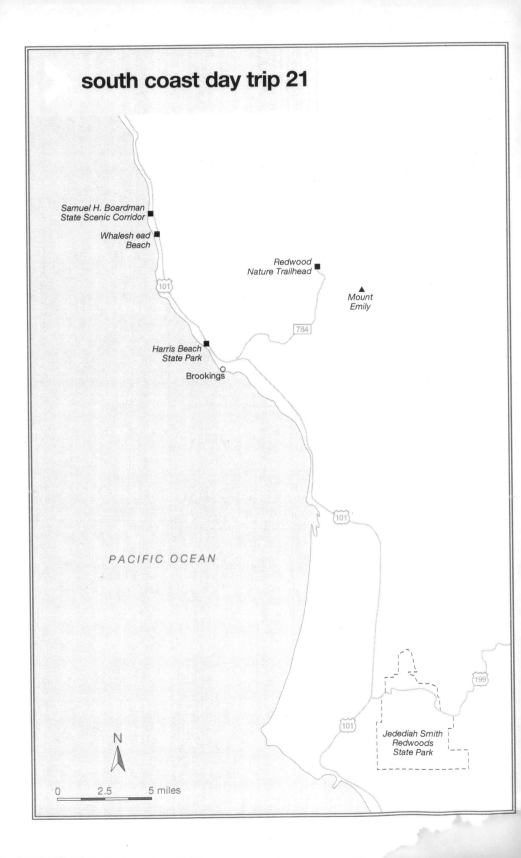

south coast day trip 21

Samuel H. Boardman
State Scenic Corridor ■

Whalesh ead ■
Beach

Redwood ■
Nature Trailhead

▲
Mount
Emily

101

784

Harris Beach ■
State Park

○
Brookings

101

PACIFIC OCEAN

101

199

101

Jedediah Smith
Redwoods
State Park

N

0   2.5   5 miles

getting there

From Grants Pass: Travel US 199 southwest 73 miles to the intersection with US 197. Follow US 197 north 7 miles to US 101. Take US 101 16.2 miles north to Brookings.

where to go

Azalea Park. 640 Old County Rd.; brookingsharbororegon.com/azalea-park. Native azaleas have been growing here since long before Brookings was platted and settled. This wonderful park is a jewel in the community, with acres of azaleas and other flora, picnic areas, a band shell, a large playground for kids, a disc golf course, and softball and soccer fields. A highlight is Capella by the Sea, a gazebo building of native wood and stone with views of the Chetco River, Port of Brookings Harbor, and the Pacific Ocean. It's a great place for events or just taking in the scenery. The park is home to many events throughout the year including live music, sporting events, and a holiday light show.

Chetco Point City Park. 901 Wharf St.; brookingsharbororegon.com/chetco-point-park. Access to this park is deceiving, as the trail begins from a parking lot at Brookings's wastewater treatment plant. Skirt that facility on a paved trail and you'll reach this 9-acre beach park with truly spectacular views. Climb a steep bluff over the sea for a great vantage point, or choose to explore two beaches on either side—Chetco Cove Beach on your left and Mill Beach on your right. The small, rugged beaches are great for beachcombing for shells, stones, and marine life. Out on the horizon to the south you'll see boats in the harbor and the St. George Reef Lighthouse near Crescent City in the distance. Picnic tables, horseshoe pits, and a few other amenities are here too.

Chetco River Redwood Trail. 8.8 miles northeast of Brookings on N Bank Chetco River Road / OR 784. This 1.2-mile loop trail offers a lot of bang for the buck. The highlight is the opportunity to see several redwood trees at their northernmost location. These grand trees are up to 250 feet tall and 10 feet in diameter, and some may be as old as 800 years. The steep and rocky trail begins on the scenic Chetco River and follows a lovely stream on a short but satisfying hike through a lush forest with amazing scenery and foliage, including wildflowers and myrtlewood.

Harris Beach State Park. Harris Beach State Park Road; oregonstateparks.org. Sandy beaches are interspersed with rocky outcroppings at this pleasant beachfront state park. Take in views of sea stacks offshore as well as Bird Island, the largest island off of the Oregon Coast and a national wildlife sanctuary and breeding site for such rare birds as the tufted puffin. Visit at low tide to explore tide pools that are home to a wide variety of marine life, and keep your eyes open for sightings of gray whales on their winter and spring migrations, harbor seals, California sea lions, and seabirds. The campground has RV sites, tent sites, and yurts for rent.

on mount emily

On September 9, 1942, a Japanese floatplane was launched from a submarine offshore, flew east, and dropped incendiary bombs in the woods near **Mount Emily,** *on a mission to start forest fires. The World War II attack fortunately caused only minimal damage. Years later, the incident would bring an opportunity for unity, forgiveness, and peace to both the people of Oregon and of Japan. The pilot, Nobuo Fujita, was invited to Brookings in 1962, where he presented the town his family's 400-year-old samurai sword in friendship, after the Japanese government was given assurances that he would not be tried as a war criminal. When Fujita came to Oregon, he also visited the site of the bombing and planted trees along the aptly named* **Bombsite Trail** *(Bombsite Trail #1118, 12 miles east of Brookings via FR 1205 and FR 240). Brookings made Fujita an honorary citizen several days before his death, in 1997.*

Samuel H. Boardman Scenic Corridor. US 101 north of Brookings for 12 miles. One scenic mile after the next comprise this scenic corridor, which stretches for 12 miles along Highway 101 and the Pacific Ocean north of Brookings. Sightseeing and exploring opportunities include access to craggy bluffs, secluded beaches, offshore rock formations, picnic areas, viewpoints, and trailheads. Some highlights not to miss are the Cape Ferrelo Viewpoint, House Rock Viewpoint, Whaleshead Beach, Natural Bridge, and Arch Rock. No matter which pullout you choose, you can't go wrong for views and sights anywhere along this journey.

where to shop

Beach Front Gifts. 16011 Boat Basin Rd.; (541) 469-8025. This gift shop carries the usual souvenirs, nautical decor, T-shirts, and more. Stop in for an order of specialty fudge, cinnamon nuts, or saltwater taffy—or all three. You'll need snacks for the road, after all!

The Market Place aka Pirate Headquarters. 668 Chetco Ave.; (541) 469-9753. Your destination for all things pirate, not to mention mermaid and dragon. This shop is worth the stop just to get your photo taken with more than one pirate statue on the premises. But you might just leave with a kite, a beach sign, or a jellyfish paperweight.

Pacific Ocean Harvesters. 16376 Lower Harbor Rd.; (541) 251-3643. Fresh fish right out of the sea is available here for you to take and cook yourself. The daily catch varies but might include lingcod, steelhead, salmon, albacore, rockfish, crab, and all of the above in a smoked version. Open from 10:30 a.m. to 6 p.m. daily, unless they run out of fish, in which case they might close up shop early.

Semi Aquatic. 654 Chetco Ave.; (503) 504-2861; artandsurf.com. Artist Spencer Reynolds brings together his two passions—the ocean and art—in the work he creates. This studio gallery features his paintings, prints, cards, and clothing, featuring themes of the Oregon Coast, surfing, the Pacific Northwest, plant life, and more. Reynolds's beautiful, colorful, and often abstract art will captivate you. Open 11 a.m. to 5:30 p.m. every day but Sun.

where to eat

Black Trumpet Bistro and Bar. 625 Chetco Ave., Ste. 220; (541) 887-0860; blacktrumpet bistro.net. This bistro specializes in regional, fresh, and house-made ingredients. The fine-dining menu features delicious locally foraged mushrooms, seared scallops, roasted duck breast, pastas, and more. Don't forget cheesecake for dessert! Black Trumpet also caters events. Open Mon through Sat for lunch and 7 days a week for dinner. $$–$$$.

Catalyst Seafood Restaurant and Lounge. 16182 Lower Harbor Rd.; (541) 813-2422. Both the family-owned boat and restaurant are named Catalyst. The Georgen family catches the fresh fish and cooks it up for guests at this restaurant on the harbor. Crab, tuna, and salmon are the mainstays, but the menu offers oysters, clams, and shrimp too at this casual, tasty eaterie. Open daily for lunch and dinner. $$.

Khun Thai. 925 Chetco Ave.; (541) 412-0555. Rich and flavorful Thai food is served here at this locally owned restaurant. Settle into a booth and try the crispy green beans, papaya salad, pineapple fried rice, or the holy basil. Mango sticky rice? Oh yeah—it's here too, as is locally made craft beers. Open daily; call for hours. $$.

O'Holleran's Steakhouse and Lounge. 1210 Chetco Ave.; (541) 469-9907. This family-run restaurant has been featuring standard steak and seafood dishes to a happy lineup of guests since the 1950s. O'Holleran's is a gathering place for the community, sometimes featuring live music and televised sporting events. Friendly service too. Open for dinner nightly. $$–$$$.

Oxenfre Public House. 631 Chetco Ave.; (541) 813-1985; oxenpub.com. Local, fresh, and organic are the buzzwords here at this friendly pub with an international flair. Korean short ribs, a Bavarian Reuben, and fried chicken and Belgian waffles grace the menu, among other delicious and creative dishes. Happy hour from 4 to 6 p.m. weeknights and a late-night menu every day round out options. Open daily 4 p.m. to close. $$.

Pacific Sushi. 613 Chetco Ave.; (541) 251-7707; pacificsushi.com. All of the usual sushi, nigiri, and sashimi delights are here as well as grill entrees, noodle dishes, rolls, and miso soup. Specialty cocktails and desserts (wasabi cheesecake, anyone?) are delicious. Late night hours continue at the adjacent Star Lounge. Open daily 11:30 a.m. to 9 p.m. $$–$$$.

Sporthaven Marina Bar & Grill. 16374 Lower Harbor Rd.; (541) 469-3301. This very casual diner on the port offers fish-and-chips and other seafood dishes surrounded by a nautical ambiance. Sit outside on nice days and nosh on lunch with fresh air and a view of the harbor; a fireplace on the patio extends the dining alfresco season. $–$$.

Zola's Pizza. 16362 Lower Harbor Rd.; (541) 412-7100; zolaspizzeria.com. Wings, salads, pasta, and all kinds of pizza pies are here for the taking. Try the Crazy Chicken (chicken, black olives, red onion, and habaneros) or the Brown Shugga (Canadian bacon, pineapple, and brown sugar). Over 100 local beers are on rotation should you choose to dine in at the restaurant, or choose Zola's wide-ranging delivery service. Open 7 days a week 11 a.m. to 9 p.m. $$.

where to stay

Best Western Beachfront Inn. 16008 Boat Basin Rd.; (541) 469-7779; beachfrontinn .com. Deluxe accommodations at this hotel near the beach feature ocean views, beach access, private balconies, and a complimentary hot breakfast. Upgrade to a suite with a Jacuzzi hot tub and kitchen and stay at the beach that much longer. An outdoor heated pool is on-site, and the hotel is also pet-friendly. $$–$$$.

Mermaid's Muse Bed and Breakfast. 18 Seascape Ct.; (541) 412-2949; mermaids musebedandbreakfast.us. The views of the sea from this beautiful cliff-top bed-and-breakfast and the beach keep people coming back. Spacious rooms, a cocktail hour at the on-site bar, a barbecue to make personal use of, a terrace for comfortable relaxation, and free use of bicycles make this place welcoming and friendly. $$–$$$.

Whaleshead Resort. 19921 Whaleshead Rd.; (541) 469-7446; whalesheadresort.com. Located 7 miles north of Brookings, perched on a hill with easy access to Whaleshead Beach, Whaleshead is a resort, destination RV park, and residential neighborhood. Book one of the many cabins sleeping 2 to 6, each a little bit different. Amenities include 2 miles of walking trails, a spa, picnic tables, communal patios and meeting spaces, and incredible views. $$–$$$.

Wild Rivers Motor Lodge. 437 Chetco Ave.; (541) 469-5361; wildriversmotorlodge.com. Comfortable and clean lodging at reasonable rates is what Wild Rivers Motor Lodge is all about. Affordable rates, pet-friendly rooms, and a fisherman's special are available too at this destination in the heart of town. $–$$.

worth more time

Just 6 miles south of Brookings is the California border. Another 16 miles travel along US 101 and you'll find yourself at **Jedediah Smith Redwoods State Park,** one of several parks in the Redwood National and State Parks systems (nps.gov/redw). Redwood trees (*Sequoiadendron*) are the largest and tallest trees in the world, and can live for thousands of years. These trees grow mainly only here, in the coastal forests of northern California. The massive, marvelous redwood trees are the main draw, but these protected parks also shelter gorgeous beaches, rugged coastline, prairies, and oak woodlands. Five visitors centers, four campgrounds, and plenty of hiking trails are all on hand. Search for agates, hike a grassy bluff with views of the sea, choose a scenic drive, watch Roosevelt elk on parade, or hug a very large tree. The nearest city is **Crescent City, California,** which offers lodgings, restaurants, and more sightseeing.

appendix a: regional information

north coast

day trip 01

Long Beach Peninsula Visitors Bureau
PO Box 562 / 3914 Pacific Way, Seaview
(360) 642-2400
visitlongbeachpeninsula.com

day trip 02

Astoria-Warrenton Area Chamber of
Commerce
111 West Marine Dr., Astoria
(503) 325-6311
oldoregon.com, travelastoria.com

day trip 03

Seaside Visitor's Bureau / Chamber of
Commerce
7 North Roosevelt Dr., Seaside
(888) 306-2326
seasideor.com

day trip 04

Cannon Beach Chamber of Commerce
207 N Spruce St., Cannon Beach
(503) 436-2623
cannonbeach.org

day trip 05

Explore Manzanita
31 Laneda Ave., Manzanita
(503) 812-5510
exploremanzanita.com

Visit Tillamook Coast
4506 3rd St., Tillamook
(503) 842-2672
tillamookcoast.com

day trip 06

City of Garibaldi
PO Box 708 / 107 6th St., Garibaldi
(503) 322-3327
visitgaribaldi.com

Visit Tillamook Coast
4506 3rd St., Tillamook
(503) 842-2672
tillamookcoast.com

day trip 07

Nestucca Valley Chamber of Commerce
PO Box 75, Cloverdale
(503) 392-4340
pcnvchamber.org

Tillamook Area Chamber of Commerce
3705 US 101 N, Tillamook
(503) 842-7525
tillamookchamber.org

Visit Tillamook Coast
4506 3rd St., Tillamook
(503) 842-2672
tillamookcoast.com

day trip 08

Visit Tillamook Coast
4506 3rd St., Tillamook
(503) 842-2672
tillamookcoast.com

central coast

day trip 09

Lincoln City Visitor and Convention Bureau
801 SW US 101, Lincoln City
(541) 996-1274
oregoncoast.org

day trip 10

Depoe Bay Chamber of Commerce
PO Box 21 / 223 SW US 101, Depoe Bay
(541) 765-2889, (877) 485-8348
depoebaychamber.org

day trip 11

Newport Chamber of Commerce
555 SW Coast Hwy., Newport
(541) 265-8801
newportchamber.org

day trip 12

Waldport Chamber of Commerce
PO Box 669 / 320 NW US 101, Waldport
(541) 563-2133
waldport-chamber.com

day trip 13

Yachats Chamber of Commerce
PO Box 728 / 241 US 101, Yachats
(541) 547-3530
yachats.org

south coast

day trip 14

Eugene, Cascades & Coast
754 Olive St., Eugene
(541) 743-8760
eugenecascadescoast.org

day trip 15

Reedsport Chamber of Commerce
2741 Frontage Rd., Reedsport
(541) 271-3495
reedsportcc.org

City of Lakeside
915 N Lake Rd., Lakeside
(541) 759-3011
cityoflakeside.org

day trip 16

Bay Area Chamber of Commerce
145 Central Ave., Coos Bay
(541) 266-0868
coosbaynorthbendcharlestonchamber.com

Coos Bay–North Bend Visitors &
Convention Bureau
50 Central Ave., Coos Bay
(541) 269-0215, (800) 824-8486
oregonsadventurecoast.com

day trip 17

Bay Area Chamber of Commerce
145 Central Ave., Coos Bay
(541) 266-0868
coosbaynorthbendcharlestonchamber.com

Coos Bay–North Bend Visitors &
Convention Bureau
50 Central Ave., Coos Bay
(541) 269-0215, (800) 824-8486
oregonsadventurecoast.com

day trip 18

Bandon Visitors Center
300 2nd St., Bandon
(541) 347-9616
bandon.com

day trip 19

Port Orford Chamber
PO Box 637, Port Orford
(541) 332-8055
portorfordchamber.com

day trip 20

Gold Beach Visitor Center
PO Box 375 / 94080 Shirley Ln.,
Gold Beach
(800) 525-2334, (541) 247-7526
visitgoldbeach.com

day trip 21

Brookings City Hall / Visitor Center
898 Elk Dr., Brookings
(541) 469-1103
brookings.or.us

appendix b: festivals & celebrations

The open road, no agenda, and free-form-type exploration of a day trip can be fabulous, but sometimes it's just more fun to go somewhere you know there's going to be action. Festivals offer the opportunity to park the car in one spot and soak up music, food, and entertainment all at once. Luckily for you, the Oregon Coast loves a good festival. No matter your interests, you're sure to find an appealing festival in this lineup. For more events, see traveloregon.com and oregonfestivals.org.

february

Newport Seafood and Wine Festival. (800) 262-7844; seafoodandwine.com. Held the last full weekend in February in Newport, this popular festival celebrates two of the things Oregonians love best—seafood and wine. Held outdoors south of town; free shuttle buses run from downtown.

march

Garibaldi Crab Races. visitgaribaldi.com. The best kind of small-town tradition, the crab races bring people together to yell, bang their heads, and even try to use psychic powers to urge their Dungeness crab cohorts toward the finish line. The races are the heart of this humorous event, and food, drink, and revelry are on the sidelines.

Savor Cannon Beach. (888) 609-6051; savorcannonbeach.com. Four days of wine tastings, culinary events, and a wine walk showcasing over 40 Northwest wineries are the heart of this event. Award-winning wines are paired with chef-designed appetizers, and restaurants, shops, and galleries all get in on the fun during this event.

april

Astoria Warrenton Crab, Seafood, and Wine Festival. (503) 325-6311; oldoregon.com. Enjoy a great spread of Northwest cuisine, arts and crafts, a selection of Oregon's and Washington's finest wines, a beer garden, and more at this annual Astoria event. Try the traditional crab dinner all weekend long. Live music is on tap too.

may

Depoe Bay Fleet of Flowers. (541) 765-2889; depoebaychamber.org. This memorable and moving ceremony honors the memories of fishermen lost at sea. An onshore ceremony at Depoe Bay Harbor features a presentation of colors, recognition of veterans, a jet fly-over, guest speakers, and musical performances. Next, a fleet of flower-laden boats passes under the Highway 101 bridge.

North Coast Culinary Festival. (503) 436-2623; cannonbeach.org. Enjoy a fabulous weekend of culinary arts in Cannon Beach in honor of legendary chef James Beard, who spent time in the area as a child. Workshops, dinners, and brunches are on hand, and the entire city rallies around the celebration. Enjoy demonstrations by local chefs, libations, and food pairings.

Rhododendron Festival. (541) 997-3128; florencechamber.com. The rhododendron blooms this time of year and deserves a festival to celebrate its beauty. See a spectacular display of hundreds of rhododendrons at the Florence Events Center, and enjoy the street vendor fair, car show, 5K run, and a carnival with rides and games. Don't miss the Grand Floral Parade featuring "Queen Rhododendra."

Seaside Downtown Wine Walk. (503) 717-1914; seasidedowntown.com. In Seaside in May, local wineries are invited into local shops to pour samples of their best wines. Each Wine Walk brings hundreds of people to the downtown area for an afternoon and evening of great wines, great food, and, of course, great fun! Buy a commemorative wine glass and join in the fun. There's a second wine walk in November.

june

Pistol River Wave Bash. internationalwindsurfingtour.com. Windsurfers from all over the globe come to Gold Beach to compete in the Pistol River Wave Bash. The action is centered around Pistol River State Park, and spectators can set up on the sandy beach to take in all of the action. This weeklong event features both pros and amateurs.

Northwest Garlic Festival. (360) 665-4448; nwgarlicfestival.com. Ocean Park on the Long Beach Peninsula knows there's a lot to love about garlic. Celebrate the passion for this exalted bulb with the faithful throngs who make their annual pilgrimage to the Northwest Garlic Festival, which is held each June in the seaside community of Ocean Park. Garlic games, garlic crafts, and—naturally—garlic food and condiments are on hand at this two-day event, as well as live music. Festival motto: It's chic to reek.

Rockaway Beach Pirate and Costume Festival. (503) 355-8108; rockawaybeach.net. This festival celebrates pirates in many ways, including with a fun and challenging treasure hunt. Experience pirate music, roving pirates, festival rides, foods and drinks, vendors selling exotic wares, musical acts, performances, and pirate-themed games.

july

Circles in the Sand. (541) 808-4496; sandypathbandon.com. Face Rock Wayside in Bandon is home to this remarkable string of events, featuring hand-drawn labyrinths in the sand. A group of volunteer artists create walkable, ephemeral art, knowing it will all be swept away with the tide. See the website for schedules.

Dory Days Weekend. (888) 965-7001; yourlittlebeachtown.com. There's no other marine fishery exactly like the one at Pacific City anywhere in the world. The modern dory fleet of today has evolved from the boats that went to sea from Cape Kiwanda more than 100 years ago. This three-day event celebrates that rich history with a parade, marine fair, and fish fry at Cape Kiwanda, and an artisan fair in the downtown area.

DuneFest. (541) 271-3495; dunefest.com. All things sand dunes are celebrated at this event in Winchester Bay each July. Camp on-site or visit for the day to see races, including a drag strip and the triple-crown shootout. A kids' riding area, freestyle show, and more entertain dunes lovers of all ages.

July Jubilee. julyjubilee.com. The town of North Bend puts on a party each year to celebrate this city's founding. Come and join the fun for live music, food, dancing, and a car cruise. Don't miss the parade featuring the Jubilee court, dancers, performers, animals, and clowns.

Oregon Coast Music Festival. (541) 267-0938; oregoncoastmusic.org. Coos Bay is home to the longest-running music festival on the Oregon Coast. Each year over 80 musicians travel from all over the country to perform three classical concerts during a weeklong event in July. Get tickets and enjoy this high-class music.

Southern Oregon Kite Festival. southernoregonkitefestival.com. Kite fliers and kite makers descend on Brookings for this free weekend event. The kite fliers choreograph their flights to music and the kite makers show, and often allow spectators to fly, some of their flying art. A demonstration of indoor kite flying is also on hand.

Yachats Celtic Music Festival. (541) 563-6210; yachatscelticmusicfestival.org. World-class traditional and nontraditional music of the Celtic countries grace the town and beaches of Yachats in the fall. Enjoy the "pub-style" format at the Yachats Commons, concerts at the Little Log Church, and Celtic-inspired workshops, speakers, storytelling, hot jam sessions, dancing, gourmet food and drinks, and whiskey tasting happening throughout the town.

august

Astoria Regatta Festival. (800) 875-6807; astoriaregatta.org. Five days of fun all about the greatest river in the West, the mighty Columbia. Sailboat races on the Columbia, live music and nightly concerts, a children's parade, fireworks over the Columbia, a salmon barbecue, a car show, and a grand parade bring out the folks in celebration.

Bay City Pearl Music Festival. (503) 377-2288; ci.bay-city.or.us. Vendors, food, and activities for the kids are on hand for this one-day festival focused on great live music. Four bands and an open-mic segment take the stage. A car show and antiques and hobby vendors entertain, and a community dance closes the event in the evening.

Charleston Seafood Beer and Wine Festival. charlestonseafoodfestival.com. Visit the Charleston Marina for food, fun, music, and crafts at this summertime festival. Over 50 vendors sell food, craft beer, regional wines, crafts, shirts, trinkets, and more at this celebration of the fruits of the sea.

Fiddle on the Beach. ootfa.org. Winchester Bay hosts this three-day free celebration of the great American musical tradition of fiddling. Jams, a stage show, and a contest are part of the fun, all around an annual theme that changes year to year.

Kool Coastal Nights. koolcoastalnights.com. Winchester Bay hosts this amazing car show each summer. Live music, vendors, a "show-and-shine," and a harbor cruise are fun for all lovers of antique cars as well as those new to the appreciation of the time-honored vehicle.

Washington State International Kite Festival. (360) 642-4020; kitefestival.com. Voted "Best Kite Festival in the World" by the Kite Trade Association, this weeklong festival on the Long Beach Peninsula includes competitions for professional and amateur kite flyers, choreographed kite flies, mass ascensions, fireworks, lighted night kite flies, vendors, and more. You can be sure the skies are full of color this week.

september

Bay Area Fun Festival. (541) 267-5008; oregonsadventurecoast.com. This weekend-long party in Coos Bay features a variety of vendors, arts and crafts, food, and a beer and wine garden. Enjoy live entertainment, Cruz the Coos featuring nearly 500 vintage automobiles, the Prefontaine Memorial Run, a parade, and much more.

Cranberry Festival. (541) 347-9616; bandon.com. This time-honored tradition celebrates local cranberry farming with entertainment for everyone, including live music and performing arts, classic cars and farm equipment, carnival rides, sports, shopping, dining, and contests. Farmers and artisans sell wares at Cranberry City and the Festival Market.

Crave the Coast. cravethecoast.org. Held under the event tent in Garibaldi on Tillamook Bay, this celebration of the region's natural bounty is a one-day extravaganza. Over 40 local chefs, business owners, winemakers, and growers are on hand to offer sips, samples, and fun cooking demos to help you create tasty dishes with local produce, fish, and more.

Earth and Ocean Arts Festival. cbgallerygroup.com. Showcasing artistic inspirations that raise awareness of the pristine coastal region through an appreciation of the arts, this event from the Cannon Beach Gallery Group includes performance and studio artists who create and perform on the beaches and in the parks and galleries of Cannon Beach to encourage sustainability and preservation.

Mill-Luck Salmon Celebration. (541) 756-8800; themillcasino.com. This celebration of Native American and Coquille tribal culture is located at The Mill Casino on Coos Bay. Events include a free outdoor festival featuring Native vendors, canoe races, canoe exhibition and rides, Native drummers and dancers, a traditional salmon bake meal, and a salmon derby.

Muttzanita. muttzanita.com. Dog lovers unite on the Oregon Coast in Manzanita each September for dog-related contests and activities, vendors, and demonstrations. Pick up tricks from trainers, get your doggy a massage, or take home a shelter pet. Dogs on leashes welcome.

SOLVE Beach Cleanup. (971) 346-2703; solveoregon.org. Be part of the solution and join many others in a big one-day clean-up of Oregon's beaches. Choose from 45 beach cleanup sites along the entire coast to participate in this family-friendly event.

october

Cranberrian Fair. (360) 642-3446; columbiapacificheritagemuseum.org. This annual fall celebration of local harvest including all things cranberry takes place on the Long Beach Peninsula. During the local cranberry harvest, visitors enjoy vendors, live music, cranberry foods and traditions, and craft demonstrations, and ride the Cranberry Trolley to bog tours.

Great Columbia Crossing. (503) 325-6311; greatcolumbiacrossing.com. The Astoria-Megler Bridge closes for one full morning for this 10K run/walk event. Cross the longest continuous truss bridge in North America on foot and experience the great Columbia River like you've never before.

Lincoln City Kite Festival. (541) 996-1274; oregoncoast.org. Held on the beach by the D Wayside, this two-day event is fun for all ages. Kite-flying demonstrations by experts, free kids' kite-making, running of the bols, and some of the most colorful "big" kites in the world are all on the lineup. Catch a free shuttle from the community center or the outlet mall.

Newport Cider Festival. (800) 262-7844; seafoodandwine.com. This family-friendly event celebrates the beauty and bounty of the Pacific Northwest and the arrival of fall. Enjoy the work of local artisans, Oregon craft brews, Pacific Northwest ciders, and wine.

Oregon Coast Jazz Party. (541) 265-2787; coastarts.org. Jazz and jazz lovers come together in Newport on the beautiful Oregon Coast each fall. Workshops and education accompany lots and lots of great jazz music at this three-day event.

november

Seaside Parade of Lights. (503) 738-6391; seasideor.com. This parade comes complete with Santa and takes place in downtown Seaside. Come and see the tree lighting, sing carols afterward, and partake of some cookies and a gift fair at the convention center on the Friday of Thanksgiving weekend.

Stormy Weather Arts Festival. (503) 436-2623; cannonbeach.org. This Cannon Beach tradition offers a deluge of artistic and musical talent. Live music plays in shops, galleries, and restaurants all over town. There is an auction and demonstrations by local artists too during this three-day festival.

december

Nature's Coastal Holiday Festival of Lights. naturescoastalholiday.com. Azalea Park in Brookings comes alive with thousands of holiday lights at this annual holiday event. The completely volunteer-coordinated-and-staffed event brings the community together as 25,000 people visit to see 500,000 lights hung in the park.

Oregon Coast Aquarium's Sea of Lights. (541) 867-FISH; aquarium.org. This holiday season tradition draws guests to the Oregon Coast Aquarium in Newport to see it adorned with holiday decorations, a large Christmas tree, and thousands of colorful lights. Enjoy face painting, holiday music, and a visit with Santa. Visitors come from all over the region to spend time together at the beach and enjoy the magic of the season.

index